THE HIKER'S GUIDE

McCall & Cascade

Scott Marchant

65 Hikes near McCall and Cascade

Published by
Hiking Idaho
P.O. Box 9498
Boise, ID 83707
Copyright © 2017 by Hiking Idaho

ISBN 978-0-9977370-0-4

All photography by Scott Marchant.
Cover Photo: Grass Mountain Lakes, hike 52
Page 1: Pond above Josephine Lake, hike 41
Page 3: Hard Butte Lake, hike 55
Page 28: Josephine Lake, hike 41
Page 238: Louie Lake, hike 17 and 18

Marchant, Scott, 1962-
Book Design: Angela R. Stewart Design, Inc.
Printed in the United States

Liability Waiver

Due to the possibility of personal error, typographical error, misinterpretation of
information, and the many changes both natural and man-made, *The Hiker's Guide
McCall & Cascade*, its author, publisher, and all other persons or companies directly and
indirectly associated with this publication assume no responsibility for accidents, injury,
death, damage or any losses by individuals or groups using this publication.

Outdoor activities are always potentially dangerous. Good decision-making skills and
astute judgment will help reduce potential hazards and risks. Prepare yourself with
proper equipment and outdoor skills, and you will have an enjoyable experience.

Every effort has been made by the author to ensure the accuracy of the information in
this guide. However, things often change once a guide is published—areas fall under
new management, trails are rerouted, private land is acquired by the public, trailhead
signs are destroyed or modified, wildfires impact areas, etc. Corrections, updates and
suggestions may be sent to the author at scott@hikingidaho.com.

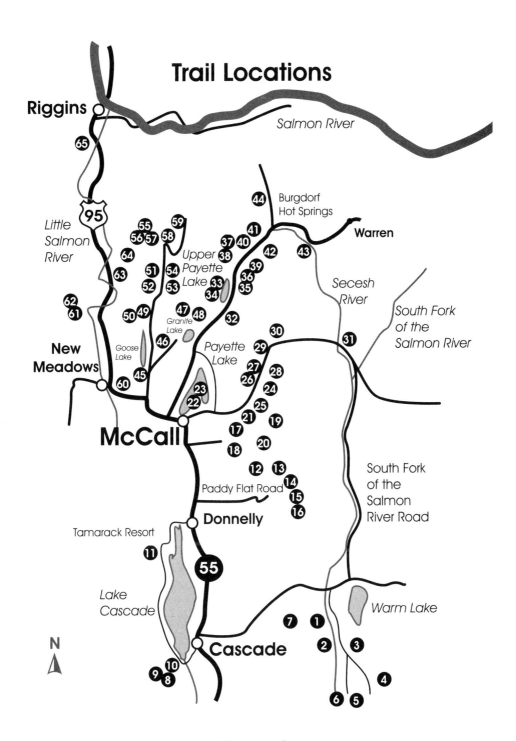

Trail Locations

Not to scale
For reference only

CASCADE

Warm Lake Area

Cascade Area

DONNELLY

Paddy Flat Road Area

Elo Road Area

Ponderosa State Park

Lick Creek Road/South Fork of the Salmon River Area

Warren Wagon Road Area

Goose Lake–Brundage Mountain Road Area

Highway 55–Between McCall and New Meadows Area

New Meadows/Highway 95 Area

Introduction

"We shall not cease from exploration, and the end of all exploring will be to arrive where we started...and know the place for the first time."

~T.S. Eliot

The rugged landscape surrounding McCall and Cascade is a complex puzzle of craggy mountains, forested ridges, open meadows and V-shaped canyons. *The Hiker's Guide McCall & Cascade* explores sixty-five hikes in this area offering a variety of destinations and journeys. You will visit the beautiful canyon cradling the lazy Fisher Creek, ascend to the top of Hard Butte Peak to discover 360° views extending over thirty miles, venture to the beautiful Buck Lake that rarely sees visitors. Most of the hikes are located in the Salmon River Mountains, a few are found in the West Mountains, west of Cascade. There are a couple of hikes northwest of New Meadows and one south of Riggins. Nearly ninety trails were explored and researched for this guidebook with the sixty-five most rewarding hikes selected.

Rapid River

This guide is for those individuals who seek out a wilderness experience on foot and offers a diverse selection of hiking experiences. Hikes were chosen for their scenic beauty. Although most of the hikes lead to a destination such as a mountain summit, lake, meadow, or other geological feature, the hikes are as much about the journey as the destination. Some of the hikes simply follow a river or creek. Most of the hikes are on maintained trails, although a few routes are to destinations where you will need to navigate faint footpaths or no trail at all. The differences in the hikes are vast and include well-established trails accessible to most hikers, to off-trail adventures that require hikers be in excellent physical condition.

The author hiked every trail mile, many of them multiple times. One of the great rewards of traveling all the routes is the chance to learn the landscape intimately—what makes one canyon or mountian landscape different from another or how they may be similar. As a result, you will find descriptions of topography, flora, fauna and scenery all based on experience. Some of the most amazing scenery near McCall and Cascade awaits you—enjoy your exploration.

USING THIS GUIDE

"The single biggest problem in communication is the illusion it has taken place."

~George Bernard Shaw

If this is your first time using this type of a guidebook, here is a brief introduction regarding how to find a hike to fit your needs. In the front of the book, there is a Location Map. Seek out the hikes in the area you wish to visit or are already near. Next, review the at-a-glance information at the top of each hike. Consider mileage, difficulty and total elevation gain. Once you have narrowed your search to a few hikes, read the brief description (under the at-a-glance information) to get a better idea of the hike you are considering.

Each hike has four primary sections:

• Twelve key, at-a-glance details (described below).

• A general description of the hike. Think of this as the sizzle—why would you want to hike this trail? Details include fauna, flora, historical references, scenery, backpacking opportunities and possibly alternate hiking options. Ideally, the description should provide you with a good impression of what it feels like to have hiked the trail. You will also find (if there are opportunities) suggestions for dispersed camping (car camping) at primitive sites or campgrounds.

• Detailed trailhead directions.

• A comprehensive description of the hike. This includes detailed information concerning mileage, unsigned and signed junctions, creek and river fords, off-trail options, specific information regarding backpack campsites, possible destinations to shorten the hike and information on flora and fauna. Cumulative distances are given so you can tailor any hike to fit your own time constraints and physical abilities.

At-a-glance details include:

• **Distance** – All distances were measured using a GPS and are reported to the closest one-tenth of a mile. Out-and-back distances were measured from the trailhead to the hike's final destination, then back to the trailhead.

• **Total Elevation Gain** – This is how much climbing you will be doing during the hike. The total elevation gain is the cumulative amount of ascending required from the trailhead to the final destination and then back to the trailhead. To compute the total elevation gain, the elevation gain is added to the elevation loss. For example, on an out-and-back hike, if you ascend 1,000 feet to a ridge and descend 400 feet to a meadow your total gain for the hike is 1,400 feet. This is because on your return, you will need to hike back up the 400 feet you descended.

- **Difficulty** – Each trip is rated for its difficulty. The rating is based on an individual in good physical condition. There is some subjectivity in the ratings with consideration given to trail conditions, route-finding, creek fords, etc. The four possible ratings are:

    Easy – 1 to 6 miles with less than 800 feet of gain.

    Moderate – 4 to 8 miles with less than 1,200 feet of gain.

    Strenuous – 6 to 10 miles with less than 2,000 feet of gain.

    Very Strenuous – 7 miles or more with more than 2,000 feet of gain.

- **Elevation Range** – These figures represent the trail's highest and lowest points not necessarily the beginning and ending elevations. Normally, the lowest elevation will be the trailhead. Elevations are given in feet and rounded to within the nearest 50 feet. For example, if a hike ends at a 6,489-foot peak, it is listed as 6,500 feet. Elevation range information is valuable if you are vulnerable to altitude sickness, which for some hikers can occur as low as 7,000 feet. Hikes ascending above this level may require an acclimation period before you set out.

- **Topographic Map** – This refers to the U. S. Geological Survey (USGS) 1:24,000 maps, which correspond to the referenced hike. The maps are the most detailed available and show forest cover, significant creeks, rivers and lakes. They also indicate steepness of terrain. You will find the maps an invaluable resource not only to identify key topographical features but also for navigation purposes if you go off-trail. Sections of the USGS 1:24,000 maps are included for each hike in the book. The route is labeled as a heavy black and white broken line. Off-trail routes are labeled as black dots.

- **Time** – It is impossible to accurately predict hiking times because everybody hikes at a different speed. Generally, the average hiker will travel 2 to 3 mph on a level trail. If you are backpacking, the pace will be slower due to the extra weight. If a trail has elevation gain, your speed drops in direct proportion to the trail's steepness.

    The times listed are within a specified range. The first time is calculated for a fast hiker averaging 3 mph on level ground. To account for elevation gain, 20 minutes is added to the total time for every 1,000 feet of gain. The second time listed is for a slower hiker averaging 2 mph on level ground. To account for elevation gain, 30 minutes is added for every 1,000 feet of gain. The vast majority of hikers' rates will fall between the two figures. The times listed are for hiking only and do not include breaks for eating, photography or resting. Many factors can slow you down such as wet trails, poor visibility, snow, difficult creek or river crossings, route-finding, poor trail conditions and altitude acclimation.

- **Seasons** – Here you will find the months that a particular hiking route is normally accessible. Obviously, it is impossible to predict when snow will melt in the high country, when creeks will be low enough to ford or when snow will appear in the fall. No two years are alike, and trails can open sooner or later than listed times. Use your own judgement when planning a hike, and contact the local ranger district office for conditions.

- **Water Availability** – This provides a list of streams, creeks and lakes where you will find water. Most sources are normally reliable throughout the year. You should purify all water before drinking.

- **Cautionary Advice** – This alerts you to possible hazards on a hike. Trail conditions may change and new, unknown cautions may emerge.

- **Additional Information** – This is the agency and phone number responsible for the area.

- **Pit Latrine** – This identifies whether a pit latrine (pit toilet) is available at the trailhead. In some instances, there may be a pit latrine at a nearby campground.

- **GPS Coordinates** – All GPS coordinates are listed as WGS84 datum. When using a GPS, make sure it is set to navigate with WGS84 datum. The coordinates for trailheads and final destinations are provided in degrees, with minutes as decimals.

- **Trail User Symbols** – The symbols above the coordinates header alerts you to the type of users allowed on a route. The Forest Service often reevaluates trail accessibility guidelines, and designations can change. On many of the trails, a user class—usually motor bikes and ATVs—may be restricted to a limited section of the trail. The motorized symbol designates both ATV and motorcycles although only the hikes to Rainbow Lake and a section of the hike to Upper and Lower Twin and Hard Butte Lakes allow ATV use.

 Hikers   Mountain bikes

 Equestrians   Motorized

- **Family-Friendly Hike Symbol** – There may be a family-friendly hike symbol too. This symbol indicates that the initial segment of a hike (usually less than 2 miles one-way) is suitable—trail is not too steep and contains no dangerous creek fords—for smaller children (ages 2 to 6). In the general description of the hike, a short turnaround destination is often given within the first 2 miles from the trailhead.

TRAILHEAD ACCESS, SIGNS AND TRAIL CONDITION

Most of the trailheads in this guide are accessible with a passenger car. If a high-clearance vehicle is recommended, it is noted in the text. Driving distances were calculated with a vehicle tripmeter. Different vehicles will vary slightly in their measurements of distances.

Many of the trails are accessed along dirt roads. Early season hikers traveling in the high country may encounter downed trees, washouts and fallen rock debris before the roads are serviced and repaired. The roads may be impassable, and you should use sound judgement when encountering road hazards. You can call the Valley County Road Department at (208) 382-7195 for road information.

Below is a list of the major access roads and their normal opening dates. These dates are approximations and can differ from year to year. Winter and spring snow accumulations, spring temperatures, fallen timber, washouts and other factors affect a road's opening.

South Fork of the Salmon Road – Open all year. Use this road to access the Secesh River before Lick Creek Road opens over Lick Creek Summit, usually around the third week of June.

Paddy Flat Road – Usually opens by the 10th of June.

Lick Creek Road – Lower elevations are normally open by mid-June. The 6,730-foot Lick Creek Summit normally opens the third week of June. The road opens once the snow has melted. Abnormal snow accumulation can push this date back to early July.

Warren Wagon Road – The road is typically plowed over the 6,434-foot Secesh Summit once the snow is less than 2-feet deep. Expect this opening to occur the first week of June.

Brundage Mountain–Goose Lake Road – The road is open to the Brundage Mountain Resort all year. Access to the Goose Lake area and beyond is usually the first week of June. Trails near the Clayburn Trailhead are usually accessible by late June.

Sometimes roads wash out during spring

Although many trailheads and trail junctions are signed, be aware that some are not. Even signs that exist today are often destroyed by weather, fire or vandalism. Many trails utilize various forms of markings such as shaved-bark blazes, cairns or weathered signs. Some of the signs are difficult to read as they have faded and are often the same color as a tree. Since the signs are often nailed to trees, they may be camouflaged and difficult to see.

A few trails through dense timber will be marked by blazes. Although not considered environmentally friendly, these markings are carved into trees and have been used for more than one hundred years to identify routes. Blazes are normally carved near eye level and look like a lowercase "i." Sometimes in a hike's text, references will be made to blazed trees.

Other trails, often those through burned forest, washouts or through areas where trees do not exist, will use rock cairns to help identify a route. A cairn is a stack of rocks, usually shaped like a pyramid, that is obviously created by human hands. Cairns are also used to identify junctions and mountain summits.

Cairns often mark unsigned junctions

The majority of the trails in this guidebook are maintained by staff from the U.S. Forest Service and volunteers. A few trails, although clearly defined due to use, are not official trails and thus do not receive any trail maintenance. Some hikes are off-trail and signs of a route are nonexistent. You will likely encounter deadfall and confusing paths (often created by game) on these hikes. High-use trails receive annual maintenance while others fall on a rotation system.

Hiking Idaho encourages readers to support the Idaho Trails Association, which organizes volunteer trail stewardship projects for the construction and maintenance of Idaho trails. Visit their website at idahotrailsassociation.org for more information.

WILDERNESS CONSERVATION

Pristine and abundant wilderness is one of Idaho's most treasured resources. It cannot be overstated how fragile the environment is at higher elevations. Plants contend with a variety of stresses including cold nights, poor soil, hot days, short growing seasons and sometimes little moisture. On top of these natural challenges, the plant community has to contend with the added impact from hikers and backpackers. What the wilderness looks like tomorrow will depend on how well the people of today take care of it.

We can do many things to protect the land for future generations. Follow these simple rules when you are in the backcountry:

• If you pack something into the wilderness, pack it out.

- Minimize campfire impacts. Backcountry stoves are very efficient, and cooking with fire is unnecessary.

- Bury human waste in a 6- to 8-inch hole at least 100 feet from other campsites, trails and water sources. Carry your used toilet paper out in a plastic bag.

- Do not cut switchbacks. This causes erosion and additional trail maintenance is then required.

- Respect wildlife.

- Be sure to leave all items—plants, rocks, artifacts, animals—as you find them.

- Minimize campsites. When camping in an established campsite, cluster the tents close, and don't expand the compacted area by spreading out. When camping at a pristine site, remove all traces of your stay.

- Hike single-file in the middle of the trail, even when it's wet or muddy, to avoid trampling vegetation.

Trailheads are often only marked with their trail number

TRAIL ETIQUETTE

Horses, Mountain Bikers, Motorized Vehicles and Other Hikers

The general rule in the wilderness is that mountain bikers and motorized vehicles yield to hikers, and hikers yield to horses and pack animals. When approached by horses or pack animals, you should get off the trail and sit or stand quietly until the animal has passed. Horseback riders will often let hikers know the habits of their animals.

Bikers are supposed to yield to hikers, but it makes more sense for a hiker to yield. When approached by a bike, especially on a steep hill, it is much easier for a hiker to step aside.

Motorized users should yield to all other users. It is unlikely you will encounter any motorized users, except where noted in the hike description.

Hiking with Dogs

- When hiking with pets, they must be under voice control or physical restraint at all times. This includes preventing your dog from pursuing wildlife and barking at other trail users. Carry a leash, and be prepared to use it when necessary. Make sure you clean up after your dog the same way you would with human waste: bury it in a hole that is 6- to 8-inches deep and 100 feet away from all campsites, water and trails.

HIKING SAFETY

"In nature, there are neither rewards or punishments; there are consequences."

~Robert Greene Ingersoll

Although hiking is relatively safe, the very nature of being outdoors is always potentially hazardous. Your greatest dangers in the backcountry are falling, drowning and getting lost. Here are a few tips to help you explore the wilderness safely.

Falls – The good news is you can usually control the situation by deciding whether you want to expose yourself to a potential fall. Be careful and use sound judgement when traversing a ledge or climbing a rock. Remember, too, it's a lot easier to climb up than down. Often a fall is not what kills you but the consequences of the fall. If you are alone, a short drop-off in which you stumble can result in a broken leg, and if you are unable to walk back to the trailhead, your chances of survival are questionable. Trekking poles can be very helpful in maintaining your balance in hazardous conditions.

Step over rocks, downed trees and roots rather than on them. These surfaces are often very slippery, and it is easy to trip or twist an ankle, especially on slopes. Although a fall happens quickly, think ahead about what you will do if you start to fall or slide. When falling, try not to land on your hands, elbow or knees. If you can land on the side of your body, it is much safer.

Dead trees make excellent bridges over creeks

If you start to slide, you can sometimes break the slide with a trekking pole or by hanging on to a tree.

Creek and River Crossings – Use good judgement when fording creeks and rivers. Don't underestimate the power of moving water, especially during spring runoff in May and June. As a rule, don't cross fast-moving water that is more than knee deep. Crossing waterways with water levels above mid-thigh gives the current a large surface area to push against. When hiking with children be very careful around moving water and teach children the dangers of high-water levels.

Tips for Safely Fording Creeks and Rivers:

• When approaching a ford, study the creek both upstream and downstream. The water will usually be the shallowest where the creek is widest.

• Walk slowly across the creek and firmly plant each foot before lifting the other.

• Consider keeping your boots on to help support your ankles and to maintain firm footing.

• Before crossing, investigate any deadfall that may bridge the creek. Remember that trees can be very slippery, especially in early morning when they could be covered with a thin layer of ice.

• If a creek has a sandy bottom, consider fording the creek in a pair of sandals. This will keep your boots dry.

• Trekking poles can provide additional stability when fording a creek.

• Make sure to place your camera and other items in watertight containers before crossing fast-moving water.

Hypothermia – Anyone who hikes should be aware of hypothermia—what it is and how to prevent it. In simple terms, hypothermia is the lowering of body temperature caused by loss of heat through the skin faster than the body is producing heat. Initial symptoms include shivering and the possible loss of physical and mental abilities. Severe hypothermia can lead to death.

Temperatures do not have to be below freezing for hypothermia to set in. Most cases occur between outside temperatures of 30°F and 50°F. Be especially cautious in windy and wet conditions since body heat is wicked away by wind and water.

The good news is, hypothermia is easy to prevent, and clothing is your best defense. Think layers—wool and synthetic clothing are best. Bring a light windbreaker, waterproof shell, gloves, a hat and wool socks. Cotton is a terrible choice because when it gets wet it can increase conductive heat loss by a factor of five.

Heatstroke/Heat Exhaustion – At the other extreme, hot weather and strenuous physical activity can cause serious heat-related problems. Heatstroke occurs when body temperature reaches 104°F or higher. Heat exhaustion is a milder heat-related syndrome that may include heavy sweating and a rapid pulse. Left untreated, heat exhaustion can lead to heatstroke, a life-threatening condition.

Fortunately, both heatstroke and heat exhaustion are preventable. Drink plenty of liquids, and wear a hat. Avoid exposed trails during the early afternoon, which is usually the hottest part of the day. If someone in your party develops

Trail signs are often faded

symptoms of heat exhaustion, have the person sit in shade or a cool place and drink plenty of fluids.

Lightning – Thunderstorms occasionally pass through the high mountains of Idaho. Storms can build quickly and hikers should constantly observe weather conditions. If lightning threatens, make it a priority to get below the treeline. Keep out of meadows and away from lone trees or rocks. If you are caught in an exposed location, discard metal objects and squat on two feet, keeping as low to the ground as possible. Stay at least 20 feet away from others in your group so one strike does not incapacitate your entire group.

Altitude Sickness – Altitude sickness is a condition caused by exposure to low air pressure, usually outdoors at high altitudes. Symptoms include headache, vomiting, fatigue, light-headedness and shortness of breath. Altitude sickness can progress to more serious conditions such as high-altitude pulmonary edema or high-altitude cerebral edema that can prove fatal. Rarely do these conditions occur below 9,000 feet.

People have different susceptibilities to altitude sickness. A few people show symptoms at elevations below 7,000 feet, but most people can hike up to 8,000 feet without problems. To help prevent altitude sickness, drink plenty of water, and do not drink alcohol before attempting a high-altitude hike. If symptoms of altitude sickness occur, descend to lower altitudes. Symptoms are usually temporary and will decrease promptly by returning to a lower elevation.

The Sun – One of the most underrated dangers in the wilderness is the effects of the sun. Prolonged exposure to the sun can cause sunburn, snow blindness, heat exhaustion, heat stroke and dehydration. Extended exposure can cause skin cancer and permanent damage to the skin. Remember, the sun's effects are more pronounced at higher altitudes. Key pieces of gear that every hiker should have include:

- A lightweight, long-sleeve shirt to provide UV protection.
- A wide-brimmed hat to protect your ears and face.
- Sunscreen with an SPF rating of at least 15.
- Polarized sunglasses to protect the eyes from UV rays.
- Water. Dehydration can easily sneak up on you while hiking. Do not underestimate your water requirements. A good rule of thumb is to carry 2 quarts of water per person.

Many packs today include a water carrier. Remember, water is heavy and 1 gallon weighs more than 8 pounds. A flexible option is to carry a water filter. There are many types of water treatment systems today. Most are relatively inexpensive, lightweight and easy to use.

Blisters – When hiking, your feet should be one of your top priorities. There is nothing like painful blisters to ruin a hiking trip. Avoid blisters by taking these precautions:

- Break in new hiking boots or shoes before you hike.
- Wear lightweight, breathable shoes.
- Wear quality socks that provide both cushion and breathability.
- Carry moleskin, and use it as soon as you feel a hot spot.

Your Ego – The vast majority of outdoor mishaps are preventable. Do not overestimate your capability whether it is fording a creek, traversing an exposed ridge, hiking off-trail or hiking long distances. The wilderness is not the place to make errors in judgement. Remember, a GPS, smartphone or high-tech watch may be the latest technological gadget, but they cannot stop you from drowning or falling and can certainly give you a false sense of security while in the backcountry. Do not underestimate the weather either—it often snows in Idaho's high mountains in summer.

Be Prepared – You should always have a first-aid kit and proper clothing. Let someone know where you are going—very important if you are hiking alone— and when you expect to return. Make sure you are in good physical health. Knowledge is your best ally when in the wilderness.

WEATHER

"There is no such thing as bad weather, only inappropriate clothing."

~Sir Ranulph Fiennes

Hikes in this book range from elevations near 2,200 feet along the Rapid River to 8,700 feet on Rice Peak near Stolle Meadows. Due to this extreme elevation range, weather conditions and accessibility are varied. A few low-elevation trails (below 5,000 feet) are accessible in April and May, but the majority of trails are

Deadfall is common on some trails in early season

at their prime in late June through early October. The Rapid River is usually accessible all year.

- **Late May and June** – In late May, a few trails may be snow free depending on the prior winter's snowfall. By the end of June, most of the trails up to 8,000 feet are snow free. High water is one of the major obstacles to travel as streams and creeks may be four times higher and wider than normal as winter snow melts in the high country. The number of people on the trails is less than later in the season. In mid-to-late May, some wildflowers begin to bloom at lower elevations, and by June flora begins to green. Average highs near McCall are around 70°F with average lows near 40°F.

- **July and August** – Mosquitoes are usually at their worst the first two weeks of July. These are the warmest months of the year—average highs are around 80°F—and the moderate temperatures are favored by most people. Consequently, the trails usually see their greatest use during this time. Wildflowers are typically at their best in July. River and creek flows begin to normalize and by mid-August, daily temperatures begin falling and mosquitoes are typically gone.

- **September and October** – By September most wildflowers have expired, but other flora begins to change to bright fall colors giving another beauty to the landscape. Aspen trees typically reach peak color the last two weeks of September. The weather is generally stable with highs near 70°F, lows a little above freezing. Creeks are at their lowest levels, and most of the intermittent streams will be dry. Hikers will have thinned dramatically, and you will have many of the trails to yourself. As October progresses, the chance of unpleasant and cold weather increases. Some trails, depending on their location, will see increased use due to hunting. If you hike during hunting season, make sure to wear bright clothing.

RECENT FIRES IN THE AREA

Over the past twenty-five years, the forests near McCall have experienced several significant fire years. In 1994, lightning caused several very large forest fires. The fires came to be known as the Corral-Blackwell Complex Fire and burned nearly 150,000 acres. Areas that are still recovering from these hot fires include Box and Sisters Lakes; Victor Creek; hikes near Upper Payette and Granite Lakes; Pearl and Brush Lakes; and Upper Hazard, Hidden and Hard Creek Lakes.

Fires often alter terrain and destroy signage

Another serious fire year occurred in 2000, when nearly 1,600 fires burned over 1.3 million acres throughout Idaho. Over 300,000 acres burned in the Payette National Forest. The largest was the Diamond Complex Fire. It started east of Big Creek and extended to the Middle Fork of the Salmon River. Closer to McCall, the 65,000-acre Burgdorf Fire burned.

Some of the most destructive fires ignited in 2007, damaging or destroying several backcountry cabins. The Cascade Complex and East Zone Complex Fires combined to burn nearly 600,000 acres. Damage from the Cascade Fire is noticable along Warm Lake Road, near Warm Lake, and most of the hikes near Stolle Meadows, especially Lodgepole Creek. The East Lake Fire burned sections of forest along the Secesh River.

The last significant fire to affect trails in the McCall area occurred in 2015 when the nearly 100,000-acre Tepee Springs Fire burned. That fire started on the west side of the Salmon River Mountains, north of Goose Lake, near Hazard Creek. The fire progressed east up the drainage and veered north getting hotter as it expanded. Some of the forest near Grass Mountain Lakes burned, but most of the burn is mosiac. Fire damage is more significant near Rainbow, Upper and Lower Twin and Hard Butte Lakes.

Although a fire might be considered destructive, it is actually beneficial to a forest's ecosystem. For example, pine needles, tree branches and fallen deadwood are consumed by fire. By removing this material, more sunlight reaches the forest floor allowing grass, flowers and young trees to grow, which creates habitat diversity. Some trees, such as the lodgepole pine, which occupies more than two million acres in Idaho, require the heat from a fire to release their seeds.

It can take many years for conifers in the forest to regenerate after high-intensity fires, and you will witness the rebirth of the forest ecosystem as you hike through burned areas. Fires greatly accelerate the return of minerals to the soil and nourish new plant growth. One of the stunning phenomena of nature's recovery from fire is the colorful display of wildflowers in late spring and early summer. Wildflowers are one of the first species to recolonize an area after a significant wildfire.

Caution is advised, especially during windy conditions, when hiking in areas of standing snags as they will eventually fall, sometimes with no warning. Be particularly wary near lodgepole pine as it has a shallow root system. If you wander off-trail in burn areas, be aware of stump holes in the ground from trees and root systems burned by fire.

THE LAND

Central Idaho possesses the most intricate geography in the state. This landscape is a result of Idaho's batholiths, which were created over seventy million years ago. Batholiths are masses of intrusive igneous rock that crystallize when magma solidifies below the crust of the earth. Over time, the batholith becomes visible due to erosion, receding glaciers and volcanic eruptions.

The central Idaho batholith stretches 200 miles long and nearly 75 miles wide. The Sawtooth, Bitterroot, Pioneer, Boulder, Clearwater and Boise mountain ranges are located within the batholith. Some of the ranges, such as the Sawtooths and Pioneers, highlight jagged summits and snow-covered apexes and exhibit the best of the Rockies. For those who have hiked and backpacked over its endless ridges and deep canyons, central Idaho is a thrilling and unique landscape.

Some lakes are well-signed

One of the largest ranges in the central batholith is the massive Salmon River Mountains, nearly 8,900 square miles of convoluted mountains, deep canyons and clear rivers. This range is generally considered the mountains extending north from Boise to the Salmon River in central Idaho. The eastern boundary is defined by the Salmon River as it meanders from Stanley to Challis to Salmon. The western border is the North Fork of the Payette River and the Little Salmon River. A vast section of the Salmon River Mountains is contained in the 2.3 million-acre Payette National Forest.

The Salmon River Mountain range is characterized by deep canyons and major mountain networks with abrupt elevation changes of nearly 5,000 feet. The highest point is the 10,442-foot White Mountain West near Challis, and the lowest is 1,400 feet near Riggins. Most of the hikes in the book are in several subranges of the Salmon River Mountains, including the Lick Creek and North Fork Ranges and the Grass Mountains.

There are hikes in the West Mountains, located to the west of Cascade and Donnelly. This relatively small range extends 75 miles north from Horseshoe Bend to New Meadows and is 15 miles wide. Its features include dense forests, large meadows, granite ridges and a high crest above 7,000 feet. This area, including the hikes south of Warm Lake Road, is managed by the 2.6 million-acre Boise National Forest.

WILDLIFE

Wildlife is abundant in central Idaho, and over three hundred different species of wildlife call the Payette National Forest home. There is a good chance you will see some on your hikes. Birds are the most common wildlife, and you will likely see a few. Look for raptors such as eagle, osprey, Cooper's hawk, owl, American kestrel and northern harriers in the deep canyons. Game birds include

Look for moose near Warm Lake

grouse, chukar, quail and turkey. Many lakes in the region provide outstanding habitat for waterfowl and shore birds and include loon, Canadian geese, ducks, grebes, Kingfisher, American avocet and the western sandpiper.

Your best opportunities to see larger animals are in early morning and late evening. Large mammals include moose, elk, deer, black bear, mountain lion, gray wolves, bobcats and the rare wolverine. Warm and Loon Lakes are excellent habitats to see moose. There are many smaller mammals too, including badgers, pine marten, beaver, otter, fox and squirrel. When you are near talus fields at higher elevations, listen for pikas and marmots. Both animals emit a shrill whistling call to alert other members of the colony of possible danger.

The likelihood of encountering a mountain lion or bear is rare. If you do run into a black bear, don't run. Avoid eye contact and slowly leave the area.

If you come upon a mountain lion, stay calm and speak in a firm voice so that the animal will know that you are not its regular prey. Appear larger than you are by raising your arms above your head. Back away slowly and ensure you give the animal a way to escape.

Don't feed the chipmunks

FLORA

The predominant tree in the area is the medium-sized lodgepole pine, forming pure stands over significant acreage. At lower elevations, look for the huge Douglas fir and ponderosa pine trees. Both can grow to heights near 200 feet and are found at elevations between 3,500 and 6,000 feet. Engelmann spruce, subalpine and grand fir and limber pine dominate at higher elevations. Quaking aspen, which is highly intolerant of shade, is often found on south-facing slopes in pure stands. The tree is one of the first to colonize an area after forest fires.

Woodland star

Look for whitebark pine at elevations above 7,500 feet. Another common tree in the McCall and Cascade area is the tamarack—a deciduous conifer. In fall, the tree's needles turn bright gold before falling to the ground.

From late spring to early fall, depending on your location and elevation, you will also find many wildflowers blooming. Wildflower communities are determined by elevation, soil type, rainfall, winds and northern or southern exposure. To make the next generation, wildflowers use pollination which is the transfer of pollen grains or male spores from the male anther of a flower to the female stigma. These pollen grains contain the genetic information to produce another plant. There are several ways to transfer the pollen grains including wind, animals, self-pollination and water. It is estimated that insect pollination accounts for about eighty-five percent of all flowering plants.

Look for wildflowers on sunny slopes, along creeks and streams, and on the floor of moist meadows. Some flowers, such as lupine, Indian paintbrush, penstemon and arrowleaf balsamroot, are common and easy to identify. Others are rare, including Macfarlane's four-o'clock and nodding saxifrage and may only exist in specific areas. Many shrubs—woody plants that are multi-stemmed—thrive on open hillsides and along riverbanks. Look for green alder, gooseberry, snowberry, elderberry, choke cherry, mountain ash and spirea.

There are some exquisite edible treats to be found in the forest including huckleberries, grouseberry and morel mushrooms. Mountain huckleberries are delicious bluish-black fruits similar in size to a blueberry that typically ripen in August. This deciduous shrub thrives in the McCall and Cascade area and is especially prevalent in old-burn areas. Grouseberry is a dwarf shrub that is common on the forest floor of coniferous forests. It produces a tasty, tiny berry that is eaten by many birds and small mammals. Grouse eat all parts of the plant, hence the name grouseberry. Morel mushrooms are an edible fungi found in the mountains in late April, May and early June, depending on elevation. A couple of species look like morels but are poisonous. Get a good mushroom book or better yet, take a friend familiar with mushroom foraging.

HUMAN HISTORY

The land around McCall was first inhabited by several Native American Indian tribes including the Shoshone, the Sheep Eaters (also known as Mountain Shoshone) and the Nez Perce. They primarily occupied the surrounding valleys and canyons during the warm summer months. The Sheep Eaters were known for inhabiting the higher country, believing that this placed them closer to a higher order of spirits called Sky People.

In 1818, a young trader, Francois Payette, and several other pioneers entered the Payette River Valley. He began trapping furs on the many lush streams and ventured as far as the Tetons in Wyoming. Payette remained in the Long Valley area until the 1840s when he returned to his homeland in Montreal, Canada. It is rumored that upon his death, his burial was on a bluff overlooking the Snake River. Today, Francios Payette's moniker is widespread throughout the area with the Payette National Forest, Payette and Upper Payette Lakes, the city of Payette, Payette Peak and Payette County bearing his name.

McCall and Cascade are located in Valley County on the opposite ends of Long Valley, which extends over 30 miles. The valley is bordered to the east by the Salmon River Mountains and the west by the West Mountains. This lush valley was formerly pasture grazing grounds for livestock for those that lived in Boise. Today, Valley County's population is close to ten thousand residents. It is a tourist destination, especially for outdoor enthusiasts in southwest Idaho.

The city of McCall was named after Tom and Louisa McCall, early homesteaders who traded a team of horses for homesteader rights to 160 acres. The family,

Payette Lake view from the Narrows overlook

which had five children, established a school, post office, saloon and hotel. Thus began the city of McCall. Today, tourism is a major foundation for the city's livelihood. The town is near Brundage Mountain Resort, which boasts the best snow in Idaho with 350 inches per year.

McCall is also home to the Winter Carnival, which began in 1924 and fizzled out by 1941. However, the carnival was revived in 1965 and continues to flourish today. Every winter, usually in late January and early February, the carnival hosts a snow sculpting championship, a snowman building contest, a Mardi Gras Parade and winter fireworks.

I hope you find this book both inspiring and a good reference. So, lace up your boots, open your mind and hit the trail. Most of all, enjoy the journey!

Scott Marchant

Twin Lakes (hike 49)

Cougar Rock (hike 1)

Vulcan Hot Springs (hike 2)

Pond at saddle on Lodgepole Creek hike (hike 3)

Monumental Peak (hike 5)

Pond along the route to Curtis Lake (hike 7)

Lost Lake (hike 10)

Louie Lake (hike 17 and 18)

Unnamed lake near Blackmare Lake (hike 15)

Box Lake (hike 27)

Summit Lake in late September (hike 29)

Secesh River (hike 31)

Anderson Lake (hike 21 and 25)

Pearl Lake (hike 32)

Crystal Lake (hike 26)

Granite Mountain Lookout (hike 50)

Hard Creek Lake (hike 53 and 54)

Hard Butte Lake (hike 55)

Upper Hazard Lake (hike 54)

One of the three Lava Butte Lakes and fireweed (hike 58 and 59)

View down to Josephine Lake after an early fall snowstorm (hike 40)

Small pond above Josephine Lake (hike 41)

North Twenty Mile Lake (hike 35)

Horton Lake in early October (hike 47)

Buck Lake after an October snow (hike 64)

Unnamed lake off-trail from the Pete Creek hike (hike 44)

First bridge over the Rapid River (hike 65)

AUTHOR'S FAVORITE HIKES

To help you find your ideal hike, the best hikes in eight categories are listed below. Hikes are in alphabetical order with their corresponding hike number.

Best Early Season Hikes

- ⑥① Cow Camp Trail to Squirrel Creek
- ⑥⓪ Goose Creek Falls from Last Chance Campground
- ⑥③ Hazard Creek Falls
- ②③ Lily Marsh Loop
- ②② Meadow Marsh Loop
- ⑥⑤ Rapid River and the West Fork of the Rapid River
- ③① Secesh River Trail
- ❷ Vulcan Hot Springs and Tyndall Creek

Best Family Friendly Hikes

- ❽ Blue Lake
- ③⑨ Deep Lake
- ③⓪ Duck Lake
- ④⑥ Fisher Creek
- ④① Josephine Lake
- ②③ Lily Marsh Loop
- ②② Meadow Marsh Loop
- ⑬ North Fork of Kennally Creek
- ③② Pearl Lake
- ②⑨ Summit Lake
- ④⑨ Twin Lakes
- ⑤④ Upper Hazard Lake

Best Wildflower Hikes

- ⑤⑧ Big Dave Trailhead to Lava Butte Lakes
- ⑰ Boulder and Louie Lakes Loop
- ②⑦ Box and Sisters Lakes
- ⑤⑨ Clayburn Trailhead to Lava Butte Lakes
- ②④ East Fork of Lake Fork Creek
- ⑤⓪ Granite Mountain Lookout
- ⑥⑤ Rapid River and the West Fork of the Rapid River
- ❻ Sixteen-to-One Creek
- ②⑨ Summit Lake
- ⑤④ Upper Hazard Lake

Best Hikes Along Creeks and Rivers

- ②⑦ Box and Sisters Lakes
- ②④ East Fork of Lake Fork Creek
- ④⑥ Fisher Creek
- ⑥③ Hazard Creek Falls
- ③⑦ Jackson Creek
- ⑫ Rapid Creek to Boulder Lake
- ⑥⑤ Rapid River and the West Fork of the Rapid River
- ③① Secesh River Trail

Best View Hikes

- **58** Big Dave Trailhead to Lava Butte Lakes
- **14** Blackmare Summit
- **64** Buck Lake
- **40** Cloochman Saddle to Squaw Point
- **9** Granite Peak to Tripod Lookout
- **56** Hard Butte Peak
- **18** Louie Lake and Jughandle Mountain
- **5** Monumental Peak
- **16** Needles Summit
- **62** Pollock Mountain Lookout
- **4** Rice Peak Loop
- **28** Snowslide Lake, Snowslide Summit and Maki Lake
- **33** Upper Payette Lake Loop

Best Fall Hikes

- **17** Boulder and Louie Lakes Loop
- **40** Cloochman Saddle to Squaw Point
- **50** Granite Mountain Lookout
- **9** Granite Peak to Tripod Lookout
- **10** Lost, Hidden and Shirts Lakes
- **18** Louie Lake and Jughandle Mountain
- **65** Rapid River and the West Fork of the Rapid River
- **31** Secesh River Trail

Best Solitude Hikes

- **11** Arling Trail
- **64** Buck Lake
- **59** Clayburn Trailhead to Lava Butte Lakes
- **61** Cow Camp Trail to Squirrel Creek
- **47** Ellis and Horton Lakes
- **9** Granite Peak to Tripod Lookout
- **37** Jackson Creek
- **42** Lake Rock Lake
- **3** Lodgepole Creek
- **5** Monumental Peak
- **38** Squaw Meadows to French Creek
- **34** Upper Payette Lake to Granite Lake

Best Backpack Destinations

- **27** Box and Sisters Lakes
- **59** Clayburn Trailhead to Lava Butte Lakes
- **26** Crystal Lake and Fall Creek Saddle
- **7** Curtis Lake
- **24** East Fork of Lake Fork Creek
- **47** Ellis and Horton Lakes
- **46** Fisher Creek
- **53** Hidden and Hard Creek Lakes
- **10** Lost, Hidden and Shirts Lakes
- **20** Rapid, Vics and Fogg Lakes and Kennally Summit
- **35** Twenty Mile Lakes
- **55** Upper and Lower Twin & Hard Butte Lakes

*A vigorous five-mile walk will do more good
for an unhappy but otherwise healthy adult
than all of the medicine and psychology in the world.*

Paul Dudley White

Cougar Rock

Distance: 2.6 miles out-and-back

Total Elevation Gain: 1,250 feet

Difficulty: Strenuous

Elevation Range: 5,750 to 7,000 feet

Topographic Map: Rice Peak

Time: 1.5 to 2 hours

Season: Mid-June through mid-October

Water Availability: None

Cautionary Advice: A high-clearance vehicle is recommended for the 1.1 mile drive on FR 483A.

Information: Boise National Forest, Cascade Ranger District (208) 382-7400

Pit Latrine: No

Coordinates

Trailhead:

N 44° 35.594'
W 115° 42.267'

Cougar Rock:

N 44° 35.913'
W 115° 42.925'

Cougar Rock

Jutting 200 feet from base to summit, Cougar Rock is one impressive piece of granite. The large outcropping sits close to 7,000 feet and is clearly visible when viewed from Stolle Meadows, nearly 2,000 feet below. This remote trail takes you to the base of Cougar Rock and continues another quarter-mile to a broad ridge near the rock, which provides stellar views of the area.

The hike to Cougar Rock is very steep and climbs a wooded ridge dotted with outcroppings and large boulders. There are only a few switchbacks, so plan on a rigorous hike. After a steep rise of 1,100 feet in about a mile, the trail comes within a few feet of Cougar Rock. It is interesting to explore the surrounding area as there are many impressive outcroppings.

On the drive to the trailhead, FR 483 passes a footbridge extending over a marshy area near the South Fork of the Salmon River. In August, chinook salmon spawn in the crystal-clear waters.

Trailhead Directions

From Cascade, drive 0.9 mile north on ID 55, and turn right onto paved Warm Lake Road. Reset your tripmeter and drive east 22.7 miles to a sign on the right side of the road "Stolle Meadows 6." Reset your tripmeter to 0 and turn south (right) onto the well-graded Stolle Meadows Road (FR 474). Drive 4.7 miles. Turn right onto FR 483, crossing a bridge near the salmon overlook, and drive 0.3 mile. Turn left onto FR 483A, and drive 1.1 miles to the signed trailhead. FR 483A is narrow and infrequently maintained. A high-clearance vehicle is recommended. If there is deadfall on the road or if you have a passenger car, you can park at the junction of FR 483 and FR 483A. You will then need to hike the road (it is a pleasant walk of 1.1 miles) and add 2.2 miles and 400 feet of gain to the hike.

The Hike

From the signed trailhead, immediately ascend in open forest. At 0.2 mile, turn through the first of four switchbacks with the faint sound of an unnamed creek heard through the woods. If you look northwest up the steep mountainside, you see Cougar Rock. The trail crests a knoll at 0.4 mile, turns left and starts a steep climb again with the help of five switchbacks. After the last switchback you are greeted with fantastic over-the-shoulder vistas down to the two-mile long Stolle Meadows. At 1.0 mile, reach the base of Cougar Rock. In the summer of 2015, the 1,200-acre Cougar Fire burned in the area, so expect deadfall.

Cougar Rock

For amazing views of this rugged terrain, follow the trail past Cougar Rock. The trail is not too steep and ascends through forest. Continue past several granite outcroppings, and turn north (right) past the last rock at 1.2 miles. Hike off-trail about 400 feet to a large outcropping (see map). The views are very good looking northwest, and many wildflowers grow in the area in late June and early July. If you are comfortable hiking off-trail, you can hike south along the wide ridge (see map) through open forest where you will discover more rock formations.

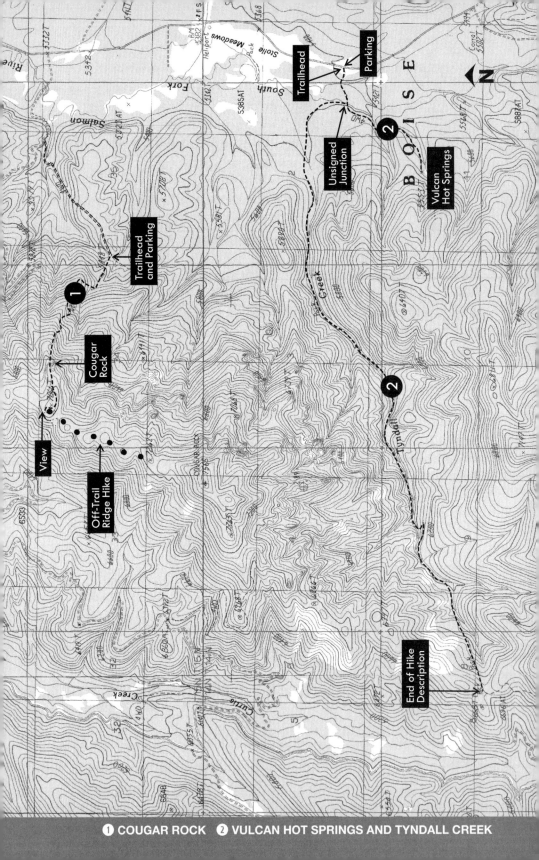

❶ COUGAR ROCK ❷ VULCAN HOT SPRINGS AND TYNDALL CREEK

Vulcan Hot Springs and Tyndall Creek

Coordinates

Trailhead:

N 44° 34.451'
W 115° 41.013'

Vulcan Hot Springs:

N 44° 34.037'
W 115° 41.714'

**Tyndall Creek
Turnaround:**

N 44° 33.725'
W 115° 45.198'

Distance: 2.2 miles out-and-back (Vulcan Hot Springs), 8.8 miles out-and-back (Tyndall Creek)

Total Elevation Gain: 150 feet (Vulcan Hot Springs) 1,300 feet (Tyndall Creek)

Difficulty: Easy (Vulcan Hot Springs) Strenuous (Tyndall Creek)

Elevation Range: 5,400 to 6,550 feet

Topographic Map: Rice Peak

Time: 1 to 5 hours

Season: Mid-May through October

Water Availability: South Fork of the Salmon River, Vulcan Creek, Tyndall Creek

Cautionary Advice: Use extreme caution with pets and children near the hot springs as temperatures can reach 190°F. Contact with water this hot can result in serious injury or death.

Information: Boise National Forest, Cascade Ranger District (208) 382-7400

Pit Latrine: Yes

Vulcan Hot Springs and Tyndall Creek

In Roman mythology, Vulcan is the god of fire. Whoever named this spring got it right for the springs can reach temperatures over 190°F. This is scorching water and obviously too hot to sit in unless you are part Vulcan. Of course, the creek below the springs allows for cooler temperatures and soakers are able to make a more inviting pool. Vulcan's greek counterpart, Hephaestus, would also be an appropriate name but many folks would be hard pressed to pronounce, spell or remember this designation for their hot spring comrades.

Although a short hike, it is an engaging jaunt. The trail passes through Stolle Meadows—a wildflower odyssey in late spring—crosses the South Fork of the Salmon River on a bridge and continues through partially burned forest to the bubbling Vulcan Hot Springs. This area burned badly in 2007, and makes for a contrasting landscape—colorful wildflowers, bright green foilage and gray snags surrounding a foggy mist rising from

Large soaking pool near Vulcan Hot Springs

the springs. In the creek, below the springs, visitors have made a couple of soaking pools.

One unique feature of Vulcan Hot Springs—in addition to the extreme water temperatures—is the springs themselves. There is enough underground pressure here that steaming water shoots up like tiny fountains through a score of fissures. Once above ground, the water cascades through narrow channels and over rock to form Vulcan Creek. Even if soaking in hot springs isn't your idea of tranquility, this geological spectacle is not to be missed.

Another option on this hike is to visit the Tyndall Creek drainage. The main trail forks at 0.3 mile, and from here, you can cross Stolle Meadows for about a mile and continue west along Tyndall Creek. The canyon is heavily forested, and there are good opportunities to see elk, deer, black bear and raptors. The low elevation of the hike is a good choice for early season hikers and is usually accessible by early June.

Trailhead Directions

From Cascade, drive north 0.9 mile on ID 55, and turn right onto paved Warm Lake Road. Continue another 22.7 miles to a sign on the right hand side of the road "Stolle Meadows 6." Turn right onto the well-graded Stolle Meadows Road (FR 474), and drive 6.4 miles to a large parking area on the left hand side of the road. The trailhead is located on the opposite side of the road. Dispersed camping is available in forest a few miles past the trailhead.

The Hike

Next to the road are a couple of interpretive signs highlighting a few of the geological features of hot springs and some of the plants and animals that exist in this unique habitat. The trail departs across a grassy meadow and crosses a bridge over Rice Creek. The route continues through an area with standing water in June, crosses another bridge over the South Fork of the Salmon River and arrives at a junction at 0.3 mile.

To visit Vulcan Hot Springs, turn left at the junction and continue through a forest of young trees. At 0.6 mile, the trail nears Vulcan Creek, crosses a bridge over a small creek and gains elevation to the steaming hot springs at 1.1 miles. There are several pools below the springs. Remember that these springs are extremely hot, and children and pets should be under close supervision. In late May and early June, look for several yellow composites, camas and Indian paintbrush surrounding the springs.

At the 0.3 mile junction, turn north (right) to see Tyndall Creek. Cross a bridge over a tiny creek and then another bridge over the South Fork of the

Vulcan Hot Springs

Salmon River. The trail continues through burned snags where wildflowers are prolific in mid-to-late June. At 1.2 miles (from the trailhead), the trail enters the canyon and starts rising near Tyndall Creek. At 1.9 miles, the canyon narrows, crosses a rocky knoll and descends to a bridge over Tyndall Creek. Beyond the bridge, the trail's grade is steep and offers good views across the canyon of impressive rock spires.

Cross another bridge over Tyndall Creek at 3.6 miles. The trail now rises another 450 feet and passes a few granite outcroppings. At 4.4 miles, the trail levels on an open hillside. While this is the end of the hike description, the trail continues about another mile to Railroad Pass on FR 409.

3 Lodgepole Creek

Distance: 7.6 miles out-and-back

Total Elevation Gain: 2,100 feet

Difficulty: Very Strenuous

Elevation Range: 5,800 to 7,800 feet

Topographic Map: Rice Peak, Tyndall Meadows

Time: 3 to 5 hours

Season: Late June through mid-October

Water Availability: Lodgepole Creek, pond

Cautionary Advice: The trail travels through extensive burn.

Information: Boise National Forest, Cascade Ranger District (208) 382-7400

Pit Latrine: No

Coordinates

Trailhead:

N 44° 34.966'
W 115° 38.965'

7,750-Foot Saddle:

N 44° 34.373'
W 115° 35.882'

Lodgepole Creek

A hike in the rugged terrain near Lodgepole Creek is eerily pristine and lonely yet has an undeniable charm—a fascinating journey through a recovering landscape of burned forest from the huge 2007 Cascade Complex fires. Other than near the trailhead and at the summit, it will be difficult to find a green tree. However, don't let this tarnish your view of the hike: abundant wildflowers, stunning views and a remarkable sense of isolation beckon the adventuresome hiker.

The trail starts on an old roadbed lined with a few trees but transitions to a singletrack within a half-mile. The steep ridges are covered with a sea of standing gray snags, although colorful wildflowers and bright green flora make an interesting contrast. After a ford of Lodgepole Creek at 1.5 miles—a good destination for a shorter outing—the hike turns into a demanding assault up a rugged canyon hemmed by steep granite ridges. As you ascend you get to see the effects of fire on hillside erosion.

The hike ends at a 7,750-foot saddle where a small pond invites an isolated backpack trip. The open forest is healthy here, and the rolling topography invites off-trail exploration. Due to the lack of shade, look to get an early start on a hot day or think early fall when the flora turns bright colors and the temperatures are cooler. Wildflower enthusiasts should look to hike in late June or early July.

Trailhead Directions

From Cascade, drive north 0.9 mile on ID 55, and turn right onto paved Warm Lake Road. Reset your tripmeter, and proceed 22.7 miles to a sign on the right side of the road "Stolle Meadows 6." Turn right onto the well-graded Stolle Meadows Road (FR 474), and continue 4.9 miles to FR 472. Turn left, and proceed 1.9 miles to its end and trailhead. There is parking for several vehicles and a couple of dispersed campsites on FR 472.

The Hike

From the signed trailhead, head east fording a couple of small creeks. At 0.5 mile, after a gain of only 100 feet, the road ends, and the singletrack trail starts. The trail rises through snowbrush, aspen and gray snags. At 0.8 mile, look south for a long stretch of granite boulders—a result of recent erosion—that parallel Lodgepole Creek. As you climb higher, the views looking back down the canyon are impressive.

At 1.5 miles, ford Lodgepole Creek. Several granite boulders line the creek and make for a perfect destination for a shorter hike. Beyond the creek ford, the trail rises 400 feet through six switchbacks and then up a steep gully to where it levels at 1.9 miles. After a short respite, continue ascending and reach a section of trail where there is a log jam. The trail weaves through the logs and makes another ford of Lodgepole Creek at 2.5 miles. Beyond the creek ford, gain another 200 feet through several switchbacks. The trail levels again at 2.8 miles. and makes a gentle descent to a couple of streams in a sandy ravine. There is a large grove of aspen nearby, and the setting is scenic for a remote backpack trip.

From the sandy ravine, the trail steepens again and rises 450 feet over the next three-quarters of a mile to where it levels near a small, shallow pond and flat summit. Look for a trail-user marker near the south side of the pond. The forest is dense, and the setting is a stark contrast from the terrain you just walked through. There are good campsites on the east side of the pond. From the summit, the trail descends into the Boulder Creek drainage and finally to FR 579 and Johnson Creek.

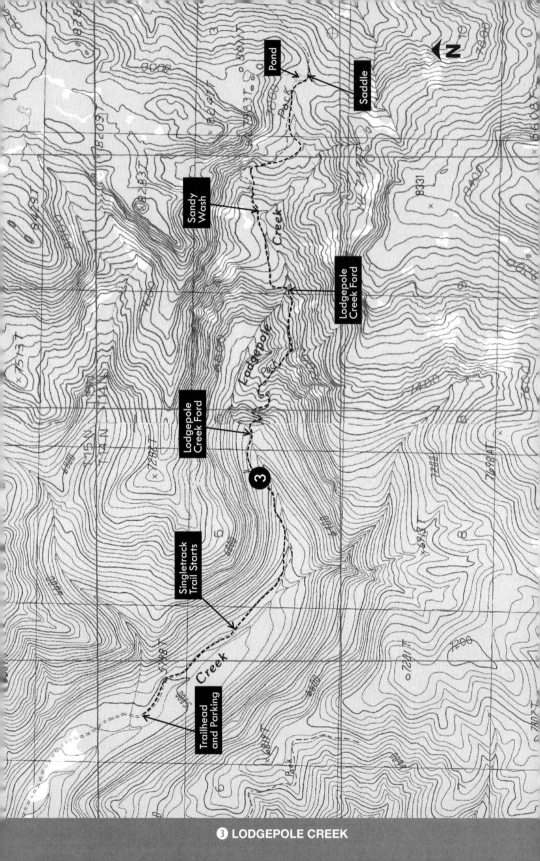

Rice Peak Loop

Distance: 9.8 miles loop

Total Elevation Gain: 2,500 feet

Difficulty: Strenuous

Elevation Range: 6,300 to 8,700 feet

Topographic Map: Rice Peak, Tyndall Meadows

Time: 4 to 6.5 hours

Season: July through mid-October

Water Availability: Rice Creek, Rice Lake, unnamed creek

Cautionary Advice: None

Information: Boise National Forest, Cascade Ranger District (208) 382-7400

Pit Latrine: No

Coordinates

Trailhead:

N 44° 32.892'
W 115° 38.248'

Rice Peak Lookout:

N 44° 30.395'
W 115° 37.678'

Rice Peak Loop

Lookouts occupy prime real estate and Rice Peak is no exception. Standing on the 8,693-foot mountain, hikers encounter exceptional panoramic vistas that extend over many ridges and to scores of smaller mountains. On a clear day even the high peaks in the Sawtooth and White Cloud Mountains are seen on the eastern horizon.

The loop hike to Rice Peak is a combination of a singletrack trail and FR 478, which is closed to vehicles. The hike has all the makings of a wonderful outing with big vistas, wildflower-covered meadows, good opportunities to see wildlife and the scenic Rice Lake. The little lake sits directly west of Rice Peak and offers several secluded campsites. On the apex of Rice Peak there is an old fire lookout—Rice Peak Lookout—that provides a good, shaded perch to take in the remarkable views.

In 2015, a massive mud and rock slide came down the west-facing canyon wall holding Rice Creek and washed out sections of FR 478. As of January 2017, the Forest Service had no plans to fix the road, and the trailhead has been moved back almost a mile from the original Blue Point Trailhead. All mileage and elevation gain is computed from the new trailhead location.

Rice Lake

Rice Peak is named after William B. Rice, a US Forest Service employee for nearly forty years.

Trailhead Directions

From Cascade, drive 0.9 mile north on ID 55, and turn right onto paved Warm Lake Road. Continue another 22.7 miles to a sign on the right hand side of the road for Stolle Meadows. Reset your tripmeter, and turn right onto the well-graded Stolle Meadows Road (FR 474). Travel 7.2 miles to a signed junction for Cupp Corral and Rice Peak. Continue straight towards Rice Peak on FR 478. Continue another 2.2 miles to the road's end and trailhead. There is parking for several vehicles.

The Hike

From the parking area, continue southeast on FR 478 fording a braided creek within 500 feet. This is the section of road that washed out in 2015. Beyond the creek, follow the road nearly a mile to the signed Blue Point Trail on the east side of the road. Turn left onto the singletrack trail. If you want to eliminate some of the elevation gain and distance or just want to visit Rice Lake, continue on FR 478 for another 2.5 miles to its end. There is a campsite here, and you can continue on the singletrack trail another quarter-mile to Rice Lake. It is a gain of about 1,100 feet.

From the Blue Point Trailead, walk east through forest, paralleling a small, unnamed creek. In late June and July, a profusion of wildflowers line the edge of the trail. Look for horsemint, Indian paintbrush, monkey flower, golden rod, yarrow, fireweed and sulfur flower.

At 1.9 miles, ford a small creek. This is a good destination for a short hike. Wildflowers and the crystal-clear creek, nestled in a narrow canyon, provide an ideal setting for a remote destination. Beyond the creek ford, ascend more than 300 feet to a signed junction with the Switchback Trail at 2.2 miles. Turn right. (The left fork travels to the Deadwood River in 4.0 miles.)

The trail continues southwest up a burned hillside. Northwest, far in the distance, is the impressive granite dome of Cougar Rock sitting high above Stolle Meadows (see hike 1). At 2.6 miles, the trail forks with the two trails coming together again in 500 feet. The trail levels near a talus-covered ridge and then enters a burned area near a large meadow at 3.0 miles.

Due to the blackened soil and infrequent use, the trail may be difficult to find here. To locate the trail, turn right and hike up the hill about 50 feet. The trail will be visible again. The route now veers south and crosses the meadow where a multitude of wildflowers bloom in early summer. Return to forest again, and ascend to the top of a knoll (elevation 8,519 feet) at 3.8 miles. In the distance, you see Rice Peak and the white Rice Peak Lookout. Descend through a little meadow, and make a final ascent of more than 200 feet to the lookout. The lookout was built in 1940 and is no longer used. After enjoying the sensational vistas, look for the trail on the south face of Rice Peak. The dusty descent winds through four switchbacks and comes to an unsigned junciton on a saddle at 4.6 miles. (The trail to the south leads to Long Lake in about 3.0 miles.)

Turn north (right) at the junction and descend below a granite ridge. At 5.1 miles, wind through five switchbacks with great views of Rice Lake and Telephone Ridge, the long mountain ridge extending north from Rice Lake. The trail levels in forest at 5.5 miles and continues below another talus-covered ridge to the north side of Rice Lake. There are several campsites along the perimeter of the lake. Cross the bridge over Rice Lake's outlet creek, and descend to the signed Rice Lake Trailhead and FR 478 at 6.3 miles. There is a campsite here next to Rice Creek. To complete the loop, follow the rocky FR 478 nearly 3.5 miles to your vehicle. The road winds through forest for much of the way, and the elevation loss is 1,100 feet.

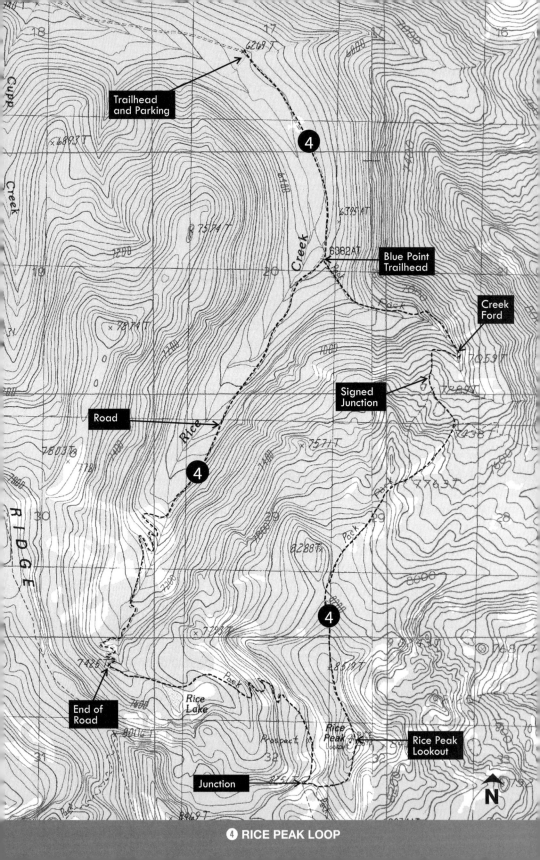

Trailhead and Parking

Blue Point Trailhead

Creek Ford

Signed Junction

Road

End of Road

Rice Lake

Rice Peak Lookout

Junction

RIDGE

N

4 RICE PEAK LOOP

5   Monumental Peak

Distance: 3.6 miles out-and-back

Total Elevation Gain: 800 feet

Difficulty: Moderate

Elevation Range: 6,700 to 7,400 feet

Topographic Map: Wild Buck Peak

Time: 2 to 3 hours (extra time is added for route-finding)

Season: Mid-June through October

Water Availability: Many seasonal streams in late spring and early summer. Mid-summer and beyond, bring water.

Cautionary Advice: This route is not maintained and you should be skilled with off-trail navigation. The last 0.6 mile of road to the trailhead requires a high-clearance vehicle. There is a parking area (0.6 mile from the trailhead) before the road gets rough.

Information: Boise National Forest, Cascade Ranger District (208) 382-7400

Pit Latrine: No

Coordinates

Trailhead:

N 44° 29.144'
W 115° 43.343'

Saddle near Monumental Peak:

N 44° 28.004'
W 115° 43.434'

Monumental Peak

Monumental Peak doesn't rank high on most hikers' must-see lists—likely because no one knows about it. But, there are so many reasons to love the pilgrimage to the 7,902-foot mountain. It is a landscape of surprising beauty including flower-filled meadows and hillsides, dramatic vistas, fertile forest and of course, the enchanting Monumental Peak. Standing high above the Bull Creek drainage, the aptly-named mountain is a sight to behold: its base is flanked by an almost limitless number of granite rocks, and this dazzling display of granite revelry proceeds over 400 feet to the rocky summit.

Although there once was a defined trail to Monumental Peak, it has not been maintained in years and is fading away in sections. In addition, some areas have been impacted by fire. The nearly 2-mile hike requires basic route-finding skills as there are segments where the trail is completely gone, and deadfall can make route-finding difficult. The hike begins near the Sixteen-to-One Trailhead and leads through a couple of meadows, up a fire-

Granite outcroppings along the off-trail ridge hike near Monumental Peak

impacted ridge and meanders through forest and open hillsides to the base of Monumental Peak.

There are many viewpoints along the route looking into this rugged and remarkable area. The hike ends at a saddle to the west of Monumental Peak where an ill-defined trail descends 2,600 feet to Bull Creek. From the saddle, you can extend the hike 0.6 mile one-way with an easy traverse west along a ridgetop adorned with impressive rock formations, early-summer wildflowers and offering stunning views. The best time to hike the area is late spring and early summer when wildflowers are prolific and seasonal creeks flow. It's a place of exceptional solitude, and the entire journey should not to be missed.

Trailhead Directions

From Cascade, drive north 0.9 mile on ID 55, and turn right onto paved Warm Lake Road. Continue another 22.7 miles to a sign on the right hand side of the road "Stolle Meadows 6." Turn right onto gravel Stolle Meadows Road (FR 474), drive 7.2 miles to a sign "Cupp Corral 7" and turn right, staying on FR 474. Follow this rocky road 5.9 miles—passable with a passenger car—to a parking area on the right hand side of the road. (If you park here, you will need to add 1.2 miles out-and-back to the hike distance.) High-clearance vehicles can proceed another 0.6 mile, the first quarter-mile of road is the worst, to the signed trailhead for Sixteen-to-One. The unsigned trailhead for Monumental Peak is located on the east side of the road (opposite side from the Sixteen-to-One Trailhead) near a dispersed campsite.

The Hike

From the unmarked trailhead, follow the trail east through a meadow sprinkled with half-buried boulders. Look for white phlox in late spring and early summer. At 0.2 mile, the trail fades. Continue east and veer south (right) along the edge of a meadow framed with forest. The faint footpath continues south across the meadow. In early summer, the meadow is blanketed with the green, large-leafed, false hellebore. At the end of the meadow, the trail becomes more prominent as it rises on an open hillside into forest.

At 0.6 mile, enter another meadow, and within 500 feet the trail is obscure again. This section of the trail is nearly non-existent and is the worst along the route to Monumental Peak. Here, veer southwest, fording a tiny stream and hike up an open, burned slope covered with deadfall (see map). You will need to negotiate a few downed trees. After an elevation gain of 200 feet, reach the top of the ridge at 1.0 mile where the trail is visible again. Views are far-reaching into the Sixteen-to-One drainage and beyond to the West Mountains. From here, continue south passing through open forest.

At 1.2 miles, the trail disappears again in deadfall at the edge of dense forest. Here, veer southeast (left) and look for the trail on the edge of an open hillside. Looking ahead, you can see the rounded, bald summit of Monumental Peak. The trail now veers southwest along the open slope and fades again in timber at 1.4 miles. Here, you can continue south either in timber or make your way to the edge of the boulder field below Monumental Peak and continue along its edge. It is 0.4 mile with a gain of 100 feet to the 7,400-foot unmarked saddle. The trail is visible the last quarter-mile to the saddle. The views south from the saddle are far-reaching looking over the Bull Creek drainage and to the distant mountains.

An easy and worthwhile side trip is to walk west from the saddle to the end of the ridge (see map). The 0.6-mile trek is relatively level and ends at a small, rock-covered knoll with sweeping vistas west to Long Valley and the West Mountains. Along the ridge are many interesting rock formations and several exquisite places to camp, although there are no water sources.

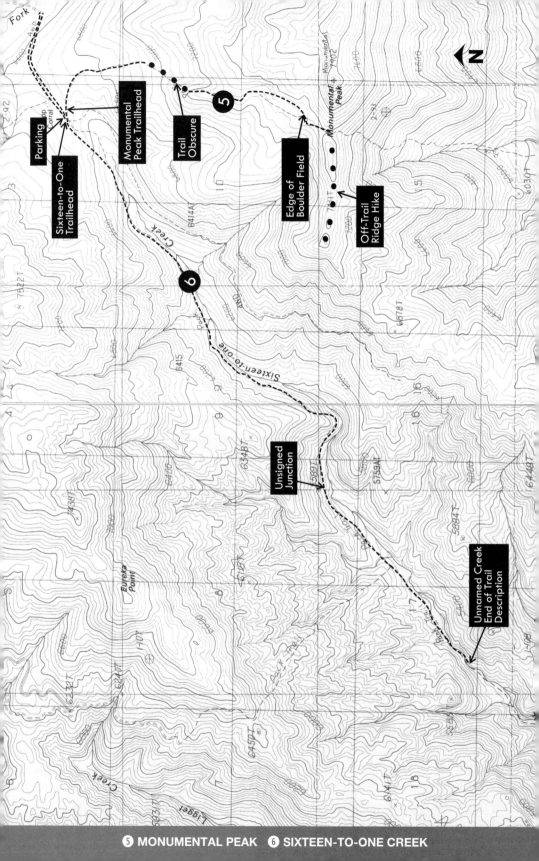

Parking

Sixteen-to-One Trailhead

Monumental Peak Trailhead

Trail Obscure

5

Edge of Boulder Field

Off-Trail Ridge Hike

6

Sixteen-to-one

Unsigned Junction

Eureka Point

Unnamed Creek
End of Trail Description

Fork

Creek

Creek

Ligget Creek

Monumental Peak

❺ MONUMENTAL PEAK   ❻ SIXTEEN-TO-ONE CREEK

Sixteen-to-One Creek

Coordinates
Trailhead:

N 44° 29.131'
W 115° 43.376'

Unnamed Creek:

N 44° 27.763'
W 115° 45.974'

Distance: 6.6 miles out-and-back

Total Elevation Gain: 1,500 feet

Difficulty: Strenuous

Elevation Range: 5,300 to 6,700 feet

Topographic Map: Wild Buck Peak, Bull Creek Hot Springs

Time: 3 to 4 hours

Season: June through October

Water Availability: Sixteen-to-One Creek, many side streams

Cautionary Advice: None

Information: Boise National Forest, Cascade Ranger District (208) 382-7400

Pit Latrine: No

Sixteen-to-One Creek

Odds are if you venture into the Sixteen-to-One Creek drainage south of Stolle Meadows in June, you'll discover countless wildflowers, ambling creeks and exceptional solitude. Butterflies and other pollinators scurry from flower to flower while songbirds flutter among the jungly forest. It is a place that is simultaneously tranquil and stirring.

Unlike many hikes, this trail starts at its high point and descends to its destination. The narrow trail stays on the west side of Sixteen-to-One Creek and continues south through dense woods. In late spring and early summer, wildflowers are a constant, especially at higher elevations. The route crosses several scenic creeks, and at lower elevations, weaves through grassy meadows with towering ponderosa pines. A few rocky knolls dispense great views allowing you to get a good perspective of this rugged topography.

The Sixteen-to-One Creek drainage is a classic V-shape. There are only a handful of quality campsites until you near the end of the hike. Here though, several small meadows with old-growth forest invite an isolated backpack outing and it is doubtful you will encounter another visitor—wild animals excluded. The hike can be extended as the trail continues south another 3.5 miles to a confluence with Bull Trout Creek and other trail systems. You will need a high-clearance vehicle for the last 0.6 mile to the trailhead. Otherwise, add 1.2 miles to the out-and-back hiking distance.

Trailhead Directions

From Cascade, drive north 0.9 mile on ID 55, and turn right onto paved Warm Lake Road. Continue another 22.7 miles to a sign on the right hand side of the road "Stolle Meadows 6." Turn right onto gravel Stolle Meadows Road (FR 474) and drive 7.2 miles to a sign "Cupp Corral 7," and turn right staying on FR 474. Follow this rocky road 5.9 miles—passable with a passenger car—to a parking area on the right side of the road. If you have a high-clearance vehicle proceed another 0.6 mile, the first quarter-mile of road is the most rocky, to the marked trailhead "16:1."

The Hike

The trail heads south in open forest and soon weaves between half-buried granite talus. White-colored phlox is prolific in June and a beautiful complement to the granite talus. At 0.2 mile, begin a gradual descent into the Sixteen-to-One Creek drainage. Looking southeast, there are good views of the rounded, granite summit of Monumental Peak (see hike 5). At 0.5 mile, cross a bridge over a small creek, and continue through open forest with hillside wildflowers.

At 1.2 miles, look west for a series of granite benches extending up the canyon face. This is an interesting place to explore off-trail and would be a fine destination for a short hike. Beyond here, the trail makes a short but steep descent to a bridge at 1.4 miles over a unnamed creek. There is room for a small tent or two on a little knoll before crossing the bridge and another possible campsite—to the west of the trail in a little grassy area—about 500 feet beyond the bridge.

Continue south along a modest decline, fording several tiny streams. Once you pass below 6,000 feet, you see many huge ponderosa pines. The trail soon fords a wide, shallow creek and at 2.4 miles crosses a rocky knoll high above Sixteen-to-One Creek. There are stellar views looking south into the drainage. Continue another quarter-mile to an unsigned junction.

From here, the trail descends another 100 feet to where it levels near a large grove of aspen at 3.0 miles. Continue through another dense stand of forest and into a small meadow where you could establish a tent site. At 3.3 miles, ford a wide, unnamed creek in a wooded area. This is the end of the hike description. To find another campsite, continue past the creek another quarter-mile into dense forest to a level area near Sixteen-to-One Creek.

Curtis Lake

Distance: 6.2 miles out-and-back

Total Elevation Gain: 1,400 feet

Difficulty: Strenuous

Elevation Range: 7,400 to 7,800 feet

Topographic Map: Oro Mountain

Time: 2.5 to 4 hours

Season: July through mid-October

Water Availability: Curtis Lake, pond and several creeks

Cautionary Advice: This trail is not maintained by the Forest Service. Expect deadfall.

Information: Boise National Forest, Cascade Ranger District (208) 382-7400

Pit Latrine: No

Coordinates

Trailhead:

N 44° 33.454'
W 115° 50.078'

Curtis Lake:

N 44° 35.162'
W 115° 48.352'

Curtis Lake

Located near the 7,759-foot Oro Mountain, this 6.2 miles out-and-back hike is a well-kept secret, likely due to its isolation from any other nearby trailheads. The trail is rarely level and twists, turns and rises through lodgepole pine forest along hillsides and over ridges. There are many opportunities to see wildlife such as deer, elk and black bear. Other highlights along the route include several meadows, hillsides blanketed with huge boulders and a picture-perfect pond.

The final destination is the circular-shaped Curtis Lake sitting in a small bowl surrounded by dense forest. Backpackers will find plenty of fine campsites strewn around the perimeter of the lake. The surrounding topography is mainly rolling ridges, enticing you with off-trail exploration.

Few hikers are aware of this gorgeous little lake, which means you'll have plenty of solitude. Although not an established Forest Service trail, the route is marked with colored tape on tree branches to help with route-finding. The hike receives enough use that the trail is clearly defined in most sections.

Trailhead Directions

From Cascade, drive north on ID 55 for 0.9 mile. Reset your tripmeter and turn right onto paved Warm Lake Road. Continue 5.9 miles to Horsethief Reservoir Road, and turn right again onto the well-graded, dirt road. Drive 1.1 miles and turn left onto Lost Basin Road (FR 433). Reset your tripmeter again and continue to a fork in the road at 3.0 miles. Take the left fork, which is a continuation of FR 433. Drive another 6.9 miles on the good dirt road (take the left fork at a Y-junction at 6.1 miles) to an unmarked trailhead on the left side of the road. There is parking for several vehicles along the roadside. The only sign at the trailhead is a trail-user marker prohibiting motorized vehicles.

The Hike

Begin ascending an old roadbed through lodgepole forest. A great number of wildflowers bloom on the partially open hillsides in July and August. After climbing 300 feet in 0.6 mile, the road levels with outstanding views southeast of the bright green Stony Meadow and beyond into the rugged Salmon River Mountains.

The crystal clear Curtis Lake

The road ends at 0.8 mile under a canopy of trees where you will find a campsite. Look straight ahead for the singletrack trail that descends to the bottom of a small ravine. In July, wildflowers—especially sego lily—are sprinkled like confetti throughout the ravine. Beyond the ravine, traverse a lodgepole pine-covered hillside that has wide-open vistas.

At 1.3 miles, ascend to a ridgetop and meander for 500 feet through partially burned forest. The trail veers north (left) and descends a steep 150 feet to an easy ford of a small stream. Continue through a small, grassy meadow to a large pond.

The trail parallels the pond, just to the east of a boulder-strewn hillside. Leave the pond behind and enter thick lodgepole pine forest. At 2.1 miles, the trail descends 200 feet and comes to a section of dense deadfall at 2.5 miles. Veer left, around the deadfall, and the trail soon becomes obvious again. Here, begin a very steep gain of 300 feet to where the trail levels at 3.0 miles. The trail braids here into several paths, one leading to the southwest side of Curtis Lake and the other to its southeast side.

Curtis
Lake

Pond

Trailhead
and Parking

Stony
Meadow

N

Blue Lake

Coordinates

Trailhead:

N 44° 25.104'
W 116° 07.948

Blue Lake:

N 44° 24.606'
W 116° 08.127'

Distance: 1.2 miles out-and-back

Total Elevation Gain: 400 feet

Difficulty: Easy

Elevation Range: 7,300 to 7,700 feet

Topographic Map: Tripod Peak

Time: 1 hour

Season: July through mid-October

Water Availability: Blue Lake

Cautionary Advice: None

Information: Boise National Forest, Cascade Ranger District (208) 382-7400

Pit Latrine: Yes

Blue Lake

Although an easy hike, a visit to Blue Lake might just take your breath away. The circular lake is nestled in a small granite basin surrounded by outcroppings, dense forest and glaciated canyon walls rising to 8,000 feet in the heart of the West Mountains. There are several granite outcroppings that extend into Blue Lake's dark blue waters and are a nice platform for swimming or just taking in the area's beauty.

Unlike most hikes, this journey starts at its highpoint and descends 400 feet to Blue Lake. Most of the short hike is through open hillside meadows covered with summer wildflowers and alpine knotweed. If you have driven to the trailhead from the Boise area the same day, you will certainly notice the thin air on your ascent back to the trailhead.

The forested terrain surrounding the lake is relatively flat and there are many private camping sites. Most are overused though as the lake sees a lot of summer visitors because of the short hiking distance and spectacular scenery. An easy walk up a granite ridge directly northeast of Blue Lake offers prime vistas looking down a forested canyon to Round Valley and beyond to rolling mountains.

Blue Lake

Trailhead Directions

From Cascade, drive south on ID 55 for 8.2 miles and turn right onto Cabarton Road (left if coming from the Boise area), between mile markers 106 and 107. Reset your tripmeter and continue west on Cabarton Road for 2.5 miles and turn left onto the well-graded Snowbank Road. Continue for 8.7 miles to the signed trailhead and large parking area on the left. Note: Snowbank Road (FR 446) is closed to all public use from November 16 to May 31.

The Hike

From the large parking area, head south on the wide trail. At 0.2 mile, cross a tiny stream and then a bridge at 0.3 mile. Soon thereafter ford another small stream and enter a grassy meadow. At the end of the meadow, at 0.5 mile, the trail forks. The left fork continues to the east side of the lake where there are several campsites. The right fork trail descends 50 feet, fords a small stream and continues to a granite outcropping on the lake's northwest edge.

There is a foot trail that circumnavigates Blue Lake where you will find many campsites scattered around the lake's perimeter. For a great perspective of the area, walk to the lake's northeast edge. From here, hike about 100 yards (with 100 feet of elevation gain) up the granite outcropping north of the lake (see map).

Passenger Car Parking

Trailhead and Parking

Blue Lake Trailhead and Parking

Trail Splits

Off-Trail View

Unsigned Junction

Blue Lake Overlook

Hangman's Tree

Off-Trail Route to Tripod Peak

Signed Junction

Granite Peak

Potters Pond

Blue Lake

Tripod Peak

Creek

GEM CO

VALLEY CO

N

❽ BLUE LAKE   ❾ GRANITE PEAK TO TRIPOD LOOKOUT

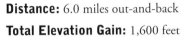

Granite Peak to Tripod Lookout

Distance: 6.0 miles out-and-back

Total Elevation Gain: 1,600 feet

Difficulty: Strenuous

Elevation Range: 7,550 to 8,100 feet

Topographic Map: Tripod Peak

Time: 3 to 4 hours

Season: July through mid-October

Water Availability: None

Cautionary Advice: Bring plenty of water as there are no reliable sources. Snowbank Road (FR 446) is closed to all public use from November 16 to May 31.

Information: Payette National Forest, Cascade Ranger District (208) 382-7400

Pit Latrine: No

Coordinates

Trailhead:

N 44° 25.247'
W 116° 08.585'

Tripod Lookout:

N 44° 23.043'
W 116° 07.699'

Granite Peak to Tripod Lookout

A journey along the backbone of the West Mountains is a chance to immerse yourself in some of the most engaging views in this part of Idaho. You can't help but be awestruck as you wander along the ridgetop, capturing vistas of the rolling hills and mountians. The terrain in undulating, passing through meadows, isolated stands of timber and along wind-swept slopes.

The trailhead is located near the apex of 8,273-foot Granite Peak. The trail leads south over open terrain and then high above Blue Lake. From here, it descends past Hangman's Tree and makes a final rise to Tripod Peak. The 360° vistas from this climactic perch are spectacular and include Long and Round Valleys, and beyond to the Salmon River Mountains. Looking south and west, the views unfold to an array of rugged canyons.

Deceivingly, the trail is rarely level. It always seems to be rising to a ridge or descending to a saddle. There are many fine destinations to shorten the hike if Tripod Peak is more than you are up for. There are lots of alpine knotweed along the open slopes and, in early fall, the plant turns to a brilliant rust color that lights up the hillsides.

Trailhead Directions

From Cascade, drive south on ID 55 for 8.2 miles, and turn right onto Cabarton Road (left if coming from the Boise area) between mile markers 106 and 107. Reset your tripmeter and continue west on Cabarton Road 2.5 miles, and turn left onto the well-graded Snowbank Road. Continue an additional 9.7 miles, and turn left (south) onto an unmarked road. Continue another 0.1 mile to its end and unsigned trailhead where there is parking for four or five vehicles. The last 0.1 mile requires a high-clearance vehicle. There is plenty of parking before the roads gets rough when you turn left at 9.7 miles, so you will need to add 0.2 mile to your out-and-back distance.

The Hike

Start south, paralleling Snowbank Road and ascend to a saddle near 8,200 feet. At 0.3 mile, you get good views of Blue Lake, Round Valley and the distant mountains and soon start a steep descent of 300 feet to a little meadow at 0.8 mile. As the trail starts to rise again, it meets with a trail coming in from the north from Wilson Meadows. From here, gain 200 feet to where the trail levels at 1.1 miles and look south for Tripod Peak.

The trail now veers southeast and comes to an open area marked with a cairn where you can hike off-trail (see map) to an overlook of Blue Lake. There is a rugged and steep footpath leading down to the lake's south edge. On the main trail, pass through a switchback at 1.6 miles and descend 250 feet to a saddle and the signed Hangman's Tree. There are conflicting stories about its history, but it seems certain that at some point a hanging rope was strung here. Whether a miscreant ever hung from the rope is up for debate.

Continue south to a signed junction with the Renwyck Trail at 2.3 miles. Proceed through open forest to a faded sign leaning on a tree, west (right) of the trail, at 2.6 miles. The quickest route to Tripod Peak is to turn east (left) here, and follow a user-created trail, faint in sections, that sidehills to Tripod Peak's apex with a gain of 400 feet in 0.5 mile (see map).

Another option, although a longer hike, is to stay on the maintained trail. This route has a bit more elevation gain. To do so, follow the trail south as it passes a muddy spring at 2.9 miles and continues through open forest to a signed junction for Tripod Lookout at 3.4 miles. Turn east (left), and ascend a steep 450 feet in a half-mile to the lookout.

Lost, Hidden and Shirts Lakes

Coordinates

Trailhead:

N 44° 26.636'
W 116° 07.932'

Hidden Lake:

N 44° 26.658'
W 116° 06.890'

Shirts Lake:

N 44° 27.503'
W 116° 07.508'

Distance: 2.6 miles out-and-back (Shirts Lake)
3.4 miles out-and-back (Lost and Hidden Lakes)

Total Elevation Gain: 850 feet (Shirts Lake)
1,150 feet (Lost and Hidden Lakes)

Difficulty: Moderate

Elevation Range: 7,050 to 8,150 feet

Topographic Map: Tripod Peak, Alpha

Time: 1.5 to 2 hours

Season: July through mid-October

Water Availability: Lost, Hidden and Shirts Lakes, several creeks

Cautionary Advice: None

Information: Boise National Forest, Cascade Ranger District (208) 382-7400

Pit Latrine: No

Lost, Hidden and Shirts Lakes

The West Mountains are a narrow-banded range stretching from Horseshoe Bend to New Meadows. The mountains are notable for dense forests on lower slopes, while the crest of the range is dotted with large meadows and several high-alpine lakes. This hike explores three of West Mountain's lakes, all near the towering 8,322-foot Snowbank Mountain, the highest in the range.

Wildflower-filled meadows, forests, granite ridges and outstanding vistas are some of the attributes of the hike. The three lakes are accessed from the same trailhead but are found on two different trails that diverge at an unsigned junction about three-quarters of a mile into the hike. South of the junction, you access Lost and Hidden Lakes. Shallow Lost Lake lies at an elevation of 7,300 feet and is partially covered by water lilies by late July. The lake is fringed by bright green grass and dense forest. The more attractive Hidden Lake is surrounded by outcroppings and a steep granite ridge rising 1,200 feet to Snowbank Mountain.

By following the trail northeast from the junction, you access Shirts Lake. Shirts Lake sits directly west of 7,982-foot Collier Peak, and its west shore is flanked by a granite ridge rising 600 feet to a flat crest. Thick forest of fir and pine, as well as granite outcroppings, surrounds most of the lake. Although this hike is shorter than Lost and Hidden Lakes, it requires a steep 450-foot descent in over a half-mile. All three lakes offer good campsites.

Trailhead Directions

From Cascade, drive south on ID 55 for 8.2 miles, and turn right onto Cabarton Road between mile markers 106 and 107. If you are traveling from Boise, Cabarton Road is 9.4 miles north of the Cougar Mountain Lodge in Smith's Ferry. Reset your tripmeter and continue west on Cabarton Road, and turn left onto the well-graded Snowbank Road at 2.5 miles. Continue an additional 11.2 miles to the top of Snowbank Mountain to a fork in the road below a large FAA radar dome. Take the left fork, and travel 0.4 mile to the unsigned parking area on the right.

The Hike

From the parking area, hike down the road about 200 feet to the unsigned trailhead on the east (left) side of the road. Look for a "no motor vehicles" sign. Hike across a large meadow where wildflowers grow profusely in July. At 0.4 mile, the trail passes beneath a large granite ridge and continues to an unsigned junction in a small meadow at 0.7 mile. The junction is not prominent, and deadfall can obscure the diverging paths. The junction is marked with a cairn. To find Lost and Hidden Lake (see below for Shirts Lake), continue east (straight) through the little meadow and veer south (right) into forest. Make a descent of 200 feet beside a small stream and arrive at the north side of Lost Lake. Several campsites are located here.

To continue to Hidden Lake, follow the trail along Lost Lake's east edge and cross the tiny outlet creek. The trail turns along the lake's south perimeter for about 500 feet where there is another campsite located beneath a granite ridge. The trail leaves the lake and crosses a small knoll at 1.4 miles. From here, descend 300 feet on the narrow footpath to a large granite outcropping above Hidden Lake. There are many good campsites on the lake's east side near the outlet creek.

Shirts Lake

At the 0.7 mile junction, take the left fork. The trail rises 100 feet through open forest to a saddle at 1.0 mile where there are excellent over-the-shoulder views of the radio towers perched on Snowbank Mountain. From here, descend a steep 450 feet beside a small flower-fringed creek to Shirts Lake. A footpath skirts the north side of the lake where you will find several excellent campsites near the outlet creek.

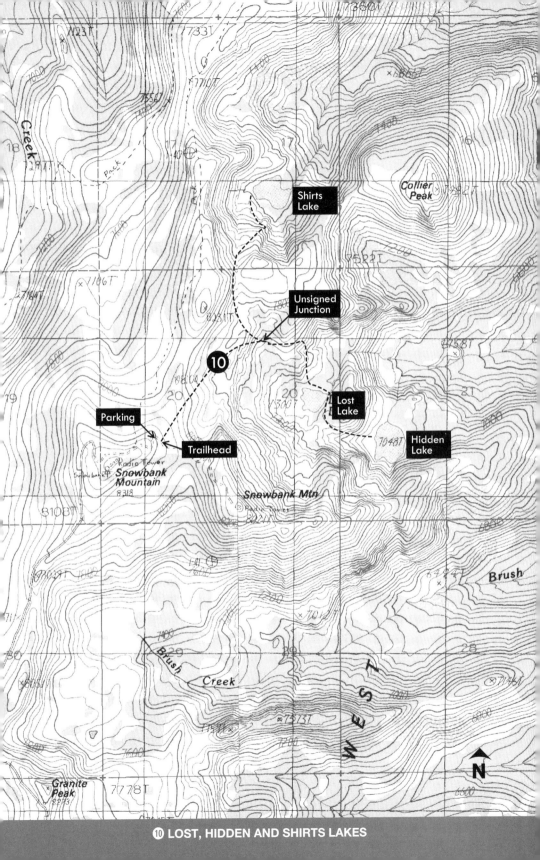

⑩ LOST, HIDDEN AND SHIRTS LAKES

Arling Trail

Distance: 4.4 miles out-and-back

Total Elevation Gain: 1,550 feet

Difficulty: Strenuous

Elevation Range: 5,650 to 7,250 feet

Topographic Map: Cold Spring Ridge

Time: 2.5 to 3.5 hours

Season: Mid-June through mid-October

Water Availability: A few small creeks

Cautionary Advice: The trail is non-existent in a couple of short sections.

Information: Boise National Forest, Cascade Ranger District (208) 382-7400

Pit Latrine: No

Coordinates

Trailhead:

N 44° 38.048'
W 116° 08.604'

Viewpoint:

N 44° 37.305'
W 116° 10.167'

Arling Trail

A few miles south of Tamarack Resort, hikers will discover a little-known trail in the West Mountains that delivers spectacular views of Cascade Lake, Long Valley and the Salmon River Mountains. Although not a long trail, the hike is worth doing if you enjoy views and a trail infrequently traveled.

From the trailhead to the crest of the West Mountains, the route is a constant climb. There is beautiful old-growth forest, a pretty meadow and several little creeks along the way. At higher elevations, the hike offers far-reaching vistas and appealing alpine scenery—stunted trees, granite outcroppings and a sprinkling of wildflowers.

The trail is clearly defined for the first mile. Beyond this point, there are a few sections—nothing more than 500 feet—where there is no trail at all. The terrain is mainly treeless though, as much of the forest is burned. There are a few sporadic cairns. Consult the map if you feel you have lost your way. Regardless, this is a wonderful hike offering stunning vistas and solitude and should not be missed.

View of Lake Cascade and Long Valley

Trailhead Directions

From Donnelly, turn onto W. Roseberry Road (heading west), and follow the signs to Tamarack Resort. At 7.0 miles, enter a traffic circle, and take the second exit. (The first exit goes to Tamarck Resort.) Beyond the traffic circle, the road (FR 422) is dirt. Continue south on FR 422 for 3.8 miles, and then turn right onto Arling Trail. Follow this road west another 1.5 miles to a switchback with parking for several vehicles. To find the trailhead, walk up the road an additional 0.2 mile to where the road ends. Although you can drive to the trailhead, there is little room to turn a vehicle around.

The Hike

The singletrack trail heads into thick forest with a dense understory of plants and soon climbs through a switchback. As you ascend, there are huge old-growth trees bordering the trail. Soon Arling Creek can be heard off in the distance. At 0.8 mile, a vague footpath veers north (right) into a small meadow with a couple of little streams. You could camp near here.

At 0.9 mile, ford Arling Creek as the trail veers southwest and gains another 200 feet of elevation in forest. At 1.2 miles, enter an old burn area where many gray snags still stand. The trail is vague here and disappears in sections. As you gain elevation, the views improve looking down to Lake Cascade.

At 1.4 miles, the trail disappears in a level, open area. Turn north (right), and walk about 1,000 feet through this badly burned area to where the route veers west again at 1.7 miles (see map for route). Look for cairns to help identify the tread. As the trail veers west, the landscape changes to a more alpine look with partially covered granite rocks, a few green firs and granite outcroppings. Looking west, you see the crest of the range as the trail becomes more prominent and rises another 400 feet to the ridgetop.

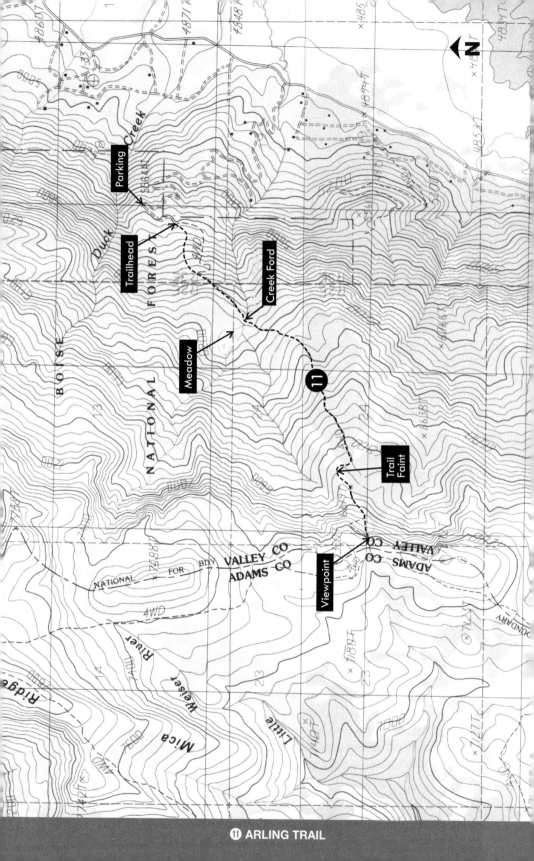

12   Rapid Creek to Boulder Lake

Coordinates

Trailhead:

N 44° 49.006'
W 115° 56.097'

Boulder Lake:

N 44° 52.056'
W 115° 56.143'

Distance: 8.4 miles out-and-back

Total Elevation Gain: 1,350 feet

Difficulty: Strenuous

Elevation Range: 5,800 to 7,050 feet

Topographic Map: Paddy Flat

Time: 3 to 5 hours

Season: Late June through mid-October

Water Availability: Rapid Creek and several small streams

Cautionary Advice: None

Information: Payette National Forest, McCall Ranger District (208) 634-0400

Pit Latrine: No

Rapid Creek to Boulder Lake

Every July, a magnificent carpet of wildflowers such as Indian paintbrush, lupine, pearly everlasting, clover, and the fragrant horsemint blanket the open hillsides near Rapid Creek. Several high peaks, including 8,457-foot Buckhorn Mountain and 8,264-foot Rapid Peak, dot the skyline with their granite apexes. The idyllic setting is enhanced by the sweet smell of the surrounding pine and fir forest bringing back memories of the holidays.

The first few miles of the hike parallel Rapid Creek as it winds through forest and meadows in a narrow canyon. You cross ambling creeks and pass a plethora of huckleberry bushes. The final segment of the hike ascends more than 1,000 feet in a couple of miles passing through open forest flanked by steep granite canyon walls. At mile four, you reach the signed junction for Boulder, Rapid, and Anderson Lakes. A quarter-mile saunter from here leads to the east side of Boulder Lake.

Although an easy trailhead to access, hikers experience an unusual degree of solitude. Boulder Lake is one of the more popular destinations in the Payette National Forest, but the majority of users access the lake from the west by way of the Boulder Lake Trail, which can feel busy on summer weekends.

Although a longer drive to the trailhead, it is unlikely you will see many people along this beautiful route to Boulder Lake. Families will find the first couple of miles to be an excellent choice for an easy hike.

Trailhead Directions

From downtown McCall, drive south 9.4 miles on ID 55. Reset your tripmeter and turn left onto paved Paddy Flat Road between mile markers 134 and 135. Follow Paddy Flat Road (FR 388) for 1.4 miles to Farm to Market Road. Cross Farm to Market Road (FR 388 turns into a well-graded road), and continue to a signed junction at Paddy Flat Summit at 5.2 miles. Take the left fork in the road and drive an additional 6.0 miles to a sign for the Rapid Creek Campground, and turn left onto FR 390. Pass the unimproved campground at 0.2 mile (with a pit latrine), and travel another 1.9 miles to the end of the road and trailhead.

The Hike

The hike starts as you walk across a wooden bridge that spans a small creek and enter a grassy meadow where many wildflowers grow. Look for monkshood, one of the most toxic plants known to man. This purple wildflower is also known as "wolfsbane" or "dogsbane" because the poison from the roots was used to kill wolves, mad dogs and other large animals in Europe and northern Asia.

Ford a larger creek at 0.2 mile and enter dense woods. Continue north and cross several bridges over small creeks. At 1.0 mile, the scenery improves as granite boulders and outcroppings become more of a constant. Huckleberries are prolific.

At 2.1 miles, pass a grassy area bordered by granite slabs. This is a superb location for a campsite or final destination if you are looking for a shorter hike. From here, the trail's grade steepens and fords three small creeks. Pass a beautiful little meadow partially surrounded by granite canyon walls at 3.2 miles. The perimeter of this meadow provides another prime location for overnighters. The path dips to another grassy meadow and climbs again. In July and early August, the open hillsides are awash with a spectacular setting of colorful wildflowers.

At 4.0 miles, reach a signed junction with trails to Anderson Lake, Rapid Lake, Summit Lake or Kennally Summit (see hikes 19 through 21). To find Boulder Lake, turn west (left) at the junction, and hike another 0.2 mile to the lake's southeast edge. The trail continues past Boulder Lake and descends 800 feet to the trailhead near Boulder Reservoir in 2.4 miles. This is a fantastic shuttle hike, although a long drive, if you have two vehicles.

Boulder Lake
6973

Signed Junction

Twin Peaks

Rapid Lake 7238

Spring

Vics Lake

Fogg Lake

⑫

Rapid Creek

P A Y E T T E

N A T I O N A L   F

Trailhead and Parking

N

⑫ RAPID CREEK TO BOULDER LAKE

North Fork of Kennally Creek

Coordinates

Trailhead:

N 44° 46.885'
W 115° 52.457'

Rock Outcropping:

N 44° 48.572'
W 115° 51.495'

Distance: 6.2 miles out-and-back

Total Elevation Gain: 650 feet

Difficulty: Easy

Elevation Range: 5,650 to 5,950 feet

Topographic Map: Blackmare

Time: 2.5 to 3.5 hours

Season: Mid-June through mid-October

Water Availability: Plenty along Kennally Creek and the North Fork of Kennally Creek

Cautionary Advice: None

Information: Payette National Forest, McCall Ranger District (208) 634-0400

Pit Latrine: Yes

North Fork of Kennally Creek

If you are looking for an easy, shaded hike with little elevation gain, the North Fork of Kennally Creek is a great destination. This 6.2-mile out-and-back hike starts from the Kennally Creek Campground and follows Kennally Creek for nearly a mile to a signed junction. Here, the trail turns north paralleling the creek's north fork, which meanders through dense forest. Eventually, you make an easy ford of the North Fork of Kenally Creek and continue on its west side passing through lodgepole forest.

The hike description ends at a stair-stepped series of granite ridges that extend up the canyon's face. You ascend an easy 150 feet over outcroppings to a huge granite slab perched high above the canyon. It's a delightful setting surrounded by open forest and granite rock formations, including fantastic vistas up and down the canyon. Backpackers will find several good campsites after the ford of North Fork of Kennally Creek. The trail continues past the outcropping another 5 miles to the Kennally Lakes and beyond to Kennally Summit. Families will find the first ford of Kennally Creek to be a great choice for a family backpack.

Trailhead Directions

From downtown McCall, drive south 9.4 miles on ID 55. Turn left onto paved Paddy Flat Road between mile markers 134 and 135. Reset your tripmeter and follow Paddy Flat Road (FR 388) for 1.4 miles to Farm to Market Road. Cross Farm to Market Road (FR 388 turns into a well-graded dirt road) and continue to a junction at Paddy Flat Summit at 5.2 miles. Take the left fork and drive an additional 9.9 miles to the Kennally Creek Campground (11 campsites). Near the junction of FR 388 and FR 390 (11.5 miles from ID 55), you will find an undeveloped campground on FR 390 and the Paddy Flat Campground, about 1.2 miles south of FR 388.

The Hike

From the signed trailhead, hike east along Kennally Creek. The trail passes a few spots providing easy access to Kennally Creek. It then rises through dense forest over a wooded knoll at 0.4 mile and drops back to the creek's edge near granite outcroppings and slabs. Those with children or out for a jaunt will find this an excellent destination. Continue through forest, crossing the bridge over Kennally Creek at 0.7 mile and arrive at a signed junction at 0.9 mile. The trail to the south (right) travels to other destinations including Blackmare Summit, Blackmare Lake, and Needles Summit (see hikes 14, 15 and 16).

At the junction, take the left fork. The trail veers northeast and turns due north in dense forest that obstruct views, but as you make your way north, the forest thins and the views improve. At 1.7 miles, ascend 100 feet over a wooded hill and descend to a ford of North Fork of Kennally Creek at 2.4 miles. Deadfall helps with the ford, although in early June hikers may find the logs underwater.

Beyond the creek ford, the mixed conifer forest transitions into predominately slender lodgepole trees. Those looking to camp will find several tent sites between the trail and the creek. At 2.9 miles, pass below granite outcroppings extending high up the canyon's east-facing wall. Turn west (left) and hike off-trail weaving up and over a couple of granite slabs to a large granite mound set 150 feet above the canyon floor. The grade is not too steep, and this is an interesting place to explore.

To extend the hike, you can continue north up the wooded canyon and ford the North Fork of Kennally Creek again in 2 miles. After the creek ford, the trail rises 1,400 feet in approximately 3 miles to the Kennally Lakes. Beyond here, it gains another 700 feet to 7,940-foot Kennally Summit and descends to Vics and Rapid Lakes and other trail systems.

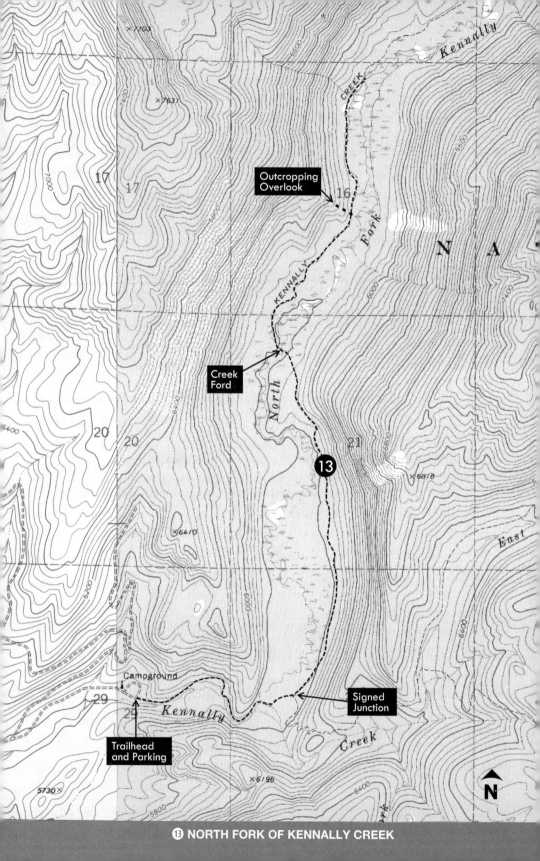

Outcropping Overlook

Creek Ford

Signed Junction

Campground

Trailhead and Parking

Kennally Creek

North Fork

Kennally Creek

East

13

⑬ NORTH FORK OF KENNALLY CREEK

Blackmare Summit

Distance: 11.0 miles out-and-back

Total Elevation Gain: 2,300 feet

Difficulty: Very Strenuous

Elevation Range: 5,650 to 7,900 feet

Topographic Map: Blackmare

Time: 5 to 7 hours

Season: July through mid-October

Water Availability: Kennally Creek, several streams and an unnamed lake near the summit

Cautionary Advice: None

Information: Payette National Forest, McCall Ranger District (208) 634-0400

Pit Latrine: Yes

Coordinates

Trailhead:

N 44° 46.884'
W 115° 52.457'

Blackmare Summit:

N 44° 48.320'
W 115° 47.773'

Blackmare Summit

Solitude, views and pristine forest are a few of the rewards along the journey to Blackmare Summit. You first hike along the densely forested Kennally Creek for 2 miles and then make an easy hike through lodgepole forest up the East Fork of Kennally Creek. The last segment of the outing is a thigh-burning 1,400-foot ascent below granite ridges to the summit.

The scenic payoffs are well worth the effort. Near the summit, over-the-shoulder views look west over twenty-five miles to Long Valley, Lake Cascade and beyond to the West Mountains. At the summit, you are rewarded with outstanding vistas east to the deep canyon of the South Fork of the Salmon River and many forested mountains. Looking north, the massive 8,724-foot Blackmare Mountain dominates the skyline. To the south, an unnamed 8,468-foot peak completes the view.

Those looking for a backpacking trip off the beaten path will find several camp opportunities along the East Fork of Kennally Creek and a couple of prime spots at a lovely unnamed lake before reaching the summit. You could also camp just over the summit in a small meadow below Cougar Creek Summit.

Trailhead Directions

From downtown McCall, drive south 9.4 miles on ID 55. Turn left onto paved Paddy Flat Road between mile markers 134 and 135. Reset your tripmeter and follow Paddy Flat Road (FR 388) for 1.4 miles to Farm to Market Road. Cross Farm to Market Road (FR 388 turns into a well-graded road) and continue to a junction at Paddy Flat Summit at 5.2 miles. Take the left fork and drive an additional 9.9 miles to the Kennally Creek Campground (11 campsites). Near the junction of FR 388 and FR 390 (11.5 miles from ID 55) you will find an undeveloped campground on FR 390 and the Paddy Flat Campground, about 1.2 miles south of FR 388.

The Hike

From the trailhead, follow the wide trail east through forest. The trail parallels Kennally Creek, which cascades over a bedrock of granite. Make a gradual ascent over a small ridge at 0.4 mile. A quick 60-foot descent leads to a picturesque setting with granite outcroppings and easy access to the creek. Hikers out for a short jaunt will find this an excellent destination.

At 0.7 mile, cross the North Fork of Kennally Creek on a bridge and come to a signed junction at 0.9 mile. (The left fork turns north up Kennally Creek – see hike 13.) Turn south (right), climbing 500 feet below a number of huge ponderosa pines to another signed junction at 1.8 miles. Grouse whortleberry is prolific along the trail. These small plants produce a tiny purple berry that is edible and flavorful.

Continue east (straight) at the junction, following the sign to Blackmare Summit. Within 50 feet, backpackers will find a small campsite on the north side of the trail. The trail remains relatively level over the next mile, meandering through lodgepole pine forest and passes more possible campsites. At 3.2 and 3.4 miles, there are two creek fords. After the last ford, the trail's grade steepens and rises high above the East Fork of Kennally Creek. Views improve as you gain elevation in the narrow, wooded canyon.

At 4.9 miles, near an elevation of 7,400 feet, you will come within 300 feet of a small unnamed lake. The lake is recessed into a small bowl and is easy to miss. There is a nice campsite on the north side of the lake with good views up to steep, granite ridges leading to the top of two 8,300-foot mountains.

Beyond the lake, ascend a steep 500 feet to the summit without the help of switchbacks. There are many baseball-sized rocks on the trail, so watch your footing. At the summit, look south (right), and hike up a small ridge dotted with lichen-covered boulders, which provide a good perch to enjoy the outstanding scenery. From the summit, you can descend to a small meadow and other trails.

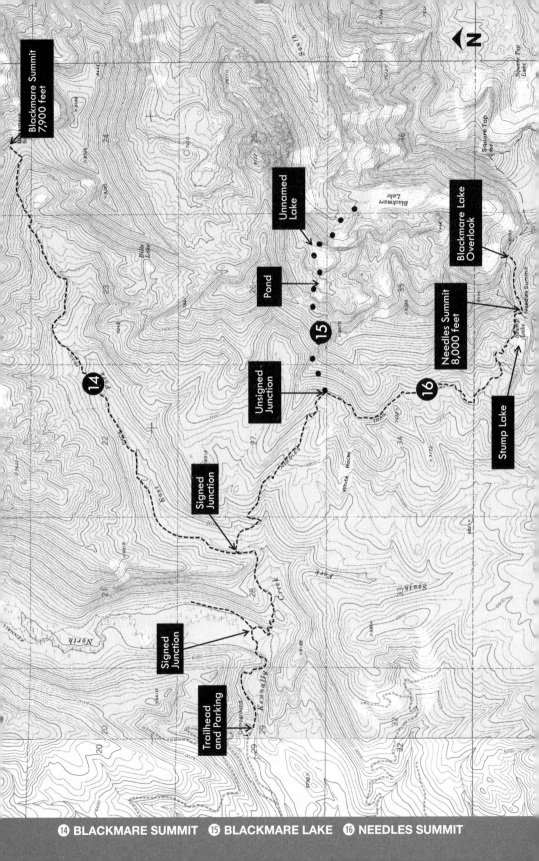

Blackmare Summit
7,900 feet

Unnamed
Lake

Pond

Signed
Junction

Signed
Junction

Trailhead
and Parking

Unsigned
Junction

Blackmare Lake
Overlook

Needles Summit
8,000 feet

Stump Lake

Blackmare Lake

Distance: 11.2 miles out-and-back

Total Elevation Gain: 2,600 feet

Difficulty: Very Strenuous

Elevation Range: 5,650 to 7,900 feet

Topographic Map: Blackmare

Time: 5 to 7 hours

Season: July through mid-October

Water Availability: Pond, Kennally Creek, two lakes and several streams

Cautionary Advice: The last two miles of the route is on an unofficial trail and is not maintained by the Forest Service.

Information: Payette National Forest, McCall Ranger District (208) 634-0400

Pit Latrine: Yes

Coordinates

Trailhead:

N 44° 46.885'
W 115° 52.451'

Blackmare Lake:

N 44° 46.215'
W 115° 48.284'

Blackmare Lake

You'll find a little piece of hiking bliss along much of this Salmon River Mountain trek. Mountain lakes? You will discover two remote beauties with secluded backcountry campsites. Wildlife? Look for deer, elk, fox, grouse, and eagles. The drainage of the South Fork of Blackmare Creek is legendary for black bear sightings. Views? The route traverses several high ridges with impressive vistas of the rugged terrain. Flora? Huckleberries, wildflowers and a lacy green canopy of forest are never in short supply. Solitude? Don't look for company once you leave the main trail and venture on an unofficial trail to the two lakes.

The 2 mile hike from the main trail requires basic route-finding skills as the trail is not maintained. Expect deadfall, braided paths and very steep grades. However, there are plenty of cairns along the route, and the path is visible most of the way. Although the first lake is not named, this beauty is surrounded by thick forest and granite outcroppings. The much larger Blackmare Lake is nestled in a granite amphitheater set directly below the towering 8,861-foot Square Top Mountain. The east edge of the lake is guarded by steep granite walls and oversized talus while the opposite side

Unnamed lake

invites exploration with granite benches and dense forest. You could easily spend hours getting lost in Blackmare's grandeur.

Trailhead Directions

From downtown McCall, drive south 9.4 miles on ID 55. Turn left onto paved Paddy Flat Road, between mile markers 134 and 135. Reset your tripmeter and follow Paddy Flat Road (FR 388) for 1.4 miles to Farm to Market Road. Cross Farm to Market Road (FR 388 turns into a well-graded dirt road), and continue to a junction at Paddy Flat Summit at 5.2 miles. Take the left fork, and drive an additional 9.9 miles to the Kennally Creek Campground. There are several confusing spur roads that fork off FR 388. Remember to follow the signs to Kennally Creek Campground (11 campsites). Near the junction of FR 388 and FR 390 you will find an undeveloped campground on FR 390 and the Paddy Flat Campground, about 1.2 miles south of FR 388.

The Hike

Follow hike 14 for 1.8 miles to the signed junction for Blackmare Summit and Needles Summit. There is a campsite just a few yards past the junction on the trail leading to Needles Summit. Turn south (right) at the junction and make a gentle descent to a ford of East Fork of Kennally Creek. A good campsite is located just before the ford. The trail's grade steepens now and rises nearly 700 feet over the next mile, passing ripened huckleberries in mid-August. At 2.9 miles, the trail levels in very dense forest. A small creek provides water. This is your last opportunity for several miles.

After a quarter-mile walk, the trail rises again and at 3.4 miles, comes to a weathered sign (west side of the trail) on a tree "Blackmare Lake No Trail." To your left, you will clearly see a trail leading up the steep ridge. Turn east (left) and ascend a steep 800 vertical feet in 0.7 mile—without any switchbacks—to the top of a high ridge at 4.1 miles. The first segment of the climb is very steep, but within 0.3 mile, it crosses a little knoll and continues through a very scenic section of trail with many cairns. Once you reach the high ridge, if you turn south (right) there are good camp spots, but no water.

From the ridge, the trail turns north and descends 300 feet to a small pond with several campsites. Follow the footpath along the north shore of the pond, crossing its outlet, and reach the unnamed lake at 4.7 miles. Several campsites are scattered around the lake's perimeter.

If you are comfortable with route-finding, continue to Blackmare Lake. A small footpath travels around the north edge of the unnamed lake and turns south toward the back of the lake. At 4.9 miles, the narrow trail leaves the unnamed lake. If you do not want to hike to Blackmare Lake, just before the trail starts descending the steep ravine, you can

Talus-covered ridge along the route to Blackmare Lake

walk about 20 yards off-trail to a good view of Blackmare Lake. To continue to Blackmare Lake, descend a very steep 400 feet in a quarter-mile to a small meadow filled with a confetti of wildflowers. The tread is faint here, but look for cairns to help with route-finding.

At 5.2 miles, turn southeast (right) at a large cairn and descend through forest, willows and deadfall to a ford of the unnamed lake's outlet creek. Beyond the creek, the intermittent footpath continues east and rises 250 feet to a grassy knoll and turns right to the north shore of Blackmare Lake.

Needles Summit

Distance: 11.2 miles out-and-back

Total Elevation Gain: 2,400 feet

Difficulty: Very Strenuous

Elevation Range: 5,650 to 7,950 feet

Topographic Map: Blackmare

Time: 5 to 7 hours

Season: July through mid-October

Water Availability: East Fork of Kennally Creek, several unnamed creeks and Stump Lake

Cautionary Advice: None

Information: Payette National Forest, McCall Ranger District (208) 634-0400

Pit Latrine: Yes

Trailhead:

N 44° 46.885'
W 115° 52.451'

Needles Summit:

N 44° 45.316'
W 115° 49.158'

Needles Summit

The trail to Needles Summit is one of the best-kept secrets near Donnelly. This long out-and-back explores remote country where you travel through a wooded forest to an 8,000-foot saddle. You will rarely see other hikers. Along the way, you tromp across ambling creeks, beside colorful wildflowers and below rocky talus ridges with opportunities to see wildlife. Before reaching the summit, backpackers will find the charming Stump Lake to be an excellent destination.

Needles Summit lies to the north of the Needles, a collection of jagged granite spires, boulders and granite outcroppings near the border of the Payette and Boise National Forests. The heart of the Needles is south of the summit, but this hike offers you wonderful panoramas of this rugged terrain. Looking east, the impressive Needles formation is visible from Highway 75, near the town of Donnelly.

From the summit, you can hike less than a half-mile to a ridge perched one thousand feet above the boot-shaped Blackmare Lake. On cloud-free days, you can see over thirty miles into the rugged Salmon River Mountains. This hike is unquestionably "off the radar."

Trailhead Directions

From downtown McCall, drive south 9.4 miles on ID 55. Turn left onto paved Paddy Flat Road between mile markers 134 and 135. Reset your tripmeter, and follow Paddy Flat Road (FR 388) for 1.4 miles to Farm to Market Road. Cross Farm to Market Road (FR 388 turns into a well-graded dirt road), and continue to a junction at Paddy Flat Summit at 5.2 miles. Take the left fork, and drive an additional 9.9 miles to the Kennally Creek Campground. There are several confusing spur roads that fork off FR 388. Remember to follow the signs to Kennally Creek Campground (11 campsites). Near the junction of FR 388 and FR 390 you will find an undeveloped campground on FR 390 and the Paddy Flat Campground about 1.2 miles south of FR 388.

The Hike

Follow hike 14 for 1.8 miles to the signed junction for Blackmare and Needles Summits. Turn south (right) at the junction, and descend to an easy ford of East Fork of Kennally Creek. A good campsite is found just before

Off-trail view of Blackmare Lake

the ford. The trail's grade steepens now and rises nearly 700 feet over the next mile, passing ripened huckleberries in mid-August, to a flat area with very dense forest at 2.9 miles. A small creek ambles close and provides water.

At 3.4 miles, there's a weathered sign nailed to a tree on the west side of the trail "Blackmare Lake No Trail." (Look at hike 15 for a description of this route.)

Continue straight on the main trail, crossing a small stream as the trail rises under a canopy of thick forest.

At 5.0 miles, the surrounding landscape transforms to high-alpine scenery with jagged boulders, outcroppings and granite ridges. Pass shallow Stump Lake at 5.4 miles, where there are several excellent campsites. Beyond the lake, the trail ascends 100 feet to the summit.

To find an off-trail view of Blackmare Lake, continue on the main trail. The route is infrequently used and is in dire need of maintenance. Rock cairns help with route-finding as the trail wanders below the ridge. After hiking 0.3 mile, turn left (see map) and scramble north to a flat knoll overlooking the lake. Look south for superb vistas of the rocky spires in the Needles.

Boulder and Louie Lakes Loop

Coordinates

Trailhead:

N 44° 52.170'
W 115° 58.225'

7,700-Foot Saddle:

N 44° 51.045'
W 115° 56.883'

Distance: 3.2 miles out-and-back (Boulder Lake)
6.8 miles loop (Louie Loop)

Total Elevation Gain: 800 feet (Boulder Lake)
1,600 feet (Louie Loop)

Difficulty: Easy (Boulder Lake)
Strenuous (Louie Loop)

Elevation Range: 6,250 to 7,700 feet

Topographic Map: Paddy Flat

Time: 1.5 to 4 hours

Season: Late June through mid-October

Water Availability: Boulder Lake, Louie Lake and several streams

Cautionary Advice: None

Information: Payette National Forest, McCall Ranger District (208) 634-0400

Pit Latrine: Yes, seasonal

Boulder and Louie Lakes Loop

You can't talk about McCall hiking without talking about Boulder Lake. The popular figure-eight-shaped lake is an easy drive from McCall and is certainly a beautiful destination. The large lake lies directly south of the 8,377-foot Boulder Mountain, surrounded by dense woods, meadows and sloping hillsides. Especially striking is the view east across the shimmering lake to the 8,457-foot Buckhorn Mountain. The trek to the lake is well-shaded and is a great choice for families.

Those seeking a more rigorous outing can continue past Boulder Lake and complete a loop hike that includes crossing a 7,700-foot saddle and descending past the beautiful Louie Lake. Along the route, the trail climbs a grassy ridge covered with many colorful wildflowers in mid-July through early August. Past the saddle, there are spectacular views south to the dark-gray cliffs of Jughandle Mountain. Meadows, boulder-dotted hillsides and great vistas make the descent from the saddle one of the hike's highlights.

There are plenty of camping opportunities at both Boulder and Louie Lakes. Both lakes see a lot of visitors though, so this is not the place for solitude. In mid-to-late August look for ripened huckleberries on the trail to Boulder

Lake. In early fall, usually the last ten days of September, the foliage along the loop hike is dramatic. You can camp near the trailhead at an undeveloped campground with many campsites.

Trailhead Directions

From downtown McCall, drive south 1.9 miles on ID 55. Turn left onto Elo Road at mile marker 142 and reset your tripmeter. Travel 2.8 miles to a fork in the road. Take the left fork, which is Boulder Lake Road. Follow Boulder Lake Road to its end at an undeveloped campground at 4.9 miles. (The road turns into a well-graded dirt road at 0.9 mile.) To find the trailhead to Boulder Lake, which can be confusing, walk east up the spur road once you enter the campground area. It is a walk of about 500 feet to the base of the small dam containing Boulder Meadows Reservoir. The Boulder Lake Trailhead is near the dam, a few feet north of the reservoir.

The Hike

The hike starts on the north side of Boulder Meadows Reservoir and continues east through forest. Several rocky boulders along the lake's shore provide perches for those looking to fish. Looking south across the lake, you see the granite apex of Jughandle Mountain. At 0.5 mile, near the end of the reservoir, the fern-lined trail gains elevation passing a lush area with wildflowers.

At 1.0 mile, reach the first of several switchbacks. As you gain elevation, the alpine scenery improves with gray walls of granite and oversized boulders. Below a polished granite rock face at 1.2 miles, ford a small creek. Downed logs assist with the crossing.

Just beyond the ford, the trail makes a sharp turn east (left). Before veering left, you will find a granite knoll providing a nice platform to look west down the forested canyon and to Long Valley. At 1.5, miles ford a creek and ascend over granite slabs to the edge of the dammed Boulder Lake. In June and early July, overflow from the lake cascades over granite slabs and is very scenic.

To continue the loop, turn south (right) at Boulder Lake and cross a tiny platform bridge over a creek. The trail meanders along the south shore of Boulder Lake, passing several campsites and crosses many streams. At 2.4 miles, at the end of the lake, several footpaths veer north (left) leading to excellent campsites along Boulder Lake's east edge.

About 500 feet beyond the lake, come to an unsigned junction marked with a cairn. Turn south (right) and ascend though open forest. At 2.9 miles, you enter a hillside meadow with great views east to 8,457-foot Buckhorn

The view of Jughandle Mountain from the 7,700-foot saddle

Mountain and 8,264-foot Rapid Peak. In late June and July, the area is awash in a confetti of color with many blooming wildflowers including monkey flower, penstemon, phlox, yellow composites and especially lupine.

At 3.4 miles, enter forest again and make a 200-foot ascent to the 7,700-foot saddle marked with a large cairn at 4.2 miles. From here, the trail begins its 700-foot descent to Louie Lake first passing a little meadow with good views south to Jughandle Mountain. If you look southwest of Jughandle's west face, you see Louie Lake. The scenic trail weaves in and out of forest and between granite boulders, finally leveling near an aspen grove at 5.2 miles.

The trail now skirts the north side of Louie Lake and reaches its outlet at 5.3 miles. Jughandle Mountain towers over the irregular-shaped lake providing outstanding photo opportunities. From here, the route follows an old Jeep road, which is also used by motorcyclists and ATV riders. The road heads north away from Louie Lake and soon veers west descending a steep grade. At 6.1 miles, the road levels. Continue another 0.2 mile, and look north (right) for a singletrack trail identified by several large granite boulders. This juction is *not* signed and is easy to miss. Turn right and descend nearly 300 feet in a half-mile through forest. Cross a log bridge over Boulder Creek and arrive at the undeveloped campground.

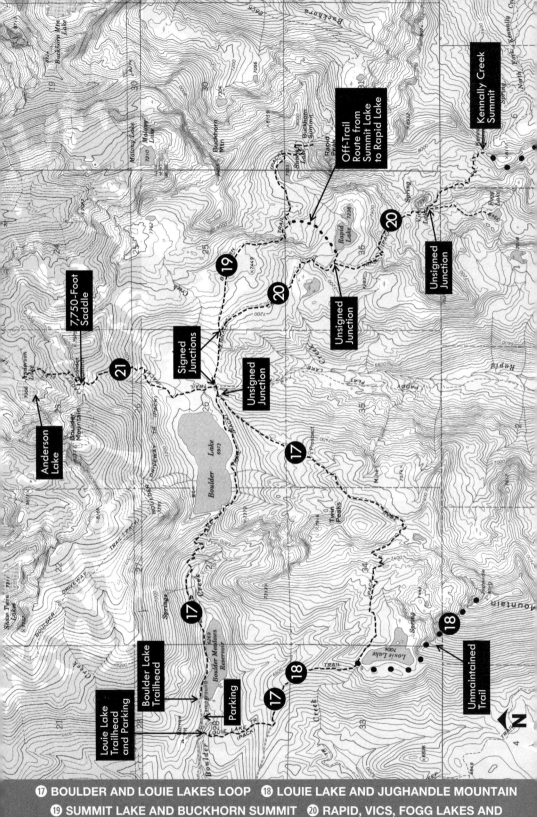

⑰ BOULDER AND LOUIE LAKES LOOP **⑱ LOUIE LAKE AND JUGHANDLE MOUNTAIN**
⑲ SUMMIT LAKE AND BUCKHORN SUMMIT **⑳ RAPID, VICS, FOGG LAKES AND**
KENNALLY SUMMIT **㉑ BOULDER RESERVOIR TO ANDERSON LAKE**

Louie Lake and Jughandle Mountain

Coordinates

Trailhead:

N 44° 52.166'
W 115° 58.495'

Jughandle Mountain:

N 44° 50.590'
W 115° 57.480'

Distance: 2.8 miles out-and-back (Louie Lake)
5.2 miles out-and-back (Jughandle Mountain)

Total Elevation Gain: 800 feet (Louie Lake)
2,200 feet (Jughandle Mountain)

Difficulty: Moderate (Louie Lake)
Strenuous (Jughandle Mountain)

Elevation Range: 6,250 to 8,300 feet

Topographic Map: Paddy Flat

Time: 1.5 to 3.5 hours

Season: July through early October

Water Availability: Boulder Creek, Louie Lake

Cautionary Advice: The footpath from Louie Lake to Jughandle Mountain is not maintained.

Information: Payette National Forest, McCall Ranger District (208) 634-0400

Pit Latrine: Yes, seasonal

Louie Lake and Jughandle Mountain

You can't help but be awed when you see Louie Lake for the first time. The dark-blue lake is nestled directly below 8,310-foot Jughandle Mountain, whose sheer north face rises 600 feet to a pointy apex. In early evening, if the wind is still and Louie Lake's surface is calm, Jughandle Mountain delivers a stunning reflection off of the lake's glass-like surface. It is an impressive sight.

Beyond Louie Lake, a user-created trail rises to the lofty perch of Jughandle Mountain. Although not a long hike, it is a vertical beast rising over 1,300 feet in a little over a mile from Louie Lake. Most of the hike is in forest and requires some boulder scrambling near the peak's apex. There are two destinations with exceptional vistas along the route to the summit, giving hikers several worthy choices for a shorter hike. The views are stunning when looking north over Louie Lake, into Long Valley and the mountains beyond.

There are good campsites around Louie Lake, but it does see a lot of visitors due to its short distance from the trailhead. ATVs and motorcycles may use a one-mile section of trail to Louie Lake, so there is a chance you might see a few. In late September, the dense foliage along the trail turns crimson red, lime green and mustard yellow—a spectacular fall pilgrimage.

Trailhead Directions

From downtown McCall, drive south 1.9 miles on ID 55. Turn left onto Elo Road at mile marker 142 and reset your tripmeter. Travel 2.8 miles to a fork in the road. Take the left fork, which is Boulder Lake Road. Follow Boulder Lake Road (it turns into a well-graded dirt road at 0.9 mile) to its end at an undeveloped campground at 4.9 miles. In the campground, turn right on a short spur road that ends at the Louie Lake Trailhead.

The Hike

From the trailhead, immediately ford Boulder Creek on a downed tree. The trail weaves through open forest and gains nearly 300 feet to an unsigned junction with an old Jeep road at 0.5 mile. Turn east (left) and hike up the road whose grade steepens at 0.7 mile. There are good views looking north into the drainage leading to Boulder Lake. At 0.9 mile, the road veers south into dense forest and, within a half-mile, arrives at the northwest edge of Louie Lake. A trail leads left rising to a saddle at 7,700 feet and descends to Boulder Lake. This is an alternative route for the Boulder and Louie Lakes Loop. (See hike 17 for a description from a clockwise perspective.)

To continue to Jughandle Mountain, turn south (right) at Louie Lake. Beyond this point, motorized users are not allowed. The trail enters dense forest, passing several campsites. At 1.5 miles, make a short descent and then pass through an area with many granite boulders. At 1.8 miles, the footpath turns east and starts a very steep climb of more than 300 feet to the first destination with a great view at 2.1 miles. To the left of the trail, there is a large, flat granite outcropping overlooking Louie Lake. There are steep dropoffs, so use caution here.

Back on the footpath, continue to gain elevation as the forest becomes more open. At 2.3 miles, you must negotiate a rock slide for about 20 feet. The terrain is fairly level so the task is managable. Beyond the rocky talus, follow cairns along the faint trail to the next destination with a wonderful view at 2.4 miles. This setting is dramatic with the 600-foot sheer face of Jughandle Mountain just east of the perch. Beyond this point, the hike is more difficult. Follow the trial another 200 feet to a large granite boulder field scattered across the upper west face of Jughandle Mountain. You will need to negotiate the large granite talus carefully. Once past the talus, it is another 500 feet with a couple hundred feet of gain to the flat top of Jughandle Mountain. The views are spectacular.

Summit Lake and Buckhorn Summit

Coordinates
Trailhead:

N 44° 52.170'
W 115° 58.225'

Summit Lake:

N 44° 51.701'
W 115° 54.282'

Distance: 8.4 miles out-and-back (Summit Lake)

Total Elevation Gain: 1,500 feet

Difficulty: Strenuous

Elevation Range: 6,250 to 7,650 feet

Topographic Map: Paddy Flat

Time: 3.5 to 5 hours

Season: July through mid-October

Water Availability: Boulder Lake, Summit Lake and several creeks

Cautionary Advice: None

Information: Payette National Forest, McCall Ranger District (208) 634-0400

Pit Latrine: No

Summit Lake and Buckhorn Summit

Directly below Buckhorn Summit, hikers will discover the diminutive, but lovely, Summit Lake. It is nestled between 8,457-foot Buckhorn Mountain and 8,264-foot Rapid Peak, encirled by grassy meadows, evergreen forest and gray granite ridges. There are many excellent campsites and several good destinations to day hike from the lake, including an easy off-trail hike to Rapid Lake.

Beyond Summit Lake, the trail rises 300 feet to Buckhorn Summit. The views are spectacular looking east and include the rugged canyon containing the headwaters of Buckhorn Creek and the glacier-carved peaks shouldering the watershed. Energetic hikers can descend to Buckhorn Creek and explore the drainage.

To access Summit Lake, you depart from the Boulder Lake Trailhead. The chances for solitude are very good, too, since most hikers tend to stop at Boulder, Anderson or Rapid Lakes since they are closer to the trailhead. Look to hike in July when the open meadows beyond Boulder Lake erupt with wildflowers, especially lupine.

Trailhead Directions

From downtown McCall, drive south 1.9 miles on ID 55. Turn left onto Elo Road at mile marker 142 and reset your tripmeter. Travel 2.8 miles to a fork in the road. Take the left fork, which is Boulder Lake Road. Follow Boulder Lake Road (it turns into a well-graded dirt road at 0.9 mile) to its end at an undeveloped campground at 4.9 miles. To find the trailhead to Boulder Lake, which is a little tricky, walk up the spur road to the left (east) once you enter the campground area. It is a walk of about 500 feet to the base of the small dam containing Boulder Meadows Reservoir. The Boulder Lake Trailhead is near the dam, a few feet north of the reservoir.

The Hike

Follow hike 17 to the east end of Boulder Lake. Beyond Boulder Lake, hike through timber, passing the unsigned junction for the Boulder and Louie Lakes Loop, and reach the signed junction with the Paddy Flat–Lake Fork Trail at 2.5 miles (from the trailhead). Continue east (straight), ascending more than 200 feet on an open ridge to the signed junction for Summit and Rapid Lakes at 2.9 miles. Turn northeast (left) at the junction for Summit Lake. (The right fork accesses Rapid, Vics and Fogg Lakes – see hike 20.)

The trail rises 200 feet on an open hillside and levels in a stand of trees. From here, pass through a gorgeous meadow bordered to the east by a granite ridge. Many wildflowers bloom here including glacier lilies and buttercups. At 3.6 miles, cross a small gully and ascend through two switchbacks to where the trail's grade lessens. To the south (right), are extensive vistas into the canyon containing Rapid Creek and beyond to Jughandle Mountain. The trail levels on a wooded knoll at 3.9 miles and descends 100 feet through timber to Summit Lake. There are many good campsites along the lake's west and south perimeters.

To reach Buckhorn Summit, follow the trail past the north side of Buckhorn Lake and ascend through four switchbacks. After a gain of 300 feet, reach the wooded summit, a little over a half-mile from Buckhorn Lake. From the summit, the trail descends more than 1,000 feet to Buckhorn Creek.

From Summit Lake, you can hike off-trail down to Rapid Lake. It is about 0.4 mile with an elevation loss of more than 300 feet. The easiest access is to return to the wooded knoll at 3.9 miles. Between here and the two switchbacks, turn south (left) off-trail and descend through open forest. As you near Rapid Lake, the forest becomes denser and there is deadfall. From Rapid Lake, you can continue south on the maintained trail to Vics and Fogg Lakes (see hike 20).

Rapid, Vics, Fogg Lakes and Kennally Summit

Distance: 7.8 miles out-and-back (Rapid Lake)
10.4 miles out-and-back (Kennally Summit)

Total Elevation Gain: 1,450 feet (Rapid Lake)
2,000 feet (Kennally Summit)

Difficulty: Moderate (Rapid Lake)
Very Strenuous (Kennally Summit)

Elevation Range: 6,250 to 8,000 feet

Topographic Map: Paddy Flat

Time: 3 to 6.5 hours

Season: Mid-June through mid-October

Water Availability: Boulder, Rapid, Vics and Fogg Lakes, many creeks

Cautionary Advice: None

Information: Payette National Forest, McCall Ranger District (208) 634-0400

Pit Latrine: No

Trailhead:

N 44° 52.170'
W 115° 58.225'

Kennally Summit:

N 44° 50.593'
W 115° 54.022'

Rapid, Vics and Fogg Lakes and Kennally Summit

Beyond Boulder Lake, hikers can explore the Kennally Creek Trail that leads southeast to several alpine lakes. The closest and largest lake is the arrow-shaped Rapid Lake, sitting at the base of the towering 8,264-foot Rapid Peak. The quarter-mile-long lake is shouldered by marsh grass, firs and an assortment of wildflowers. By August, water lilies bloom on the lake's west and south shorelines. There are several excellent campsites scattered around the lake's perimeter.

Beyond Rapid Lake, the maintained trail continues another three-quarters of a mile to the diminutive and lily-covered Vics Lake. Although tiny, the lake is attractive and is surrounded by a dense forest of green firs and granite outcroppings. Near Vics Lake, a spur trail descends 250 feet in a half-mile to the larger Fogg Lake.

The Kennally Creek Trail continues past Vics Lake and rises 350 feet to the 7,940-foot Kennally Summit. To the south of the trail, an easy scramble up a granite knoll dispenses some of the best views in the area. From this vantage point, there are excellent views to several of the high peaks in the vicinity including Rapid Peak and Green and Jughandle Mountain. Twenty miles

Meadow and talus-covered ridge along the hike to Rapid Lake

to the southwest and over 3,000 vertical feet below, Lake Cascade stretches towards the town of Cascade. Looking east, the views stretch for miles and miles to an almost limitless number of ridges and mountains in the Salmon River Mountains.

Trailhead Directions

From downtown McCall, drive south 1.9 miles on ID 55. Turn left onto Elo Road at mile marker 142. Follow Elo Road 2.8 miles to a fork. Take the left fork in the road, which is Boulder Lake Road. Follow Boulder Lake Road 4.9 miles to its end. (The road turns to dirt in 0.9 mile.) The road ends at an undeveloped campground. To find the trailhead, which is a little tricky, walk east about 500 feet from the campground to the base of the small dam of Boulder Meadows Reservoir. The Boulder Lake Trailhead is to the left of the reservoir.

The Hike

Follow hike 17 to the east side of Boulder Lake. Beyond the lake, continue past the unsigned junction for the Boulder and Louie Lakes Loop, and reach the signed junction with the Paddy Flat–Lake Fork Trail at 2.5 miles (from the trailhead). Continue straight, ascending an open ridge to the signed junction for Rapid Lake at 2.9 miles. At the junction, turn right on Trail 102 towards Rapid Lake. (The left fork trail rises to Summit Lake and Buckhorn Summit – see hike 19.)

Hike south along a wildflower-covered hillside that offers fantastic views west into the Rapid Creek drainage and beyond to Twin Peaks and Jughandle Mountain. At 3.1 miles, ford a small stream, often dry by fall, and descend 200 feet to a small meadow.

Beyond the meadow, ascend about 75 feet through forest to a ford of Rapid Creek at 3.7 miles. Beyond the creek, the trail gains another 50 feet and arrives at a prominent, unsigned fork in a grassy meadow at 3.8 miles. Veer east (left), enter timber and reach Rapid Lake. A footpath, faint in spots, circumnavigates the lake. There are several excellent campsites.

To continue to Vics and Fogg Lakes, back at the unsigned fork at 3.8 miles, continue south (right fork). The trail rises 400 feet through forest to where it levels and then makes a descent to Vics Lake at 4.6 miles. Although close to the trail, there is an excellent campsite here.

To find Fogg Lake, ford Vics Lake's tiny outlet creek, and come to an immediate unsigned junction. Take the right fork, and descend 250 feet in a half-mile beside talus and through forest to Fogg Lake. The trail ends at the north side of the beautiful and remote lake where there are several good campsites.

Rapid Lake and Rapid Peak

Back at Vics Lake, take the left fork to continue to Kennally Summit. The trail's grade steepens right away and crosses a tiny stream in a little meadow at 4.9 miles. Beyond the meadow, it is a thigh-burning climb through forest to the signed summit at 5.2 miles. For breathtaking vistas, look southwest (right) for a rocky knoll. Hike along the right side of the knoll, and gain 100 feet to its top. From here, you can walk another quarter-mile along the ridgetop enjoying the outstanding views. From Kennally Summit, the maintained trail descends to Kennally Lakes and continues along the North Fork of Kennally Creek to the Kennally Creek Trailhead (approxiamately 11.0 miles). With two vehicles, this would be an excellent 16-mile shuttle hike.

Boulder Reservoir to Anderson Lake

Distance: 8.2 miles out-and-back

Total Elevation Gain: 2,050 feet

Difficulty: Strenuous

Elevation Range: 6,250 to 7,750 feet

Topographic Map: Paddy Flat, Fitsum Summit

Time: 3.5 to 5.5 hours

Season: Late June through mid-October

Water Availability: Boulder Meadows Reservoir, Boulder and Anderson Lakes and several creeks

Cautionary Advice: There is lots of standing water near Anderson Lake and mosquitoes can be atrocious in late June and early July.

Information: Payette National Forest, McCall Ranger District (208) 634-0400

Pit Latrine: No

Coordinates

Trailhead:

N 44° 52.170'
W 115° 58.225'

Anderson Lake:

N 44° 53.194'
W 115° 55.795'

Boulder Reservoir to Anderson Lake

Crowds thin less than two miles into this 8.2-miles out-and-back hike that explores Boulder Lake, Boulder Summit and Anderson Lake. Past Boulder Lake, the route climbs to Boulder Summit on a steep hillside dotted with colorful wildflowers in midsummer. The treeless slope offers superb views of pastoral meadows, deep ravines and forested ridges. You also see Boulder Lake, glistening 1,000 feet below the summit.

Your reward for the steep climb over the summit is the beautiful Anderson Lake. This high alpine lake is nestled in a small bowl below the dark gray-cliffs of the 8,377-foot Boulder Mountain. Dense forest surrounds the lake, and a huge granite outcropping extends into its dark waters. Backpackers will find several shaded campsites on the lake's perimeter.

Another route to Anderson Lake is from the East Fork of Lake Creek Trail off Lick Creek Road. From this trailhead, it is a longer hike but one that is infrequently traveled. If you are backpacking, the Boulder Reservoir Trailhead makes more sense, but for those out for an exciting day hike with plenty of solitude, look to hike from Lick Creek Road.

Trailhead Directions

From downtown McCall, drive south 1.9 miles on ID 55. Turn left onto Elo Road at mile marker 142, and reset your tripmeter. Travel 2.8 miles to a fork in the road. Take the left fork, which is Boulder Lake Road. Follow Boulder Lake Road, which turns into a well-graded dirt road at 0.9 mile, to its end at an undeveloped campground at 4.9 miles. To find the trailhead to Boulder Lake, which is a little confusing, walk east (left) up the spur road once you enter the campground area. It is a walk of about 500 feet to the base of the small dam containing Boulder Meadows Reservoir. The Boulder Lake Trailhead is near the dam a few feet north of the reservoir.

The Hike

Follow hike 17 to the end of Boulder Lake. Beyond the lake, hike through timber, passing the unsigned junction for the Boulder and Louie Lakes Loop, and reach the signed junction with the Paddy Flat–Lake Fork Trail at 2.5 miles (from the trailhead). At the junction, turn north (left) to Anderson Lake. The trail meanders through a grassy meadow and makes an easy ford of Boulder Creek. At 2.9 miles, reach the first of four switchbacks, and ascend a very steep 700

Anderson Lake

feet on an open hillside. In July, many wildflowers bloom here including penstemon, Indian paintbrush, lupine and arrowleaf balsamroot. As you ascend, make sure to look behind you at the fantastic vistas looking south.

Reach a signed saddle (7,750 feet) at 3.5 miles between Boulder Mountain and Boulder Summit. A user-created footpath leads west, gaining 400 feet, to the 8,377-foot Boulder Mountain. From the saddle, make a steep descent of 300 feet over the next half-mile to the signed junction for Anderson Lake. Turn west (left), and descend 150 feet to the lake's northeast side where you will find several excellent campsites.

PONDEROSA STATE PARK OVERVIEW

Ponderosa State Park is less than two miles from downtown McCall, located on a 1,000-acre peninsula extending two and one-half miles into Payette Lake. Named after the ponderosa pine, which can grow up to 150 feet tall, the park contains an assortment of hiking and biking trails. The trail system within the park allows for a wide range of hikes. The terrain is diverse with marshes, dense forest, cliffs and arid hillsides. Wildflowers are prolific in midsummer and huckleberries ripen in late summer.

In addition to the ponderosa pine, other tree species found in the park include Douglas fir, lodgepole pine, western larch and grand fir. Wildlife is present, presenting opportunities to spot Canadian geese, bald eagles, wood ducks, osprey, woodpeckers, deer, moose, muskrats, beaver and an occasional black bear.

This area is frequented by hikers, mountain bikers and trail runners. Horses and motorized vehicles are prohibited on the trails in the park. A few of the trials allow mountain bikes while others allow foot traffic only. Interpretive signs can be found near trailheads and along several of the trails. Two loop hikes are highlighted in this guidebook.

The park offers several camping opportunities, including cabins. Reservations are accepted nine months in advance and are highly recommended. Peak visitation begins on Memorial Day weekend and tapers off after Labor Day. September and October are excellent times to visit the park as there are few visitors, and the fall foilage is beautiful. If you enjoy snowshoeing, check out the twelve miles of groomed trails and over three miles of designated snowshoe trails. To obtain more information on this fantastic state park or to make camp reservations, visit *parksandrecreation. idaho.gov/*. There is a $5.00 day use entrance fee per vehicle.

Ponderosa State Park
Meadow Marsh Loop

Coordinates

Trailhead:

N 44° 56.465'
W 116° 04.503'

**Junction of Meadow
Marsh and Fox Run Trail:**

N 44° 56.321'
W 116° 04.497'

Distance: 1.8 miles loop

Total Elevation Gain: 50 feet

Difficulty: Easy

Elevation Range: 5,000 to 5,050 feet

Topographic Map: McCall

Time: Up to 1 hour

Season: Mid-June through October

Water Availability: None

Cautionary Advice: None

Information: Ponderosa State Park (208) 634-2164

Restroom: Yes, at the visitor's center

Meadow Marsh Loop

This is a short, well-marked, loop hike through dense forest for the majority of the trek. There are interpretive signs along many sections of the trail that provide interesting information on the local flora and fauna. There is very little elevation gain, so anyone looking for an easy hike will enjoy this outing. The trailhead is located near the Peninsula Campground. Mountain bikes are prohibited on the trail.

Trailhead Directions

From downtown McCall, drive south on ID 55 for 0.1 mile, and take an immediate left onto Railroad Avenue. Continue straight at the first stop sign. At 0.4 mile, reach a four-way stop sign. Turn left onto Davis Avenue to another four-way stop sign at 1.1 miles. Travel through the four-way intersection entering the park and reaching the pay station at 1.3 miles. Once in the park, follow the main road 0.7 mile to the signed Meadow Marsh Trailhead on the right.

Look for deer in Ponderosa State Park

The Hike

The hike starts in dense forest and quickly arrives at a signed junction in 0.2 mile. Turn north (left) on the Meadow Marsh Trail. At 0.5 mile, arrive at the Fir Grove Cut-Off junction. (The trail to the right cuts back to the Meadow Marsh Trail in 0.2 mile where a right turn will make a mini-loop of 1.1 miles.)

Meadow Marsh is a good snowshoe hike

Continue straight at the Fir Grove junction passing an interpretive sign and then Meadow Marsh. Reach the first of two junctions at 0.9 mile. Follow the signs for the Meadow Marsh Trail through both junctions. At 1.3 miles, the trail bypasses the Fir Grove Cut-Off and comes to the first junction near the beginning of the hike. Turn left to the trailhead.

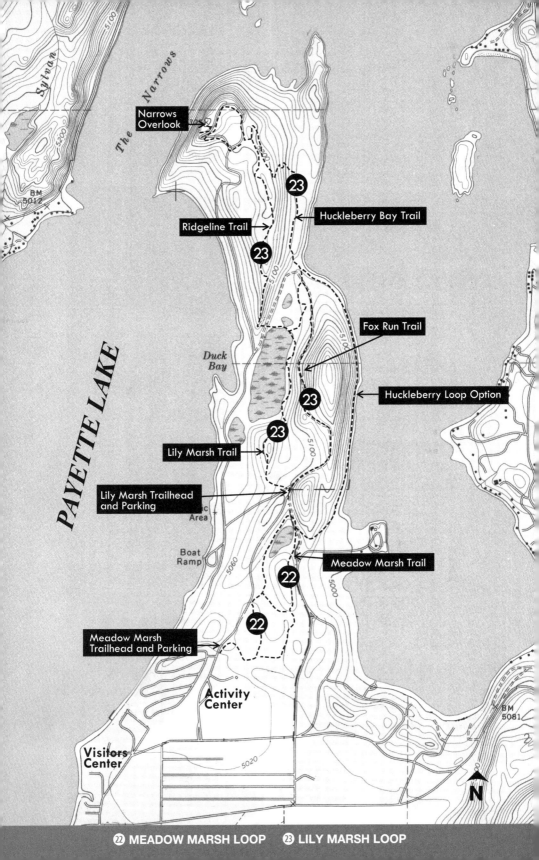

The Narrows

Sylvan

BM
5012

Narrows
Overlook

Ridgeline Trail

23

23

Huckleberry Bay Trail

Fox Run Trail

PAYETTE LAKE

Duck
Bay

Huckleberry Loop Option

23

23

Lily Marsh Trail

Lily Marsh Trailhead
and Parking

...ic
Area

Boat
Ramp

Meadow Marsh Trail

22

22

Meadow Marsh
Trailhead and Parking

Activity
Center

Visitors
Center

BM
5081

N

23 Ponderosa State Park
Lily Marsh Loop

Coordinates

Trailhead:

N 44° 56.465'
W 116° 04.508'

Junction of Ridgeline and Huckleberry Trails:

N 44° 57.683'
W 116° 04.670'

Distance: 4.0 miles loop

Total Elevation Gain: 500 feet

Difficulty: Easy

Elevation Range: 5,000 to 5,250 feet

Topographic Map: McCall

Time: 1.5 to 2.5 hours

Season: Mid-June through October

Water Availability: Lily Pond and Payette Lake

Cautionary Advice: None

Information: Ponderosa State Park (208) 634-2164

Restroom: Yes, at the visitor center

Lily Marsh Loop

Create a diverse loop hike that is easily tackled by the entire family by combining four different trails. Along the way, ramble past the scenic Lily Marsh, up the wildflower-lined Ridgeline Trail, down the heavily forested Huckleberry Bay Trail and back to the trailhead on the Fox Run Trail. There are plenty of detours along the way, including a short hike from the Ridgeline Trail to the Narrows Overlook where there are sensational views of Payette Lake.

Trailhead Directions

From downtown McCall, drive south on ID 55 for 0.1 mile and take an immediate left onto Railroad Avenue. Continue straight at the first stop sign. At 0.4 mile, reach a four-way stop sign. Turn left onto Davis Avenue to another four-way stop sign at 1.1 miles. Travel through the four-way intersection, entering the park and reaching the pay station at 1.3 miles. Once in the park, follow the paved road an additional 1.4 miles to the signed Fox Run Trailhead on the right.

Lily Marsh is a good destination for a family hike

The Hike

From the trailhead, descend to a small ravine and ascend to an open ridge dotted with yellow arrowleaf balsamroot in late spring. Continue through forest arriving at the edge of Lily Marsh at 0.4 mile. The marsh has several ponds covered with bright yellow water lilies in July and August.

From here, the trail ascends to a small knoll near the east side of the marsh. At 0.9 mile, reach a signed junction with the Huckleberry Trail. Turn west (left), crossing a footbridge and then a small road. At the road junction, look for a sign for the Ridgeline Trail.

The Ridgeline Trail ascends 100 feet through forest and then meanders along a ridge that has many wildflowers in late June and early July. There are huge ponderosa pines along this section of trail. At 2.0 miles, reach the signed junction with the Huckleberry Bay Trail. (Turn left here for a scenic detour. Within 100 feet, turn right onto the dirt road and continue 0.4 mile to the Narrows Overlook. The spectacular views are worth the extra walk.)

To continue the loop, turn north (right) at the junction with the Huckleberry Bay Trail. The trail enters dense forest and descends past a little marsh. Continue through forest to an unsigned junction at 2.9 miles. A small footpath turns left towards the edge of Payette Lake. Continue straight on the Huckleberry Loop Trail, and make an immediate right at a sign for the Fox Run Trail. Within 10 feet, turn left on the gravel road (Fox Run Trail). It is a mile through dense forest, with an elevation gain of nearly 200 feet, back to the Lily Marsh Trailhead.

(If you want a longer hike, instead of turning right for the Fox Run Trail, continue straight on the Huckleberry Loop Trail that heads south 1.3 miles along Payette Lake and intersects with the Fox Run Trail again. Turn north (right) and walk 0.3 mile to your vehicle.)

East Fork of Lake Fork Creek

Coordinates

Trailhead:

N 44° 56.213'
W 115° 56.479'

Junction with trail to Maki Lake:

N 44° 58.325'
W 115° 53.992'

Distance: 12.6 miles out-and-back

Total Elevation Gain: 1,100 feet

Difficulty: Strenuous

Elevation Range: 5,450 to 6,400 feet

Topographic Map: Fitsum Summit

Time: 4.5 to 7 hours

Season: Mid-June through mid-October

Water Availability: North and East Fork of Lake Fork Creek, Idler Creek, many streams

Cautionary Advice: None

Information: Payette National Forest, McCall Ranger District (208) 634-0400

Pit Latrine: No

East Fork of Lake Fork Creek

You won't find a more beautiful McCall getaway than the creekside hike along the East Fork of Lake Fork Creek. Although this long hike visits no alpine lakes, the easy stroll wanders through a majestic, glaciated canyon with towering granite ridges, sparkling creeks and lush meadows. Shade is provided by an evergreen forest. Near the upper elevations of the hike, precipitous granite walls tower more than 2,000 feet along both sides of the canyon to many unnamed peaks between 7,500 feet and 8,500 feet.

What really separates this excursion from many others is the outlandish show of wildflowers in the upper canyon. In July and early August, penstemon, lupine, Indian paintbrush, clarkia, flax, avens and glacier lily cover the open hillsides with a flurry of color. It is a real spectacle.

Most hikers stop at the creek ford near Idler Creek 4.7 miles into the hike. This is a worthy destination as the creek is shouldered by huge boulders and includes several blue pools that invite a swim. Beyond the ford of Idler Creek, the canyon narrows, and the alpine landscape only gets better. This hike's description sends hikers to a beautiful meadow set below an unnamed 8,151-foot granite peak. Backpackers will find many prime campsites once they have hiked about 3 miles from the trailhead.

Trailhead Directions

From downtown McCall, drive 0.1 mile south on ID 55, and turn left onto Railroad Avenue. Continue straight at the first stop sign. At 0.4 mile, reach a four-way stop sign. Turn left onto Davis Avenue to another four-way stop sign at 1.1 miles. Turn right onto Lick Creek Road. At 3.2 miles, the road will fork. Reset your tripmeter, and continue straight on Lick Creek Road for 7.2 miles. (It turns into a well-graded dirt road in 3.3 miles.) Take an immediate right, after crossing the North Fork of Lake Fork Creek, onto a short spur road to the trailhead. There is parking for five or six vehicles.

The Hike

The trail starts in open forest parallelling the North Fork of Lake Fork Creek. At 0.2 mile, ford a small stream, ascend over a small knoll, and then ford a much wider stream at 0.5 mile. The trail's grade soon steepens and comes to an unsigned junction at 0.7 mile. Take the left fork and ascend through forest. (The right fork descends to the North Fork of Lake Fork Creek.)

At 1.1 miles, turn through a switchback, and ascend to a level area where the trail passes to the left of a huge granite boulder. At 1.5 miles, reach a signed junction. (The right fork fords the East Fork of Lake Fork Creek and ascends through dense forest to Anderson Lake in 3.8 miles – see hike 25.)

Continue east (straight) through forest and soon turn north, passing a multitude of huckleberry bushes and lichen-covered boulders. At 3.0 miles, enter the first of several small meadows, which you will pass through over the next mile. At 4.0 miles, cross two streams and enter a large meadow. At the end of the meadow, ford the East Fork of Lake Fork Creek, just north of its confluence with Idler Creek. This a great destination for a shorter hike.

Beyond the ford, the trail moves away from the creek and steepens. The views of the mountains improve, especially looking east into the narrow canyon containing Idler Creek. At 5.0 miles, ford a small stream, bypass a huge gray outcropping and continue along a steep grade through forest.

At 5.9 miles, the grade becomes more moderate as it runs beside large slabs of granite. The trail eventually levels at 6.3 miles near a large meadow on the opposite side of the East Fork of Lake Fork Creek. With the meadow, granite slabs, lofty canyon ridges and cascading East Fork of Lake Fork Creek nearby, this is a great place to spend a few hours.

As shown on the Fitsum Summit map, the trail to Maki Lake fords the creek here. The trail is infrequently maintained and leads one mile with 900 feet of gain to the lake. The main trail continues north and then veers west to the 7,900-foot Snowslide Summit in 3 miles.

Snowslide Peak

Maki Lake

End of Trail Description

Golden Lake

East Fork Creek Ford

Idler Creek

F A Y E T T E

F O R E S T

Trailhead and Parking

Unsigned Junction

Signed Junction

Campground

Lake Fork Forest Service Station
Footbridge

East Fork

Middle

N

East Fork of Lake Fork Creek to Anderson Lake

Coordinates

Trailhead:

N 44° 56.213'
W 115° 56.479'

Anderson Lake:

N 44° 53.194'
W 115° 55.795'

Distance: 10.6 miles out-and-back

Total Elevation Gain: 2,200 feet

Difficulty: Very Strenuous

Elevation Range: 5,450 to 7,400 feet

Topographic Map: Fitsum Summit

Time: 4.5 to 6.5 hours

Season: Late June through mid-October

Water Availability: East, South and North Fork of Lake Fork Creek, Anderson Lake and many streams

Cautionary Advice: The trail is infrequently maintained and can get brushy. Long pants are recommended. Mosquitoes are very bad around Anderson Lake from late June to mid-July.

Information: Payette National Forest, McCall Ranger District (208) 634-0400

Pit Latrine: No

East Fork of Lake Fork Creek to Anderson Lake

If you want to experience a truly remote and secluded trail that leads to a beautiful lake, try this route to Anderson Lake. The East Fork Trail starts at Lick Creek Road, near North Fork of Lake Fork Creek, and continues about 1.5 miles to a signed junction. Here, adventuresome hikers turn south on the Paddy Flat–Lake Fork Trail and ford the East Fork of Lake Fork Creek. It is doubtful you will see any horse or mountain bike traffic beyond this point as it is very rugged.

The trail continues up the South Fork of Lake Fork Creek and eventually leaves the canyon making a steep 1,500-foot ascent in a narrow drainage to Anderson Lake. This entire area teems with a thick understory of plants, bushes and wildflowers, and the forest is incredibly dense. As you wind your way through this foliage paradise, you get the distinct feeling that few travel here and at any moment, a wild critter might jump onto the narrow trail.

Although Anderson Lake is an excellent backpacking destination, there are only a couple of spots along the entire route where you will find enough level

Looking north from the 7,200-foot saddle

ground to set up camp for the night. You can also access Anderson Lake from the Boulder Lake Trail. This route is heavily traveled but is shorter. If you are looking for serenity though, you just found your hike.

Trailhead Directions

From downtown McCall, drive 0.1 mile south on ID 55 to Railroad Avenue and turn left. Continue straight (east) at the first stop sign. At 0.4 mile, reach a four-way stop sign. Turn left onto Davis Avenue to another four-way stop sign at 1.1 miles. Turn right onto Lick Creek Road. At 3.2 miles, the road will fork. Take the right fork (Lick Creek Road) and reset your tripmeter. Continue on Lick Creek Road for 7.2 miles—the road turns into a well-graded dirt road in 3.3 miles—to the bridge over the North Fork of Lake Fork Creek, and take an immediate right onto a short spur road leading to the trailhead. There is parking for five or six vehicles.

The Hike

The trail starts in open forest and parallels the North Fork of Lake Fork Creek on level ground. At 0.2 mile, ford a small stream, ascend over a small knoll and then ford a much wider stream at 0.5 mile. The trail's grade soon steepens and comes to an unsigned junction at 0.7 mile. Take the left fork and ascend through open forest. (The right fork descends to the North Fork of Lake Fork Creek where you can ford the creek—difficult in early season—and hike to the Lake Fork Campground.)

At 1.1 miles, turn through a switchback, and ascend to where the trail levels near a huge granite boulder. Continue through forest to a signed junction at 1.5 miles. Turn south (right) and descend to a ford of the East Fork of Lake Fork Creek. In late June and early July, use caution as the creek is about knee deep. (If you continue straight at the junction, the trail continues up the East Fork of Lake Fork Creek – see hike 24.)

Beyond the ford, follow the trail as it weaves around thick brush and gains 100 feet to where it levels. Here, descend past a little bog, and ascend another 200 feet to where the trail levels again at 2.3 miles. The trail stays fairly level over the next half-mile and veers west to a ford of the sandy-bottomed South Fork of Lake Fork Creek at 2.8 miles. Although the creek is not that deep, there is deadfall to assist with the ford. About 100 feet beyond the ford, there is a level area in timber near the trail where you can establish a campsite.

At 2.9 miles, begin a very steep 400-foot gain through four switchbacks. The old-growth forest is very dense along this stretch. The trail levels momentarily at an elevation of 6,300 feet, just east of Anderson Lake's outlet creek at 3.3 miles. Here, the trail turns south paralleling the creek and starts rising again. After another gain of 200 feet, ford Anderson Lake's outlet creek at 3.9 miles.

Past the creek ford, continue the grinding ascent, passing to the right of a granite outcropping at 4.2 miles. The outcropping dishes out steller views looking north and makes for a great excuse to enjoy a rest. The forest is still dense as you make your way south to a final ford of Anderson's outlet creek at 4.5 miles. Beyond the ford, pass below a granite ridge, and ascend an open hillside covered with alpine knotweed and a few firs. After a couple of tight switchbacks, the trail levels near an open saddle at 7,200 feet. The views from here are spectacular looking across the canyon and beyond to the west-facing granite ridges.

From the saddle, the trail's grade becomes moderate and ascends through beautiful, open forest to a ford of two small creeks at 5.0 miles and a signed junction at 5.2 miles. The signage is on the opposite side of the tree, so if you're lightheaded after all of the elevation gain, you could miss it. Turn right, and zigzag down 150 feet to the east edge of Anderson Lake. There are good campsites here and beyond the outlet creek.

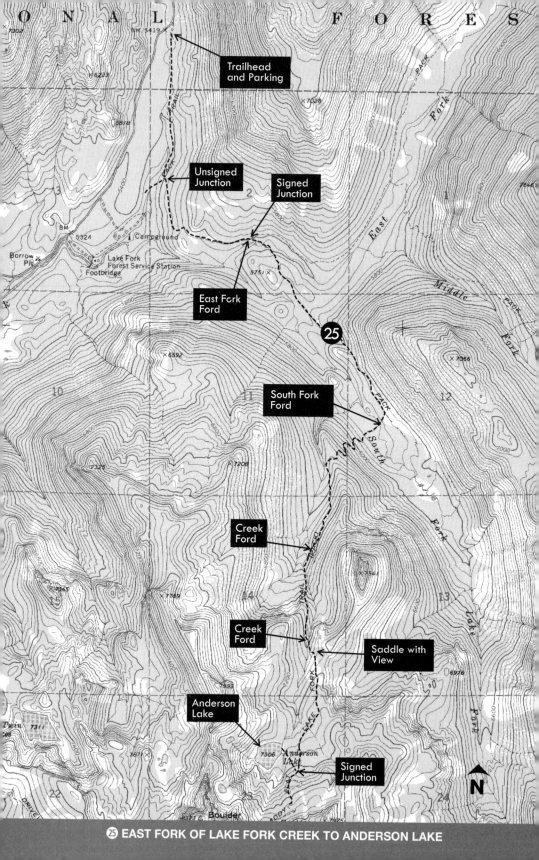

Trailhead and Parking

Unsigned Junction

Signed Junction

East Fork Ford

South Fork Ford

Creek Ford

Creek Ford

Saddle with View

Anderson Lake

Signed Junction

N

㉕ EAST FORK OF LAKE FORK CREEK TO ANDERSON LAKE

Crystal Lake and Fall Creek Saddle

Trailhead:

N 44° 58.536

W 115° 57.371'

Crystal Lake:

N 44° 57.190'

W 115° 57.848'

Distance: 5.2 miles out-and-back (Crystal Lake)
5.4 miles out-and-back (Fall Creek Saddle)

Total Elevation Gain: 1,800 feet (Crystal Lake)
2,200 feet (Fall Creek Saddle)

Difficulty: Strenuous

Elevation Range: 5,550 to 7,700 feet

Topographic Map: Fitsum Summit

Time: 2.5 to 3.5 hours

Season: Late June through mid-October

Water Availability: Crystal Lake, several creeks

Cautionary Advice: Part of the route to Crystal Lake
is on an unmaintained footpath. Expect deadfall and
some route-finding.

Information: Payette National Forest, McCall Ranger
District (208) 634-0400

Pit Latrine: No

Crystal Lake and Fall Creek Saddle

Between Fall Creek Saddle and Slick Rock—one of the longest continuous
technical rock routes in the state of Idaho—lies the oval-shaped Crystal
Lake. This breathtaking beauty is recessed in a granite bowl surrounded by
outcroppings, forest and steep ridges. Adventurous hikers can ascend another
250 feet above Crystal Lake to a small pond near a granite ridge with
outstanding views.

Although not a long hike, the route is steep. The trail snakes through
burned forest from the 1994 fires, along a meandering creek and into a
scenic meadow. From here, you can head off-trail for three-quarters of a
mile to Crystal Lake. Expect deadfall and some route-finding. Another
destination option is to continue southwest through the meadow on the
maintained trail and ascend a rocky ridge to Fall Creek Saddle. An easy
off-trail hike south along a footpath leads to a treeless ridge with spectacular
views 700 feet down to Crystal Lake, the deep canyon of the North Fork
of Lake Fork Creek and beyond into the Salmon River Mountains. The
views west into Long Valley of the sprawling Cascade and Payette Lakes
are equally breathtaking.

Pond above Crystal Lake

In July and early August there are many wildflowers along the route. They are especially prolific on the high ridge south of Fall Creek Saddle. Backpackers will find several good campsites in the large meadow before reaching Fall Creek Saddle or at Crystal Lake.

Trailhead Directions

From downtown McCall, drive 0.1 mile south on ID 55 to Railroad Avenue, and turn left. Continue straight at the first stop sign. At 0.4 mile, reach a four-way stop sign. Turn left onto Davis Avenue to another four-way stop sign at 1.1 miles. Turn right on Lick Creek Road. At 3.2 miles, the road forks. Reset your tripmeter and continue straight on Lick Creek Road for 9.9 miles. (It turns into a well-graded dirt road in 3.3 miles.) On your left will be a sign "Fall Creek Trail." A large parking area is on the opposite side of the road.

The Hike

Start in dense forest and immediately ford a creek and then a couple of tiny streams. Reach a switchback at 0.5 mile as the trail's grade intensifies and rises in and out of burned forest through a set of additional switchbacks. At 0.9 mile, weave between head-high snowbrush. This evergreen shrub is quite fragrant when it blooms in late June. Amazingly, the fire-resistant seeds of the plant can survive in soil for 200 years before fire stimulates germination.

The trail's grade diminishes at 1.2 miles but still climbs another half-mile beside an unnamed creek to a large meadow. Before entering the meadow at 1.7 miles, look for a faint footpath that branches south (left) off the main trail (see map). There are several campsites in the immediate area. To continue to Crystal Lake, follow the footpath south navigating deadfall. At 1.9 miles, ascend a burned slope weaving between deadfall and granite rocks. After a gain of 250 feet, at the top of the saddle, the tread becomes more prominent. Follow the footpath down the east side of the saddle as it veers south into forest and makes a final gain of 100 feet to Crystal Lake.

To find a small pond and a great overlook of Crystal Lake, turn northwest (right) at Crystal Lake and continue up a talus-covered ridge, veering due west after a gain of about 200 feet. There is a granite ridge south of the pond that is worth exploring.

To continue to Fall Creek Saddle from the 1.7 mile unsigned junction near the meadow, follow the trail south. At 1.9 miles, the grade steepens and after an arduous gain of nearly 500 feet in a half-mile reaches the forested 7,350-foot saddle. The trail is braided in spots, so look for cairns to help with route-finding as you zigzag up the steep hillside. At the saddle, views to the west are obscured by dense forest, but hiking north up a series of granite knolls, the vistas to Long Valley and Payette Lake dramatically improve.

Crystal Lake

For outstanding views of the area, turn south (left) at the saddle on a footpath. It rises 250 feet through forest with remarkable views down into the meadow you passed through earlier. At 2.6 miles, leave the forest behind on an open ridge and ascend another 100 feet to the edge of a grassy knoll carpeted with summer wildflowers. Several granite outcroppings provide platforms to observe the sparkling Crystal Lake, 700 feet below.

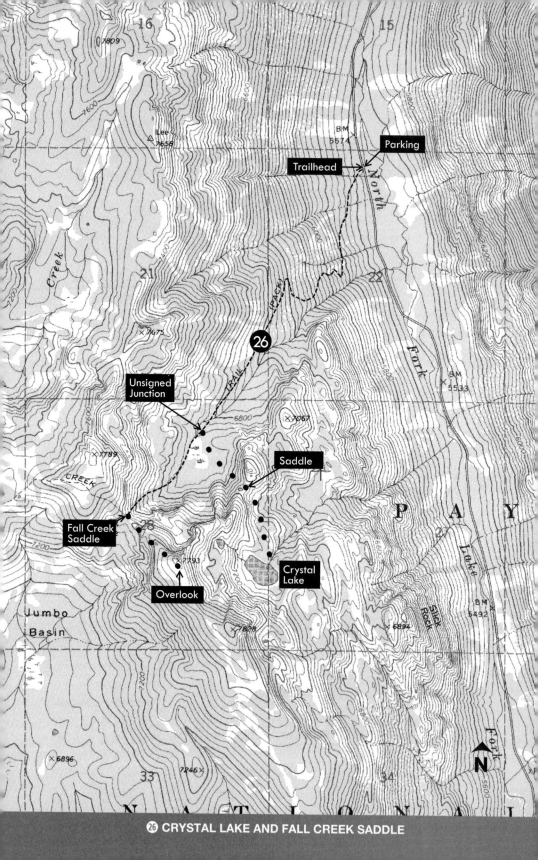

CRYSTAL LAKE AND FALL CREEK SADDLE

Box and Sisters Lakes

Distance: 6.0 miles out-and-back (Box Lake)
8.8 miles out-and-back (Sister Lake)

Total Elevation Gain: 2,200 feet (Box Lake)
2,350 feet (Sister Lake)

Difficulty: Strenuous to Very Strenuous

Elevation Range: 5,700 to 7,550 feet

Topographic Map: Fitsum Summit, Box Lake

Time: 3 to 4.5 hours (Box Lake)

Season: Late June through mid-October

Water Availability: Black Lee Creek, Box and Sister Lakes

Cautionary Advice: None

Information: Payette National Forest, McCall Ranger District (208) 634-0400

Pit Latrine: No

Coordinates

Trailhead:

N 44° 59.355'
W 115° 57.265'

Box Lake:

N 45° 00.769'
W 115° 58.938'

Box and Sisters Lakes

Most of the trailheads near Lick Creek Road lead to spectacular scenery. However, many of the lakes are close to the road, which tends to draw weekend crowds. This out-and-back hike sees its fair share of hikers, but the size of Box Lake (nearly a mile long) gives you the opportunity to find solitude. The majority of hikers come to the lake's edge and make a beeline back to the trailhead.

By continuing around the lake's west edge, you access the remote north side of Box Lake. Excellent campsites look south across the dark-blue water, perfectly framed in a glaciated amphitheater. A half-mile jaunt west, on a faint trail, takes you to one of the two Sister Lakes. The shallow, picturesque lake shelters a couple of remote campsites. Cross-country hikers can explore the other Sister Lake.

The 3-mile trek to Box Lake is steep. Most of the route parallels Black Lee Creek, a tributary of the North Fork of Lake Fork Creek. From July through mid-August, much of the terrain is awash with colorful wildflowers including lupine, penstemon, sego lily, columbine, scarlet gilia, Indian paintbrush, lousewort, goldenrod and beargrass. On the ascent, there are sprawling

View from granite outcropping above Black Creek drainage

views down to the winding canyon of the North Fork of Lake Fork. Lush flower-filled meadows, steep granite ridges, the picturesque Box Lake and sensational vistas guarantee lasting memories.

Trailhead Directions

From downtown McCall, drive 0.1 mile south on ID 55 to Railroad Avenue, and turn left. Continue straight at the first stop sign. At 0.4 mile, reach a four-way stop sign. Turn left onto Davis Avenue to another four-way stop sign at 1.1 miles. Turn right onto Lick Creek Road. At 3.2 miles, the road will fork. Take the right fork (Lick Creek Road), and reset your tripmeter. Continue on Lick Creek Road for 10.9 miles, which turns into a well-graded dirt road in 3.3 miles, to the trailhead on the left side of the road. Look for a sign "Box Lake Trail." Parking is limited to five or six vehicles.

The Hike

From the trailhead, ascend through a series of switchbacks through lodgepole, Douglas fir and Engelmann spruce forest, gaining more than 400 feet in a half-mile. The trail enters a hillside of gray snags from the 1994 fires, showcasing spectacular views of the surrounding rugged mountains. At 0.9 mile, the trail levels as you cross a small meadow.

Beyond the meadow, cross Black Lee Creek at 1.1 miles on a downed tree. The trail rises again, passing a series of impressive granite benches where you will find alpine knotweed, a shrub-like perennial, peppered on the open hillsides. This plant turns a beautiful shade of burgundy in the fall. Ford Black Lee Creek again at 1.4 miles and once more at 1.6 miles, entering burned forest as the grade intensifies, ascending beside a collection of huge outcroppings. At 2.0 miles, near an elevation of 7,400 feet, the trail passes a granite outcropping just a few feet off-trail providing outstanding views south down into the Black Creek drainage.

After a bit more gain, the trail finally levels at 2.4 miles in a lovely meadow flanked by steep granite ridges. There are a multitude of potential campsites in the area. At the end of the meadow, Box Lake comes into view and

Sister Lake

sparkles 400 feet below in a glaciated bowl. Descend through six switchbacks to the edge of the lake at 3.0 miles. Several well-used campsites are found here.

To continue to the north side of the lake and beyond to Sister Lake, follow the trail into forest. The trail is sketchy in spots along the lake's west shore. Make sure you stay near the lake's edge as several game trails lead up the ridge. At 3.8 miles, near the end of the lake, enter a grassy meadow. Campsites with fine views across Box Lake are along the lake's north edge.

To continue to the smaller Sister Lake, turn northwest (left) in the meadow. The trail is difficult to see but is prominent once you leave the small meadow. Descend 100 feet in 0.4 mile, and turn south (left) over deadfall to the small, shallow Sister Lake in 150 yards. A shady campsite is located on a rocky knoll near the lake.

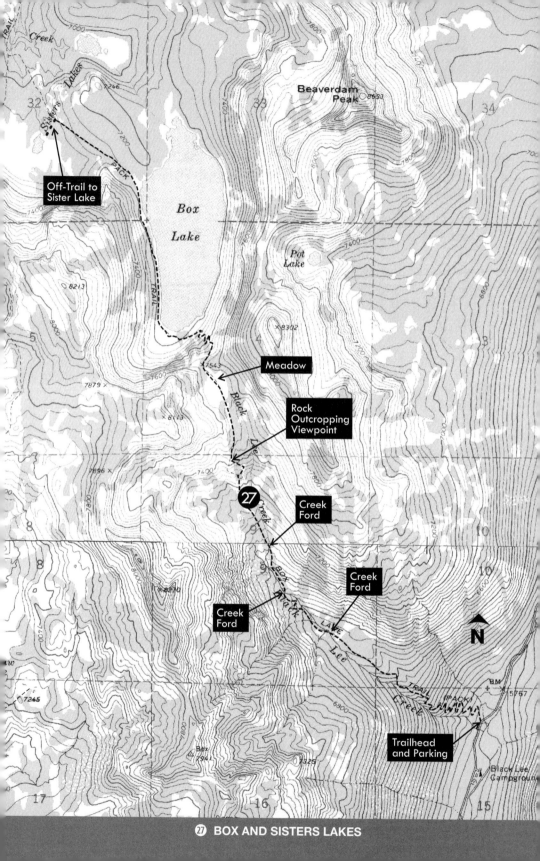

Off-Trail to
Sister Lake

Box
Lake

Beaverdam
Peak

Pot
Lake

Meadow

Rock
Outcropping
Viewpoint

27

Creek
Ford

Creek
Ford

Creek
Ford

N

Trailhead
and Parking

Black Lee
Campground

Snowslide Lake, Snowslide Summit and Maki Lake

Coordinates

Trailhead:

N 44° 59.927'
W 115° 56.830'

Snowslide Lake:

N 44° 59.033'
W 115° 55.971'

Distance: 4.6 miles out-and-back (Snowslide Lake)
6.6 miles out-and-back (Maki Lake)

Total Elevation Gain: 1,300 feet (Snowslide Lake)
2,600 feet (Maki Lake)

Difficulty: Strenuous (Snowslide Lake)
Very Strenuous (Maki Lake)

Elevation Range: 5,900 to 7,900 feet

Topographic Map: Fitsum Summit

Time: 2 to 3 hours (Snowslide Lake)

Season: July through mid-October

Water Availability: Snowslide Lake, Maki Lake, several creeks

Cautionary Advice: The North Fork of Lake Fork Creek may be impassable in late spring. Trekking poles help with the steep descent on the return.

Information: Payette National Forest, McCall Ranger District (208) 634-0400

Pit Latrine: No

Snowslide Lake, Snowslide Summit and Maki Lake

Although Snowslide Peak is only a mile east of Lick Creek Road, it's impossible to see the peak's impressive face due to dense forest. The 8,522-foot mountain is topped with a half-mile-wide granite face cresting nearly 1,400 feet above the beautiful Snowslide Lake. Granite ridges stair-step the lake's east perimeter and enhance this spectacular mountain haven.

From Snowslide Lake, the steep trail rises 700 feet to Snowslide Summit for some of the best views in the area. Breathtaking vistas await including the rugged canyon of the East Fork of Lake Fork Creek and the many impressive mountains in the area: Beaverdam, Fitsum, Sawtooth, Snowslide and Nick Peaks. Beyond the summit, adventuresome hikers can extend the journey by descending on a maintained trail 1,100 feet to the East Fork of Lake Fork Creek or hike off-trail to the isolated Maki Lake.

Make no mistake, any section of this hike is steep. Although the closest destination is Snowslide Lake, you are still looking at a gain of 1,300 feet in

Open hillside and granite ridge, southeast of Snowslide Lake

1.6 miles. Backpackers will find many quality campsites at both Snowslide and Maki Lakes. The hike to Snowslide Lake is mainly in forest with an occassional open hillside dotted with summer wildflowers. For wildflower aficionados, the hillside meadows to the southeast of Snowslide Lake are a spectacular destination in late July. Be forewarned: the marshy terrain southeast of Maki Lake results in a lot of mosquitos in early-to-mid July.

Trailhead Directions

From downtown McCall, drive 0.1 mile south on ID 55, and turn left onto Railroad Avenue. Continue straight at the first stop sign. At 0.4 mile, reach a four-way stop sign. Turn left onto Davis Avenue to another four-way stop sign at 1.1 miles. Turn right onto Lick Creek Road. At 3.2 miles, the road will fork. Reset your tripmeter, and continue straight on Lick Creek Road for 11.6 miles. (It turns into a well-graded dirt road in 3.3 miles.) Look for a sign "East Fk. Lake Fork Tr. " on your right. Turn right into the parking area that can accommodate three or four vehicles.

The Hike

From the trailhead, make an immediate ford of the North Fork of Lake Fork Creek. In late spring, use caution in high snowfall years as the ford can be challenging. Beyond the ford, enter forest and start a zigzag ascent. As you ascend, views improve looking west into the the deep canyon of the

North Fork of Lake Creek and to the high peaks beyond. At 0.9 mile, cross two streams, and look ahead for filtered views of Snowslide Peak. The trail traverses a hillside and makes a final steep climb of 200 feet to the north side of Snowslide Lake. There are campsites along the lake's east and north sides.

To continue to Snowslide Summit, follow the trail around Snowslide Lake's east side. At the southeast side of the lake, come to a nice campsite near Snowslide's inlet creek. Look for a sign on a tree "Snowslide Lake." Here, the trail to the summit turns east and rises on an open hillside. Dense grass and wildflowers can obscure the trail, although it is well-defined as you continue to ascend.

At 1.9 miles, turn through a switchback where there are spectacular views down to Snowslide Lake. Continue paralleling a talus-covered ridge and make one last steep ascent in forest. At the summit, look south (right) for a rocky knoll that provides a prime perch to enjoy the scenery.

To extend the hike, you can descend on the signed trail to the East Fork of Lake Fork Creek. This trail descends 1,100 feet into lodgepole forest and meanders on a gradual grade nearly 11.0 miles to Lick Creek Road near the Lake Fork Campground. Another option, if you are comfortable hiking off-trail, is to go southeast from the summit, and descend 600 feet to Maki Lake. To find Maki Lake, turn right at the summit on a footpath descending the open ridge. The faint trail fades as it enters dense forest, but there are sporadic cairns to help with route-finding.

Snowslide Lake

At 2.8 miles (from the trailhead), pass a beautiful grassy meadow (this would be a nice place to camp), and cross an unnamed creek that empties into Maki Lake. Here, the forest is thick, and it is difficult to get a sense of your location. Follow the unnamed creek downstream, and reach Maki Lake's grassy edge at 3.3 miles. Maki Lake is a beauty with several white sandy beaches surrounded by dense forest and a sloping 8,151-foot unnamed peak cresting above its north side.

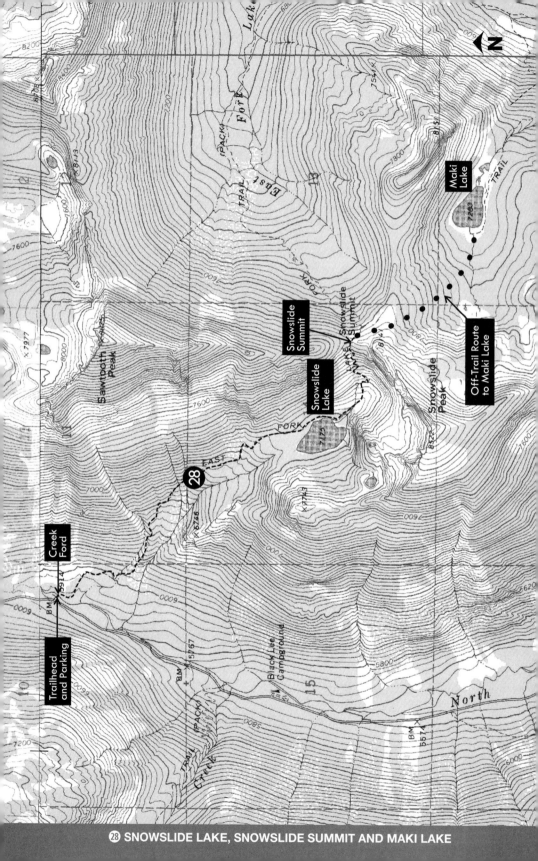

28 SNOWSLIDE LAKE, SNOWSLIDE SUMMIT AND MAKI LAKE

29 Summit Lake

Coordinates

Trailhead:

N 45° 02.159'
W 115° 55.957'

Summit Lake:

N 45° 02.114'
W 115° 56.038'

Distance: Up to 1.0 mile loop

Total Elevation Gain: 50 feet

Difficulty: Easy

Elevation Range: 6,850 to 6,900 feet

Topographic Map: Box Lake

Time: 30 minutes

Season: Late June through mid-October

Water Availability: Summit Lake

Cautionary Advice: None

Information: Payette National Forest, McCall Ranger District (208) 634-0400

Pit Latrine: No

Summit Lake

Access to a beautiful high alpine lake usually requires at least a few miles of hiking. The oblong-shaped Summit Lake is a rare exception where hikers will find beauty and an effortless walk within minutes of their vehicle. The diminutive lake sits less than 500 feet from Lick Creek Road, near the 6,879-foot Lick Creek Summit. However, it is easy to miss since the little jewel is recessed into a granite bowl and the lake is not marked with a road sign. From the parking area, it is a short walk over granite slabs to the lake.

Although much of the forest around the lake burned in 1994, the numerous granite outcroppings, ridges and rocks make for a beautiful landscape. There are a few green trees and wildflowers are prolific in midsummer. From the lake's edge, there are excellent views southeast to the sheer north face of Snowslide Peak and southwest to the pointy Beaverdam Peak.

There are no trails around the lake. However, it is fairly easy to circumnavigate the lake, weaving around deadfall and over granite outcroppings. The west side of the lake has many granite benches and outcroppings which makes for a pleasurable experience to explore off-trail.

Summit Lake looking north

Trailhead Directions

From downtown McCall, drive 0.1 mile south on ID 55 and turn left onto Railroad Avenue. Continue straight at the first stop sign. At 0.4 mile, reach a four-way stop sign. Turn left onto Davis Avenue to another four-way stop sign at 1.1 miles. Turn right onto Lick Creek Road. At 3.2 miles, the road will fork. Reset your tripmeter and continue straight on paved Lick Creek Road for 14.8 miles to Lick Creek Summit. (It turns into a well-graded dirt road in 3.3 miles.) At the summit, there is a small parking area on the left for two or three vehicles.

The distant Snowslide Peak

The Hike

From your vehicle, veer southwest (left) across several granite slabs. Within 500 feet, Summit Lake comes into view. There is a small peninsula on the lake's south edge providing a good destination to enjoy the stunning scenery. The north side of the lake is marshy in early summer. The granite benches on the west side of the lake are an interesting place to explore.

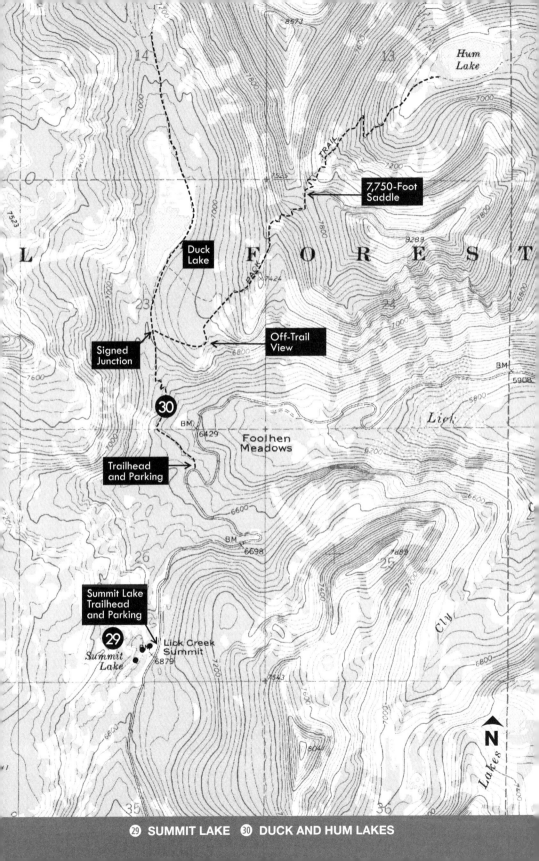

8573

14

13

Hum Lake

7750

7000

7600

7523

7700

TRAIL

7200

7200

7,750-Foot Saddle

7800

7800

Duck Lake

L

F   O   R   E   S   T

8289

7424

23

24

1000

6600

Off-Trail View

BM 5908

6800

6800

Signed Junction

5800

7600

Lick

30

BM 6429

Foolhen Meadows

6200

6600

Trailhead and Parking

7000

6600

BM 6698

7888

26

7200

Summit Lake Trailhead and Parking

Cly

6800

29
Summit Lake

Lick Creek Summit
6879

7200

7543

7600

7000

6800

35

36

804

Lakes

N

Duck and Hum Lakes

Coordinates

Trailhead:

N 45° 02.698'
W 115° 55.807'

Duck Lake:

N 45° 03.455'
W 115° 55.944'

Hum Lake:

N 45° 04.145'
W 115° 54.503'

Distance: 2.4 miles out-and-back (Duck Lake) 8.6 miles out-and-back (Hum Lake)

Total Elevation Gain: 300 feet (Duck Lake) 2,300 feet (Hum Lake)

Difficulty: Very Strenuous (Hum Lake)

Elevation Range: 6,600 to 7,750 feet

Topographic Map: Box Lake

Time: 4 to 5.5 hours (Hum Lake)

Season: July through mid-October

Water Availability: Duck and Hum Lakes, several creeks

Cautionary Advice: Travels through extensive burn

Information: Payette National Forest, Krassel Ranger District (208) 634-0600

Pit Latrine: Yes

Duck and Hum Lakes

From the 20 Mile Trailhead, near Lick Creek Summit, hikers can access two different lakes. About a mile into the hike, the trail forks and an easy trek through forest leads to the arrow-shaped Duck Lake. The beautiful lake is surrounded by granite ridges, forest and a lovely meadow. In late June and July, the wet meadow produces a profusion of colorful wildflowers including purple penstemon, pink elephant's head, red Indian painbrush and white American bistort. There are plenty of good campsites at the lake and the hike's short distance and easy elevation gain makes for a compelling backpack outing for families.

For a more challenging hike with a lot of elevation gain, look to hike to Hum Lake. From the 1-mile junction, it's a tale of two hikes: nearly 1,100 vertical feet up to a 7,750-foot pass and then 1,000 vertical feet down to Hum Lake. Unlike many trails in the area, the grade is not bad as there are many switchbacks—the descent alone has twenty-four.

The entire trek is a visual feast with an endless amount of granite boulders, outcroppings and rocky cliffs. And if wildflowers make your spirit dance, get

Duck Lake

ready to frolic from July into early August. You will find scores of wildflowers lining the well-maintained trail. They include mountain bluebells, Indian paintbrush, beargrass, lupine, valerian, penstemon, phlox, aster and arrowleaf balsamroot. At the 7,750-foot pass, Hum Lake glimmers 1,000 feet beneath you in a cavernous granite cirque, offering an exceptional photo opportunity. Several unnamed 8,000-foot plus peaks surround the lake.

Much of the forest to the pass was burned by the 1994 fires, and the lack of trees allows for exceptional vistas. Fortunately, the basin containing Hum Lake escaped the fire's carnage. The forest surrounding Hum Lake is dense and provides many good campsites. If the hike to Hum Lake is too demanding but you want outstanding vistas, the 7,750-foot pass is a beautiful destination.

Trailhead Directions

From downtown McCall, drive 0.1 mile south on ID 55, and turn left onto Railroad Avenue. Continue straight at the first stop sign. At 0.4 mile, reach a four-way stop sign. Turn left onto Davis Avenue to another four-way stop sign at 1.1 miles. Turn right onto Lick Creek Road. At 3.3 miles, the road will fork. Reset your tripmeter, and continue straight on Lick Creek Road for 16.0 miles. (It turns into a well-graded dirt road at 3.3 miles.) On your left will be a sign "Duck Lake Hum Lake." Turn left into the large parking area where you will find the trailhead and pit toilet.

The Hike

From the trailhead, hike north through partially burned forest. At 0.2 mile, the trail crosses a bridge over a fork of Lick Creek and continues past a huge granite outcropping. Looking east, there are superb vistas into the beautiful canyon shouldering Lick Creek. At 0.6 mile, turn through a switchback near the outlet creek of Duck Lake. The trail makes a moderate rise, crosses a bridge over the outlet creek and reaches the signed junction for Hum and Duck Lakes at 0.9 mile.

To find Duck Lake, continue north. The trail parallels the outlet creek through forest and arrives at the south side of Duck Lake in 0.3 mile. The north side of the lake has the most private campsites. If you are looking to extend the hike, the trail continues three-quarters of a mile past Duck Lake to a junction. Here, the 20 Mile Trail continues into the canyon with Twenty Mile Creek and beyond to Warren Wagon Road near Upper Payette Lake. The trail to the right rises 900 feet to an 8,000-foot saddle and descends to Loon Creek and beyond to Loon Lake.

Rocky tread near 8,000-foot saddle

To see Hum Lake, turn east (right) at the 0.9-mile junction. The trail enters burned forest and makes a gentle rise with impressive views of the 8,875-foot Sawtooth Peak. Continue along a modest grade, and turn through a switchback. At the switchback (see map), you can walk off-trail about 100 yards to a granite slab perched high above the Lick Creek drainage. Back on the trail, the scenery improves as you ascend alongside granite slabs, large boulders and wildflowers. Look southwest for a impressive view of the triangular 8,653-foot Beaverdam Peak.

At 1.5 miles, reach the first of fourteen switchbacks that grind to the summit. The trail passes wildflowers, outcroppings and granite boulders. During early morning and late evening, deer are almost guaranteed to be foraging in the vicinity. Reach the 7,750-foot saddle at 2.7 miles. The views looking north are spectacular, but standing snags hinder the view southwest.

From the saddle, descend below granite ridges through twenty-four switchbacks. At the bottom of the descent, thread through a grassy meadow, and ford a small creek before reaching Hum Lake. Several campsites are located near here. To find a couple of private campsites, bushwack along a small footpath paralleling Hum Lake's south shore. The campsites are near the lake's outlet creek.

Secesh River Trail

Distance: 9.4 miles out-and-back

Total Elevation Gain: 1,400 feet

Difficulty: Strenuous

Elevation Range: 4,050 to 4,950 feet

Topographic Map: Enos Lake

Time: 4 to 5.5 hours

Season: April through November

Water Availability: Secesh River and several creeks

Cautionary Advice: Watch for rattlesnakes during summer months.

Information: Payette National Forest, Krassel Ranger District (208) 634-0600

Pit Latrine: Yes, at Ponderosa Campground

Coordinates

Trailhead:

N 45° 03.764'
W 115° 45.565'

Campspot on River near Tobacco Can Creek:

N 45° 06.657'
W 115° 45.420'

Secesh River Trail

The spectacular thirty-mile long Secesh River snakes its way through the rugged Salmon River Mountains to a confluence with the South Fork of the Salmon River. This trek begins near the confluence and journeys up canyon along the east side of the Secesh River. The scenery is stupendous as the wide river is bordered by steep canyon walls dotted with open forest of towering Douglas firs and ponderosa pine. In late spring and early summer, the canyon is at its best with a picturesque parade of wildflowers.

The river is undeveloped and remote and has very few access points. There is a good fish species mix including steelhead, Chinook salmon and bull and cutthroat trout. The surrounding mountains harbor an abundance of wildlife including moose, black bear, mountain lion, elk, deer, boreal owl, three-toed woodpecker and wolverine.

The low elevation of the terrain allows for spring hiking. Temperatures are mild, and the melting snow in the high country turns the wide river into a thunderous revelry of Class IV and V whitewater. September is another beautiful time to hike when the riverbank understory transforms to beautiful hues of red, yellow and orange. Odds are you will have the trail to yourself.

The beautiful Secesh River

Overnighters will find very few campsites on the river as the topography is rarely level. The trail follows the contours of the riverbank, occasionally along its rocky shore and sometimes 150 feet above the river. However, there is an excellent campsite at the end of this hike description. The location is near a wide section of the canyon just beyond the confluence of Tobacco Can Creek with the river. There is a white sandy beach north of the campspot where the river is calm, allowing for a swim. Near the trailhead, there are two secluded campgrounds—Ponderosa and Horse Camp.

The history of the Secesh River is interesting. About twelve miles east of the river is the historic gold-mining town of Warren. During the Civil War, residents of the small town became divided. Some of the residents who favored the south moved to the banks of the river. As a result, the waterway became known as the Secessionist River, and the moniker was eventually shortened to the Secesh River.

Trailhead Directions

From downtown McCall, drive south on ID 55 for 0.1 mile and turn left onto Railroad Avenue. Continue straight at the first stop sign. At 0.4 mile, reach a four-way stop sign. Turn left onto Davis Avenue to another four-way stop sign at 1.1 miles. Turn right onto Lick Creek Road. At 3.2 miles, the road will fork. Reset your tripmeter, and continue straight on Lick Creek Road for 25.9 miles. (It turns into a well-graded dirt road in 3.3 miles.) On your right will be a sign "Horse Camp Trailhead Secesh." Turn left on FR 469, and drive 0.1 mile to the parking area at the entrance of the Horse Camp Campground. To find the trailhead, take a small footpath back to Lick Creek Road. Turn left and cross the bridge over the Secesh River. The trailhead is on the north side of the road.

Early season hikers and those from the Boise area will want to access the trail from Cascade. Lick Creek Summit is not usually passable until late June. From Cascade, turn right onto paved Warm Lake Road, and travel 23.7 miles to the South Fork of the Salmon River Road (FR 474). Turn left, and follow the single lane paved road north approximately 31.0 miles to the junction with FR 412. Turn left, and follow FR 412 approximately 6.0 miles to the Secesh Trailhead on the north side of the road. Parking is available just past the Secesh River at the Horse Camp Campground.

The Hike

From the trailhead, hike north through partially burned forest. In June, wildflowers are prolific in this area. At 0.8 mile, the path follows a bend in the river and the canyon narrows. Continue north, paralleling the river over a set of small ridges, leaving the burned forest behind.

Secesh River Trailhead

At 2.4 miles, enter another burn area with distant views upstream of the cascading river. The trail crosses Butterfly Creek at 3.1 miles as the forest transitions from burn to green forest. Ascend a knoll and drop to the river again. From here, the trail makes a dramatic rise of more than 150 feet beneath beautiful granite outcroppings and talus.

The trail descends again and continues north along a modest grade. At 4.5 miles, ford Tobacco Can Creek. There is a waterfall along the creek. To find it, before the creek ford, turn right and scramble through brush about 75 feet to the base of the falls. Beyond the ford of Tobacco Can Creek, the canyon widens and passes a fine campsite on the banks of the river. This is the end of this hike. (The trail continues upstream, with similar terrain, nearly 11.0 miles to the Chinook Campground Trailhead.)

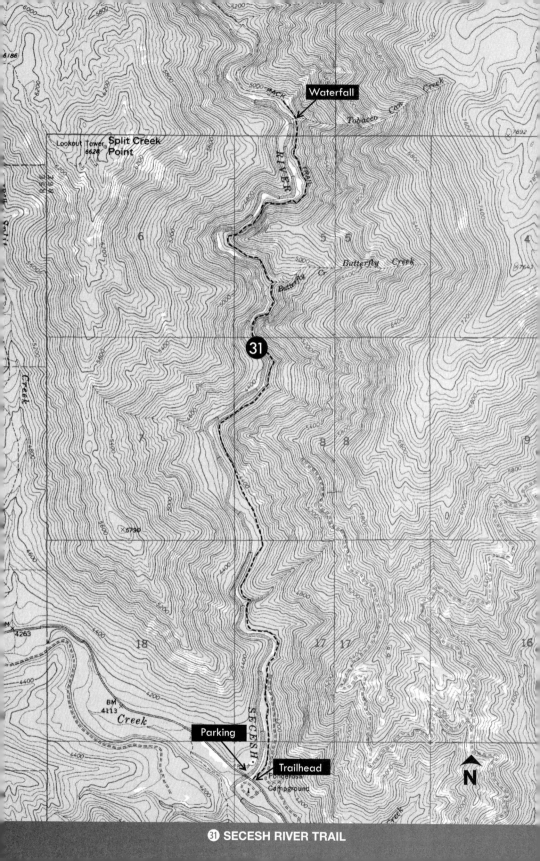

Waterfall

Split Creek Point

Lookout Tower 6628

Butterfly Creek

31

Parking

Trailhead

Ponderosa Campground

N

32 Pearl and Brush Lakes

Coordinates

Trailhead:

N 45° 05.282'
W 115° 59.431'

Brush Lake:

N 45° 03.125'
W 115° 59.348'

Distance: 3.8 miles out-and-back (Pearl Lake)
8.4 miles out-and-back (Brush Lake)

Total Elevation Gain: 300 feet (Pearl Lake)
1,600 feet (Brush Lake)

Difficulty: Easy (Pearl Lake)
Strenuous (Brush Lake)

Elevation Range: 6,700 to 7,450 feet

Topographic Map: Box Lake

Time: 2 to 5 hours

Season: Late June through mid-October

Water Availability: Pearl and Brush Lakes, many creeks

Cautionary Advice: FR 432 to the trailhead is extremely rocky and requires slow travel. Mosquitoes are very bad in early July.

Information: Payette National Forest, McCall Ranger District (208) 634-0400

Pit Latrine: No

Pearl and Brush Lakes

Pearl Lake is a superb destination for a short hike or backpack. Hikers with children will find the one-way distance of 1.8 miles quite manageable. The route winds past lush forest, granite ridges and several mountain meadows. In midsummer, there are many blooming wildflowers. Although the 1994 fires burned much of the forest near Pearl Lake, the lake is still exquisite. It is surrounded by bright green grass, wildflowers and gray granite peaks. Fortunately, a few stands of forest were spared and provide sheltered campsites on the lake's east side.

The much larger Brush Lake is located a few miles south of Pearl Lake. Unlike Pearl Lake, the forest surrounding Brush Lake burned extensively; it is difficult to find an old-growth tree anywhere near it. Gray snags are everywhere, and the setting is surreal. East of the lake, several unnamed peaks between elevations of 8,200 and 8,550 feet dot the horizon. Fishing is very good at the lake, and there are a few campsites on the lake's west shore.

Marge Lake

If you are experienced with route-finding, you can hike 1.5 miles from Pearl Lake (off-trail) to Marge Lake. The route requires negotiating deadfall and granite outcroppings, but the scenic lake is certainly worth a visit. The lake is positioned directly below an unnamed 8,755-foot peak that rises over 1,000 feet from the lake's south shore. The forest surrounding the lake burned badly in 1994. There are several spots to establish a campsite and you will likely have the lake to yourself.

Trailhead Directions

From downtown McCall, go west on ID 55. At 1.2 miles, turn right onto Warren Wagon Road. Go north on Warren Wagon Road 13.8 miles, and look for a sign "Crestline Trhd 7" on the right side of the road. Turn right onto the rocky FR 432, crossing a bridge over the North Fork of the Payette River. Continue approximately 7.0 miles to the road's end and trailhead. Note: this road is extremely rocky; plan on a slow forty-five-minute drive. FR 432 intersects with five other forest roads on the way to the trailhead. Most of the roads are marked. At the first two junctions, continue straight and make sure to veer right at the next three junctions. With careful navigation, passenger cars can make it to the trailhead.

The Hike

The scenic landscape near the trailhead provides you with an idea of what's ahead. From the trailhead, cross a bridge over a small creek, a tributary of the North Fork of Pearl Creek. The trail continues east through a forest of young trees and arrives at the shallow, lily pad-covered Teardrop Lake at 0.6 mile. The lake is surrounded by wet meadows and is very buggy in early summer.

From Teardrop Lake, make a gentle ascent along a grassy hillside sprinkled with gray snags, and crest a hill at 0.9 mile. Descend to a couple of meadows and an easy ford of Pearl Creek at 1.4 miles. Just beyond the creek, arrive at a signed junction for Pearl Lake (the trail south—Crestline Trail—continues to Brush Lake). If you are going to Pearl Lake, turn east (left), soon passing an excellent campsite with good views across the meadow. At 1.5 miles, the trail rises 150 feet in a quarter-mile to Pearl Lake near its outlet creek. There are good campsites along the perimeter of the lake with some of the best on the lake's northeast edge.

Another lake, Marge Lake, is found by traveling about 1.5 miles east of Pearl Lake. The route to Marge Lake is off-trail with no cairns or tread. You should be experienced with route-finding. You will need to negotiate deadfall most of the way. To find Marge Lake, walk to the northeast side of Pearl Lake.

Turn east, and continue through open forest. Over the next mile, gain 450 feet to a saddle at 7,950 feet where you can see the sizable Marge Lake to the southeast (see map). From the saddle, descend a steep 300 feet in 0.4 mile to Marge Lake's north side. Out-and-back distance from Pearl Lake is 3.0 miles with a total gain of an additional 750 feet.

Teardrop Lake

Back at the signed junction at 1.4 miles, continue south to find Brush Lake. The trail rises nearly 150 feet up a steep hill to a saddle with good views and then descends a hillside sprinkled with colorful wildflowers in midsummer. At 2.3 miles, pass a lush meadow, and descend through six switchbacks to a ford of Brush Creek at 2.8 miles.

Beyond Brush Creek, the trail rises again along a hillside and comes to a small sign on a tree "Brush Lake" at 3.7 miles. The sign is weathered and easy to miss, so keep alert. The lake cannot be seen from here. Turn east (left) at the sign, and walk around deadfall for 0.4 mile to the lake.

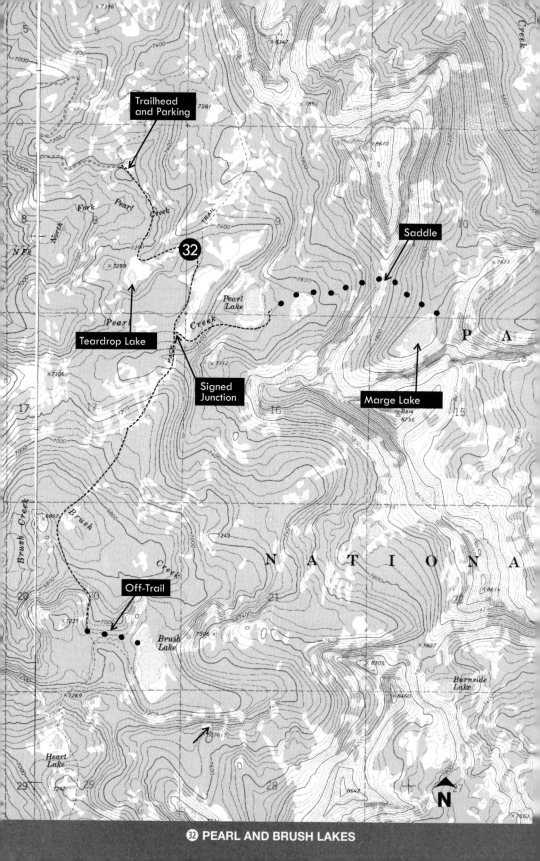

Trailhead and Parking

Saddle

32

Teardrop Lake

Signed Junction

Marge Lake

Off-Trail

N

33 Upper Payette Lake Loop

Coordinates

Trailhead:

N 45° 08.125'
W 116° 01.323'

Payette Lake Connector Trail Junction:

N 45° 08.101'
W 116° 02.532'

Distance: 4.6 mile loop

Total Elevation Gain: 1,300 feet

Difficulty: Strenuous

Elevation Range: 5,550 to 6,800 feet

Topographic Map: Granite Lake

Time: 2 to 3 hours

Season: Mid-June through mid-October

Water Availability: Cougar and Camp Creeks, several small creeks

Cautionary Advice: The trail is brushy in sections. Long pants are recommended.

Information: Payette National Forest, McCall Ranger District (208) 634-0400

Pit Latrine: Yes, at the Upper Payette Lake Group Campground

Upper Payette Lake Loop

This loop hike utilizes the Cougar Creek Trail (336), the Upper Payette Lake Connector Trail and a three-quarter-mile hike along FR 495 to complete a 4.6 miles loop. Most of this hike is through burned forest from the historic 1994 fires that burned nearly 300,000 acres in the Payette National Forest. The lack of large trees allows for outstanding vistas along much of the hike. The flora is slowly recovering with evergreen saplings, aspen groves, snowbrush and other shrubs.

Along the route, there are a couple of off-trail destinations. The easiest is along the first part of the loop to the south-facing granite ridges above the Cougar Creek watershed. This area is stunning with oversized, lichen-covered boulders strewn about on gray granite slabs. From here, you get incredible views to Upper Payette Lake and the surrounding mountains. The other setting is on the return where you can scramble over deadfall about 600 feet to a granite ridge perched high above Cougar Creek. Either destination will long be remembered.

Granite benches north of the trail

Backpackers will find remote camping in grassy terrain near the ford of Cougar Creek. Off-trail adventure seekers can explore the headwaters of Cougar Creek by continuing northwest up the glaciated canyon directly below Black Tip. There is no clear advantage regarding which direction you complete the loop. It is described counter-clockwise.

Trailhead Directions

From downtown McCall, go west on ID 55. At 1.2 miles, reset your tripmeter and turn right onto Warren Wagon Road. Go north on Warren Wagon Road 15.5 miles, and turn left onto FR 495. Follow the well-graded dirt road 0.9 mile. (Look to your left for the Upper Payette Lake Connector Trail.) Proceed another 0.8 mile (1.7 miles total) to the signed trailhead on the west (left) side of the road. There is parking for three or four vehicles.

The Hike

Head west through open forest, weaving between many evergreen saplings. The views are good looking up the canyon as the trail's grade steepens. Pass a tiny spring and ford a small creek at 0.5 mile, having gained 350 feet from the trailhead. Continue through a switchback and sidehill a brushy slope that has outstanding views to Upper Payette Lake and the rugged mountains beyond. At 0.7 mile, the trail comes within yards of the slanted granite benches leading north up the canyon face. If you want to explore this area, bushwhack about 20 feet to the edge of the granite bedrock and from here, it is an easy walk up the slickrock.

The trail levels at 1.0 mile and makes a 50-foot descent to a wide ford of Cougar Creek at 1.2 miles. Although this area burned, the open meadow north of the trail is spectacular in July thanks to its blooming wildflowers. There are a couple of places to camp. For a good off-trail adventure, turn north (right) at Cougar Creek and continue up canyon nearly 2 miles exploring the Cougar Creek headwaters. Beyond the ford, the trail is vague in some sections due to the dense, grassy landscape. Look for cairns. Continue up the grassy hillside climbing through a switchback at 1.5 miles. The views are outstanding looking east into the wide canyon cradling Twenty Mile Creek. At 1.7 miles, reach a signed junction with the Upper Payette Lake Connector Trail. ("Trail" signs are nailed to a tree stump.) Turn east (left). If you continue south the trail leads to Granite Lake – see hike 34.

From the junction, the trail descends about 300 feet over the next half-mile along a burned slope to a wooden bridge and large granite outcropping. About 500 feet past the bridge, the trail levels. Look northeast (left) for a

View southeast from the granite benches

large granite mound. Here, you can hike over deadfall for about 600 feet to find a wonderful perch to take in the magnificent scenery.

The trail continues to descend and snowbrush encroaches on some sections of the narrow path.

At 2.8 miles, cross another wooden bridge, and pass a large pyramid-shaped, granite rock. Continue past aspen groves and dense flora to the bridge over Camp Creek at 3.6 miles. Enter dense forest, and descend to an unsigned junction with an old roadbed. Turn right (south) crossing a wooden bridge, and reach the connector trailhead on FR 495. Turn north (left) and hike along the dirt road three-quarters of a mile to your vehicle.

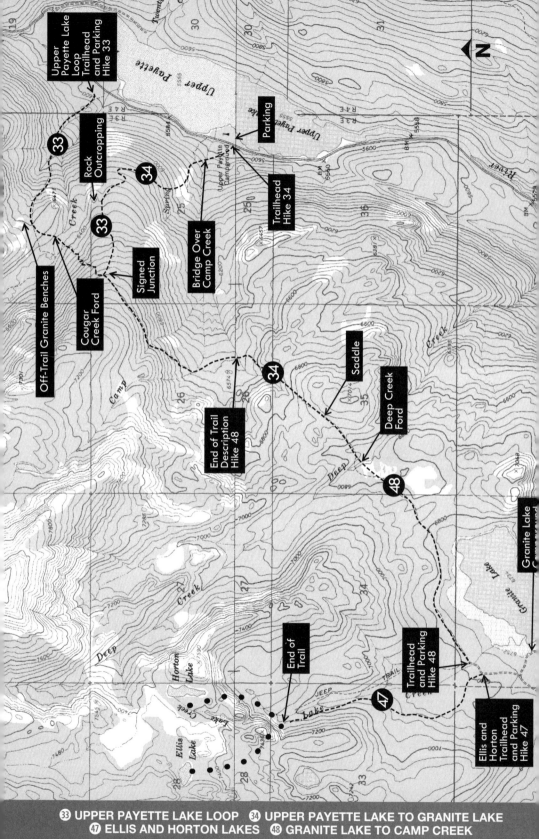

33 UPPER PAYETTE LAKE LOOP **34 UPPER PAYETTE LAKE TO GRANITE LAKE**
47 ELLIS AND HORTON LAKES **48 GRANITE LAKE TO CAMP CREEK**

Upper Payette Lake to Granite Lake

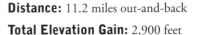

Coordinates

Trailhead:

N 45° 07.492'
W 116° 01.737'

Granite Lake:

N 45° 06.387'
W 116° 05.002'

Distance: 11.2 miles out-and-back

Total Elevation Gain: 2,900 feet

Difficulty: Very Strenuous

Elevation Range: 5,650 to 6,950 feet

Topographic Map: Granite Lake

Time: 4.5 to 6.5 hours

Season: Late June through mid-October

Water Availability: Deep, Camp and Lake Creeks, several unnamed creeks

Cautionary Advice: The first 2 miles of trail can be brushy. Long pants are recommended.

Information: Payette National Forest, McCall Ranger District (208) 634-0400

Pit Latrine: Yes, at Upper Payette Lake Campground

Upper Payette Lake to Granite Lake

Upper Payette Lake sees a fair number of visitors in the summer months not only because of its scenic setting but because of the many lakeside camping opportunities. However, the masses tend to stay near the lake, and those who venture from it will find plenty of solitude in the gorgeous mountain's high-country meadows and old-growth forest laced with pristine creeks.

This description takes the hiker up the steep east-facing slopes above Upper Payette Lake, gaining 1,100 feet, to a signed junction with the Cougar Creek Trail. This two-mile section of trail burned back in the Blackwell Fire of 1994, although saplings are now taking hold. There are very good views down to Upper Payette Lake. Snowbrush is prolific along the steep hillside and can encroach on the trail. Past the signed junction though, the trail enters dense forest and travels south past Camp and Deep Creeks to Granite Lake. Beautiful meadows, far-reaching views and good opportunities to see wildlife make this an outstanding segment of the hike.

If you want to shorten your outing, there are several good choices. One option is to hike about 1.5 miles, and then turn off-trail about 600 feet to a huge granite knoll with spectacular panoramic views. Or look to turn around

Upper Payette Lake

at Camp Creek for an invigorating 6.2 miles out-and-back hike. There are no good campsites until Camp Creek. From Deep Creek to Granite Lake, there are many outstanding selections.

Trailhead Directions

From downtown McCall, go west on ID 55. At 1.2 miles, reset your tripmeter, and turn right onto Warren Wagon Road. Continue north for 15.5 miles, and turn left onto FR 495. Follow the well-graded dirt road 0.9 mile, and turn right into a large parking area near Upper Payette Lake Campground. The trailhead is located on the opposite side of FR 495 (west) and marked with a green trail sign.

The Hike

The narrow trail starts in dense forest and crosses a wooden bridge within 200 feet. Just beyond the bridge, veer west (left) where the trail splits. (The other trail continues down to FR 495.) At 0.2 mile, cross another bridge over the beautiful Camp Creek. This is a great destination if you have young children. There are many huckleberry bushes in the area too. The grade steepens and climbs past a couple of small meadows with many wildflowers during July and soon enters old burn. Continue past a few aspen groves, and at 0.9 mile, pass a huge granite boulder. Here, there are excellent views down to Upper Payette Lake and to the high mountains beyond. This is another good destination for a short hike with about 500 feet of elevation gain.

Beyond this point, snowbrush becomes prolific and often crowds the trail. Continue over another bridge at 1.0 mile and weave higher through snowbrush, aspens and evergreen saplings. At 1.5 miles, the trail levels in a little clearing. Look north (right) and you will see a large granite outcropping (see map). It is about 600 feet off-trail to reach the outcropping, and it is a worthy destination for the spectacular views. (You must bushwhack a bit to reach the outcropping.)

On the main trail beyond the clearing, continue past a large granite outcropping and over another wooden bridge. From here, the trail rises 300 more feet in a half-mile to a signed junction with the Cougar Creek Trail. The junction is marked with several "trail" signs nailed to a tree stump. If you turn north (right), the trail descends to a ford of Cougar Creek and continues to the trailhead at Upper Payette Lake near the group campground (see hike 33).

At the junction, turn south (left) as the trail levels at 2.2 miles in old-growth forest. Many ferns grow in the area. From here, continue south in dense forest, a big contrast from the first part of the hike. After crossing a little stream, descend a steep 200 feet to a ford of a creek at 2.8 miles where the trail levels again. Here, amongst the thick forest, several grassy settings offer good campsites until the ford of Camp Creek at 3.1 miles.

Beyond Camp Creek, ascend a wooded hillside—the trail becomes less obvious—to a tree with a "trail" sign. The sign is difficult to see as it is nailed on the west side of the tree. Turn right at the tree as the trail becomes more prominent and rises 350-feet to a wooded and rocky saddle at 3.8 miles. Now descend 150 feet through forest to a large meadow and a ford of Deep Creek at 4.2 miles. The perimeter of the meadow offers many excellent camp options.

Continue through the meadow into open forest and traverse a smaller meadow. The trail continues southwest in open forest and winds past another large meadow. At 4.6 miles, ascend an open hillside to a lone tree with a "trail" sign. The trail is a little faint on the hillside. From the lone tree, the trail (very prominent now) enters forest again and makes a gentle descent of 100 feet over the next half-mile to the north side of Granite Lake. The last half-mile is fairly level. The trail ends at a wooden bridge over Lake Creek (marked with a green "Trail 336" sign). If you continue down the road another quarter-mile, you can veer left on a spur road to the undeveloped campground near Granite Lake.

35 Twenty Mile Lakes

Distance: 11.6 miles out-and-back

Total Elevation Gain: 2,500 feet

Difficulty: Very Strenuous

Elevation Range: 5,600 to 7,950 feet

Topographic Map: Black Tip, Victor Peak, Box Lake

Time: 5 to 7 hours

Season: July through mid-October

Water Availability: Twenty Mile and the North Fork of Twenty Mile Creeks, several streams and the four Twenty Mile Lakes

Cautionary Advice: Travels through extensive burn

Information: Payette National Forest, McCall Ranger District (208) 634-0400

Pit Latrine: Yes

Coordinates

Trailhead:

N 45° 08.065'
W 116° 00.604'

North Twentymile Lake:

N 45° 07.531'
W 115° 55.730'

Twenty Mile Lakes

East of Upper Payette Lake and Warren Wagon Road, hikers will find the four Twenty Mile Lakes in a glacial cirque resting at 7,800 feet. The cirque is ringed by several peaks cresting near 9,000 feet, with the 9,026-foot Storm Peak soaring the highest. All four lakes—North, South, East and Long—are nestled within a half-mile of one another and offer many outstanding campsites.

The nearly 6-mile hike unfolds with two very different experiences. The journey starts near Upper Payette Lake and wanders through the wide canyon containing Twenty Mile Creek. Most of the canyon escaped the big fires of 1994, so most of the walk is well-shaded through mixed-conifer forest. Amazingly, you only gain about 300 feet in the first two and one-half miles. The trail splits at the confluence of the North Fork of Twenty Mile and Twenty Mile Creeks and here begins an entirely new hike: more scenic, much harder and less traveled.

From the junction, the trail gains a steep 2,000 feet in 3 miles. Motorized travel is prohibited along this stretch and the steep, rough terrain discourages even the hardiest mountain bikers. You will likely see few people. Although

The large North Twenty Mile Lake

much of the North Fork Canyon is burned, the lack of dense forest allows hikers to better experience the soaring granite walls shouldering the beautiful canyon. If you are a lover of wildflowers, try to time your hike in mid-July through early August when the canyon lights up with color.

The lake basin did not escape the fire's fury. The north side of Long Lake and much of North Lake caught the brunt of the fire, yet there is still plenty of green forest in the basin. Anglers will find rainbow and cutthroat trout.

Trailhead Directions

From downtown McCall, go west on ID 55 for 1.2 miles. Reset your tripmeter and turn right onto paved Warren Wagon Road. Go north on Warren Wagon Road 17.3 miles, and look for a sign "Twenty Mile Lakes." Turn right into the large parking area.

The Hike

The hike starts in burned forest, but within a half-mile the forest is dense and lush. At 1.0 mile, skirt the edge of a shallow pond, usually dry by the end of summer. The trail continues east through thick forest for another 1.5 miles. Look for grouse whortleberry, also known as red or grouse huckleberry, growing along much of the route. This small plant, related to the huckleberry, produces a edible berry that is very flavorful. The fruit typically ripens in late July but is difficult to gather in quantity because of its tiny size, about 3–6 mm in diameter.

Arrive at a junction at 2.6 miles. The right fork crosses a small bridge over the North Fork of Twenty Mile Creek within 500 feet and continues south over 5 miles to Duck Lake. The bridge is a prime destination if you are looking for a short hike.

At the junction, turn north (left) where a sign indicates motorized travel is prohibited. The trail starts a steep ascent at 2.7 miles, with the first of twelve switchbacks. Fortunately, the forest is dense and provides shade on a hot day. At 3.0 miles, the grade becomes moderate and enters burned forest. Ford several small streams as you continue east up a modest grade. The North Fork of Twenty Mile Creek parallels the trail, and backpackers will find several flat campsites near it. Storm Peak dominates the skyline near the end of the canyon.

At 4.4 miles, the trail turns southeast, crosses a bridge over a small creek and rises a steep 500 feet to the marshy confluence of two streams. The Victor Peak USGS map is incorrect, as it shows the trail going to Long Lake. The trail actually travels to North Twenty Mile Lake. Make one last climb of 200 feet in a half-mile to the west side of North Twenty Mile Lake, where there is a large campsite.

To visit the other lakes, the easiest route is to head south (right) on a footpath. The footpath travels over a small knoll and arrives at South Twenty Mile Lake in 0.4 mile. From here, go along the outlet stream of South Lake to Long Lake in 0.2 mile. To reach East Lake from South Lake, hike along South Lake's north shore, and climb 100 feet in 0.4 mile. All four lakes have multiple campsites.

South Twenty Mile Lake

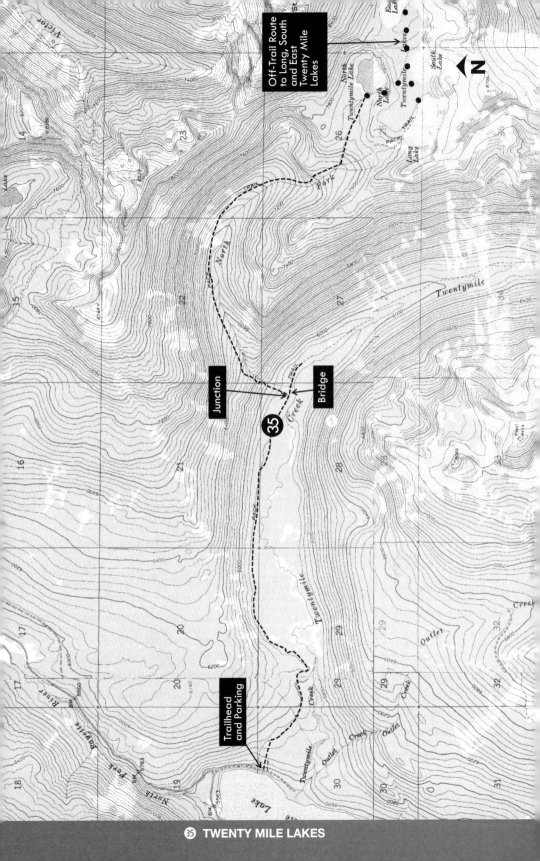

Off-Trail Route to Long, South and East Twenty Mile Lakes

Junction

Bridge

Trailhead and Parking

N

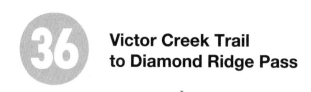

36 Victor Creek Trail to Diamond Ridge Pass

Distance: 7.6 miles out-and-back

Total Elevation Gain: 2,000 feet

Difficulty: Strenuous

Elevation Range: 6,000 to 8,000 feet

Topographic Map: Victor Peak

Time: 3 to 4.5 hours

Season: July through mid-October

Water Availability: Several small streams and a pond

Cautionary Advice: There is no reliable water the first 3 miles of the hike. The trail is through extensive burn.

Information: Payette National Forest, McCall Ranger District (208) 634-0400

Pit Latrine: No

Coordinates
Trailhead:

N 45° 09.963'
W 115° 59.439'

Saddle:

N 45° 09.049'
W 115° 56.221'

Victor Creek Trail to Diamond Ridge Pass

This steep trail is all about the views. If ever there was doubt regarding the outstanding scenery of the Salmon River Mountains, the Victor Creek Trail puts it to rest. As you ascend on the open hillside, the views to the west are spectacular. The Salmon River Mountains unfold with their rocky summits, including 8,478-foot Granite Mountain, 8,225-foot Slab Butte and 8,292-foot Black Tip. Far below, the North Fork of the Payette River begins its journey south through Squaw Meadows en route to Upper Payette Lake.

The first few miles of trail are through burnt forest from the 1994 fires and the trail is sometimes rutted. However, the sensational views and abundance of wildflowers more than compensate for the lack of shade. Interestingly, a little beyond 3 miles into the hike, the fire was contained and the high mountain landscape is stunning. Meadows, granite outcroppings, creeks and dense forest welcome the hiker.

At the pass, brace yourself for breathtaking vistas. To the north, the pointy tips of Diamond Ridge command your attention. To the east are two of the larger peaks in the area—the triangular 9,100-foot Storm Peak and the rugged 8,718-foot Victor Peak. In the valley below, Victor Creek meanders to its confluence with the Secesh River.

Trailhead Directions

From downtown McCall, go west on ID 55. At 1.2 miles, turn right onto Warren Wagon Road. Reset your tripmeter and travel north on Warren Wagon Road 20.0 miles and look for a sign "Victor Cr. Tr. No. 117" on the right side of the road. Beyond the sign is the trailhead and a small pullout with parking for two or three cars. There is additional parking at another pullout on the opposite side of the road.

The Hike

Begin hiking through burned forest and within a quarter-mile enter an area with many saplings. The trail continues to gain elevation, crosses an old road and turns through two switchbacks. At 0.7 mile, arrive at an unsigned junction. Turn right, ascending a grassy hillside through two more switchbacks. In summer, wildflowers flourish here including sego lily, penstemon, pearly everlasting and lupine.

Climb through five more switchbacks with views improving looking west to Squaw Meadows and the rugged mountains beyond. The trail levels at 1.5 miles. Here, go north (left) and take a short 50-yard hike to see Frog Lake in the basin below. The grade intensifies again, reaches another flat knoll at 2.0 miles and makes one last climb of 400 feet.

Beyond this point, the trail meanders through an interesting landscape of deadfall and granite boulders. Soon pass a tiny pond and boulder hop across a small stream. Here you will find spectacular scenery with lush forest, granite ridges and several small meadows. This area would make an excellent destination for a short backpack trip.

At 3.5 miles, cross another small stream and look left for a superior view down to Trail Lake. With the help of three tight switchbacks, make one final ascent of 250 feet to the 8,000-foot pass. From the saddle, you can hike north along the ridgeline for about a quarter-mile with nearly 400 feet of gain to an unnamed peak at 8,386 feet. The maintained trail continues with a steep descent to Victor Creek and eventually intersects with the trail from Chinook Campground to Loon Lake.

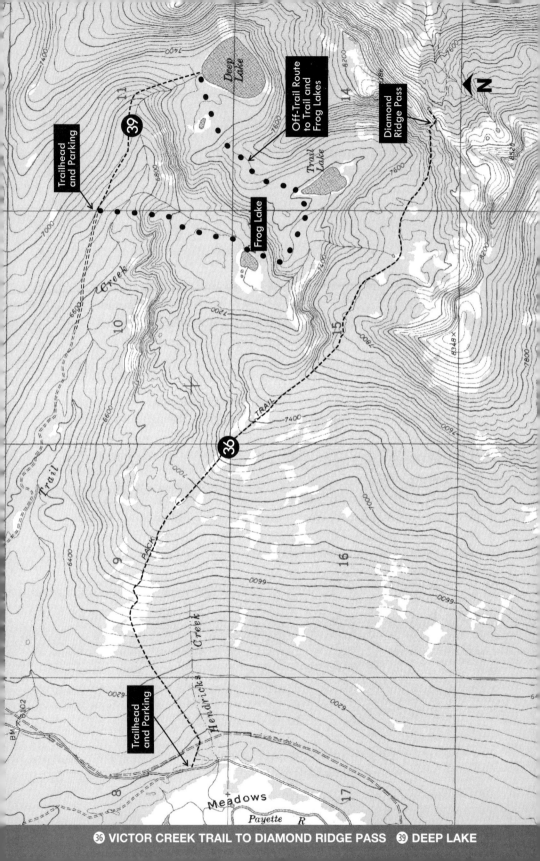

Deep Lake

Off-Trail Route to Trail and Frog Lakes

Diamond Ridge Pass

Trailhead and Parking

39

Trail Lake

Frog Lake

N

Creek

10

11

14

15

16

17

9

8

Trail

36

Hendricks Creek

Pack Trail

Trailhead and Parking

Meadows

Payette R.

BM 6402

37 Jackson Creek

Coordinates

Trailhead:

N 45° 11.196'
W 116° 00.292'

Viewpoint:

N 45° 13.835'
W 116° 01.566'

Distance: 7.8 miles out-and-back

Total Elevation Gain: 650 feet

Difficulty: Strenuous

Elevation Range: 5,550 to 6,000 feet

Topographic Map: Black Tip

Time: 3 to 4 hours

Season: June through October

Water Availability: Jackson and Pond Creeks, several unnamed creeks

Cautionary Advice: None

Information: Payette National Forest, McCall Ranger District (208) 634-0400

Pit Latrine: No

Jackson Creek

If you are looking for a lengthy adventure through a wild and untamed landscape without much elevation gain, make sure to visit the Jackson Creek watershed. This hike is mostly through dense forest: the trees are often so closely packed it is difficult to see the sky. Small meadows, rushing creeks and good opportunities to see wildlife add to the hiker's experience. The hike description ends at a granite outcropping near the trail with inspiring vistas into the French Creek drainage. Here, the landscape was burned many years ago, and the lack of trees provides great views of French Creek and the rugged mountains beyond.

There are many opportunites to camp along the route, and adventuresome hikers can hike off-trail less than a quarter-mile from the final destination to the banks of Jackson Creek. Due to the trail's low elevation, this area is often accessible from early June into late October. There are many springs along the route. Sections of the trail can get boggy, so make sure to wear good boots.

Trailhead Directions

From downtown McCall, go west on ID 55. At 1.2 miles, reset your tripmeter, and turn right onto Warren Wagon Road. Go north on Warren Wagon Road 20.5 miles and turn left on FR 260. There will be a sign for the French Creek Trailhead. Follow the well-graded dirt road 3.0 miles to a fork. Take the right fork, and proceed another 500 feet to the trailhead. There is parking for two or three vehicles.

The Hike

The hike starts in open forest just north of Squaw Meadows. The trail makes an easy rise up a wooded hill, passing a huge granite outcropping, and levels at 0.7 mile. From here, descend into thick forest with many types of conifers and an abundance of shrubs. At 1.3 miles, Jackson Creek can be heard through the timber as the little creek is only yards away. Continue another quarter-mile, and ford a shallow creek, soon passing to the east of a grassy meadow. At 1.8 miles, the trail meanders through a tiny meadow, your first opportunity to establish a campsite.

Beyond the small meadow, enter dense forest again and pass several springs. The trail is often boggy near the springs, and you must hike around standing water to avoid wet boots. At 2.2 miles, ford a narrow unnamed creek and then the larger Pond Creek at 2.6 miles. There is a good campsite just beyond the ford of Pond Creek. From here, the forest transitions into skinny lodgepole pine and passes several more secluded camp possibilities. At 3.3 miles, ford the first of two more creeks and arrive at a signed junction at 3.7 miles. The foot trail to the left is no longer maintained and ventures a few yards over deadfall to the edge of Jackson Creek.

Continue north as the landscape transitions into burned forest. After about 300 yards, look to the left for a granite outcropping. With an easy bushwhack of 20 feet, walk to the outcropping to see the far-reaching vistas to French Creek and the rugged topography beyond. From here, you can hike west off-trail over deadfall about a quarter-mile to Jackson Creek.

(If you want to continue the hike, the main trail gains another 100 feet from here and then descends 200 feet to a ford of Ditch Creek at 4.5 miles. It then continues north high on a forested hillside and eventually descends to the edge of French Creek in approximately 4.0 miles.)

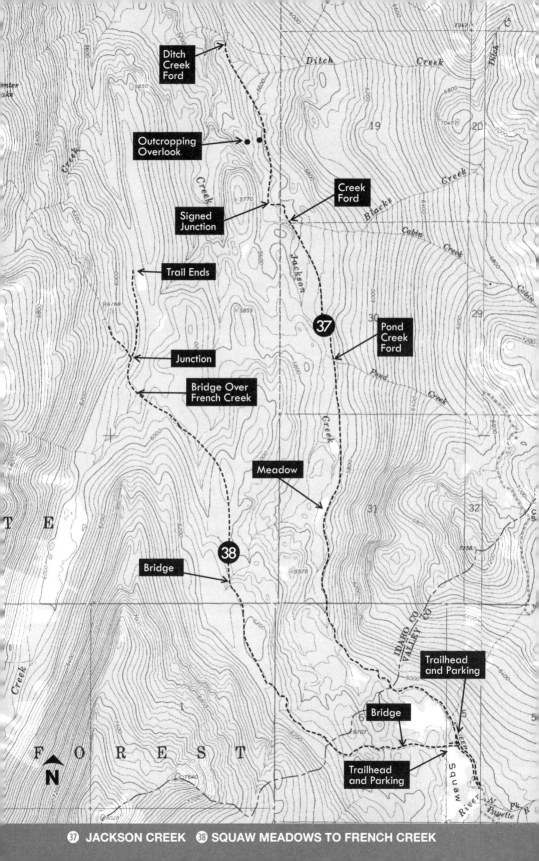

Ditch
Creek
Ford

Outcropping
Overlook

Creek
Ford

Signed
Junction

Trail Ends

Junction

Pond
Creek
Ford

Bridge Over
French Creek

Meadow

Bridge

Trailhead
and Parking

Bridge

Trailhead
and Parking

37

38

N

37 JACKSON CREEK   **38** SQUAW MEADOWS TO FRENCH CREEK

Squaw Meadows to French Creek

Coordinates

Trailhead:

N 45° 11.081'
W 116° 00.295'

French Creek:

N 45° 12.704'
W 116° 02.403'

Distance: 6.8 miles out-and-back

Total Elevation Gain: 900 feet

Difficulty: Moderate

Elevation Range: 5,850 to 6,200 feet

Topographic Map: Black Tip

Time: 2.5 to 4 hours

Season: Early June through mid-October

Water Availability: French Creek, many creeks and several small streams

Cautionary Advice: Long pants are recommended as the trail can get brushy.

Information: Payette National Forest, McCall Ranger District (208) 634-0400

Pit Latrine: No

Squaw Meadows to French Creek

This moderate hike (along Trail 504) starts near the north side of Squaw Meadows and travels northwest to the beautiful French Creek. Unlike the nearby trail along Jackson Creek, this hike is mostly through burned forest from the 1994 fires. There are a few sections of old-growth forest that the fires missed, but you are mainly walking near gray snags, green saplings and a dense understory of bushes.

The trail does not get a lot of use. If you are looking to camp, there are not many places to establish a campsite until you get to French Creek. The forest near French Creek did burn, but it is more mosiac and the creek is placid, clear and beautiful. This is a great trail to hike in early morning or late evening to see wildlife.

Although the hike has about 900 feet of total gain, the accumulation is mainly through rolling terrain with easy 50-foot segments. The entire hike feels very remote. If you are seeking solitude this is the trail for you as it is doubtful you will see anyone else along the trail.

Trailhead Directions

From downtown McCall, go west on ID 55. At 1.2 miles, reset your tripmeter, and turn right onto Warren Wagon Road. Go north on Warren Wagon Road 20.5 miles, and turn left on FR 260. There will be a sign for the French Creek Trailhead. Follow the well-graded dirt road 3.0 miles to a Y-junction. Take the left fork of the road, and proceed another 100 feet to the trailhead. There is parking for several vehicles.

The Hike

From the trailhead, cross a bridge over a creek, and ascend a small hill. At 0.3 mile, cross another bridge over an unnamed creek, and gain 150 feet near saplings to where the trail levels. Now make an easy descent, and ford several streams beginning at 0.9 mile.

The terrain and landscape are similar over the next mile, with the trail undulating over several small hills. At 2.0 miles, cross a bridge over an unnamed creek, and wind through an area that is thick with bushes. At 2.4 miles, the scenery changes as the trail enters dense, old-growth forest and starts a modest descent. At 3.2 miles, look to the north (right) for a campsite on a wooded knoll. The trail descends 100 feet to the bridge over French Creek. In late spring, just prior to reaching the bridge, the trail will likely be waterlogged due to melting snow. The grassy bank along the creek is a great destination to enjoy this remote locale.

French Creek

Trail 504 continues beyond French Creek and gains nearly 1,500 feet to Center Ridge. It then descends to Little French Creek, about 5.8 miles from French Creek. This area gets very little trail maintenance. Beyond French Creek, you can also hike down the unmarked Trail 308, which continues north, paralleling French Creek. There is a campsite at 0.4 mile, and the trail disappears in dense deadfall at 0.8 mile.

39   Deep Lake

Map located on page 156

Coordinates

Trailhead:

N 45° 10.346'
W 115° 56.614'

Deep Lake:

N 45° 09.968'
W 115° 55.913'

Distance: 1.8 miles out-and-back

Total Elevation Gain: 550 feet

Difficulty: Easy

Elevation Range: 6,800 to 7,350 feet

Topographic Map: Victor Peak

Time: 1 hour

Season: Late June through mid-October

Water Availability: Deep Lake

Cautionary Advice: None

Information: Payette National Forest, McCall Ranger District (208) 634-0400

Pit Latrine: No

Deep Lake

The easy hike to Deep Lake delivers a lot of eye candy within a short distance: outstanding vistas, a rugged canyon lined with granite ridges, summer wildflowers and the beautiful Deep Lake. Deep Lake sits at an elevation of 7,300 feet. Two unnamed peaks, one at 8,618 feet and the other at 8,386 feet, rise more than 1,000 feet above Deep Lake's edge. Although the 1994 fires burned much of the forest to the lake, the lack of trees allows unobstructed views along the trail to this otherworldly adventure.

Deep Lake is accessible from a trail at the end of FR 431. From the trailhead, it is nearly a 1.0-mile hike up a burned ridge sprinkled with saplings and granite rocks. Although most of the forest near the lake burned, there are stands of timber sheltering campsites. Many granite boulders fringe the lake's perimeter, and the surrounding topography is interesting to explore off-trail.

If you are comfortable hiking off-trail, you can complete a 3.2-mile loop hike, visiting the smaller Trail and Frog Lakes. Much of the forest north of Trail Lake escaped the fire adding to its appeal. Both lakes offer a few campsites. An added bonus for late August hikers, huckleberries flourish along the trail to Deep Lake.

Trailhead Directions

From downtown McCall, go west on ID 55. At 1.2 miles, reset your tripmeter, and turn right onto Warren Wagon Road. Go north on Warren Wagon Road 21.7 miles, and turn right onto unmarked FR 431. Follow the dirt road 1.9 miles to its end. The trailhead is marked with a cairn at the east end of the parking area. There is parking for five or six vehicles.

The Hike

From the trailhead, head east up the narrow trail as it weaves through saplings. Over the next half-mile, the trail rises 200 feet and veers south on a burned slope. The views here are good looking west into the canyon and beyond to Squaw Meadows and the distant mountains. With a keen eye, you can also see the 8,292-foot Black Tip Mountain, a noteworthy peak that is the headwaters for eight drainages. Reach the north side of the lake at 0.9 mile near its outlet creek. Here you will find a few parcels of green forest that shelter a couple of fine campsites.

If you are skilled with map reading or with a GPS, you can hike off-trail and complete a 3.2 miles loop back to your vehicle. There are signs of a footpath along the hike, but most of the route is ill-defined. Ford Deep Lake's outlet creek, and hike west across deadfall. The route passes to the south of a small pond and rises 150 feet up a charred ridge. From here, descend southwest (left) as the landscape transitions from burn to dense forest. The lake is

Trail Lake

not visible due to forest, but continue south and you will eventually arrive at Trail Lake's north side.

To finish the loop, walk around Trail Lake to its west side (see map). Before you reach Trail Lake's outlet creek, turn northwest (right), and hike a quarter-mile across a burned slope to a rocky knoll perched 250 feet above Frog Lake. From here, descend 250 feet on an open hillside to Frog Lake's outlet creek where you will find a campsite. Continue north, paralleling Frog Lake's outlet creek, to the edge of the canyon containing Trail Creek. Look across the drainage where your vehicle is visible near the trailhead. A footpath descends more than 300 feet to a ford of Trail Creek and then an easy ascent to the trailhead.

40   Cloochman Saddle to Squaw Point

Trailhead:

N 45° 12.142'
W 115° 59.751'

Squaw Point:

N 45° 13.065'
W 115° 58.294'

Distance: 6.4 miles out-and-back

Total Elevation Gain: 1,400 feet

Difficulty: Moderate

Elevation Range: 6,950 to 8,200 feet

Topographic Map: Victor Peak

Time: 3 to 4 hours

Season: July through mid-October

Water Availability: None

Cautionary Advice: The trail is through extensive burn. The last half-mile is off-trail.

Information: Payette National Forest, McCall Ranger District (208) 634-0400

Pit Latrine: No

Cloochman Saddle to Squaw Point

You would be hard-pressed to find more stunning views in the McCall area than those that are a constant on the Bear Pete Trail from Cloochman Saddle. The vistas unfold from nearly your first step until you finish your journey atop Squaw Point. The views of the French, Jackson and Summit Creek watersheds, vast open space of Squaw Meadows and beyond to Upper Payette Lake and the rough-hewn Salmon River Mountains are spectacular.

The first half-mile of the hike weaves between granite outcroppings and open forest. Beyond this point, the trail begins a moderate climb through burned forest, crossing several outstanding viewpoints and leads to a high ridge where Josephine Lake rests 600 vertical feet below. Although the views are stupendous, an easy half-mile walk off-trail takes you to the 8,286-foot Squaw Point, delivering unrivaled panoramas.

Beyond Josephine Lake, those looking for a longer hike can continue north on the Bear Pete Trail. The path rarely dips below 8,000 feet as it meanders on a high ridge that offers impressive views. After a hike of 2.5 miles, it arrives at Frosty Meadow. There is no reliable water source on this hike, so make sure to bring plenty of water as much of the hike is exposed. The trail was rerouted in the summer of 2016 and is nearly a mile longer (one-way) than it once was.

Trailhead Directions

From downtown McCall, travel west on ID 55 for 1.2 miles. Reset your tripmeter, and turn right onto the paved Warren Wagon Road. Travel north on Warren Wagon Road for 21.8 miles. Look for a sign on the side of the road "Cloochman Saddle 3, Bear Pete Trail 3," and turn left onto the well-graded FR 492. Follow FR 492 for 2.9 miles to the road's end. There is parking for six or seven vehicles. There are a couple of dispersed campsites along FR 492.

The Hike

The trail starts in open forest and turns through a switchback under a granite ridge at 0.1 mile. Continue over a seasonal creek, and gain about 100 feet of elevation along a west-facing granite rockface. At 0.5 mile, make an easy descent into burned forest with many gray snags. The trail stays fairly level for about a half-mile and turns through the first of several switchbacks at 1.0 mile. At 1.5 miles, come to the edge of a hillside with great vistas looking down into the Jackson Creek watershed (see hike 37).

The trail now turns northeast and climbs 200 feet to an open saddle with good vistas, looking both east and west, at 2.0 miles. Beyond here, the trail continues northeast, turns through another switchback and finally turns north towards Josephine Lake. This final stretch of trail is in open, beautiful forest.

View from saddle above Josephine Lake

At 2.7 miles, reach the high saddle above Josephine Lake. The views are far-reaching, looking north over Josephine Lake and to the mountains beyond. To find Squaw Point, turn southeast (right) at the saddle, and hike across a grassy meadow. Enter open forest and ascend more than 200 feet to the rocky apex of Squaw Point, marked with a cairn. The views are sensational in all directions.

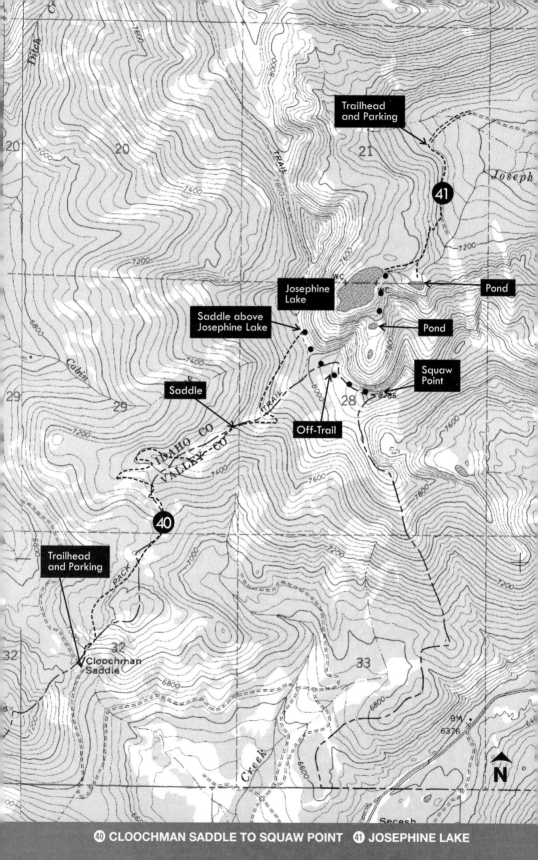

Trailhead and Parking

41

Joseph

Pond

Josephine Lake

Saddle above Josephine Lake

Pond

Squaw Point

Saddle

Off-Trail

IDAHO CO
VALLEY CO

40

Trailhead and Parking

Cloochman Saddle

BM 6376

Creek

Secesh

N

40 CLOOCHMAN SADDLE TO SQUAW POINT   41 JOSEPHINE LAKE

Josephine Lake

Coordinates

Trailhead:

N 45° 13.931'
W 115° 58.005'

Josephine Lake:

N 45° 13.493'
W 115° 58.274'

Distance: 1.6 miles out-and-back

Total Elevation Gain: 350 feet

Difficulty: Easy

Elevation Range: 7,050 to 7,400 feet

Topographic Map: Victor Peak

Time: 1 hour

Season: Mid-June through mid-October

Water Availability: Josephine Lake, pond

Cautionary Advice: None

Information: Payette National Forest, McCall Ranger District (208) 634-0400

Pit Latrine: No

Josephine Lake

You will certainly be awestruck when you first see Josephine Lake. The small lake is flanked by steep, granite ridges rising more than 600 feet. Directly south, the 8,286-foot Squaw Point looms over the translucent, emerald-colored lake while nearby granite boulders provide flat perches for admiring the area's beauty. Although this area burned in 1994, there are pockets of forest near the lake and a few worthy campsites.

The jaunt from the trailhead to Josephine Lake leads up an old roadbed and transforms to a singletrack trail about halfway to the cirque. Before reaching the lake, a large pond bordered by a steep granite wall offers a worthy diversion. Experienced off-trail hikers can follow a faint footpath along the steep hillside south of Josephine Lake to a couple of beautiful ponds perched below a granite rampart. The views enroute to the ponds offer a bird's-eye perspective of glistening Josephine Lake.

Trailhead Directions

From downtown McCall, go west on ID 55. At 1.2 miles, turn right onto Warren Wagon Road. Travel north 25.1 miles, and turn left on FR 316.

Josephine Lake

Follow FR 316 for 3.1 miles to where the road ends at the trailhead. Although rough, a passenger car can manage the road. There are a couple of dispersed camping sites along FR 316 and near the trailhead.

The Hike

From the trailhead, ford a small stream and veer south along a modest grade. This area burned badly and there are few trees. However, without the trees, the views are far-reaching, looking both east and south. At 0.3 mile, ford a tiny stream as the trail turns west and turns into a singletrack. Ascend through two switchbacks, and after a gain of 200 feet look for a small pond at 0.6 mile, to the south of the trail. There is a narrow footpath leading down to the pond, although dense foliage makes access to the pond's edge difficult. The brush is not as dense on the pond's west side.

On the main trail, continue another 500 feet, reaching the signed Josephine Lake at 0.7 mile. A footpath continues east to the lake's rocky north side. Look for several campsites along this stretch. To find two small ponds—only attempt if you are experienced hiking off-trail—cross Josephine's outlet and ascend the steep ridge south of Josephine Lake. There is a faint footpath, but it is braided in spots and is easy to lose. After an elevation gain of 200 feet in a quarter-mile, you will reach the first pond. The second pond is another 500 feet but requires careful scrambling over large talus.

42   Lake Rock Lake

Distance: 3.2 miles out-and-back

Total Elevation Gain: 1,500 feet

Difficulty: Strenuous

Elevation Range: 6,150 to 7,300 feet

Topographic Map: Victor Peak

Time: 1.5 to 2.5 hours

Season: Late June through mid-October

Water Availability: Lake Rock Lake, several small streams, Lake Rock Lake's outlet creek

Cautionary Advice: This trail is not maintained. Expect deadfall and steep grades.

Information: Payette National Forest, McCall Ranger District (208) 634-0400

Pit Latrine: No

Coordinates

Trailhead:

N 45° 13.404'
W 115° 55.725'

Lake Rock Lake:

N 45° 12.438'
W 115° 55.154'

Lake Rock Lake

It is as good as guaranteed that you won't see many hikers here. The unmaintained trail to Lake Rock Lake is not well known and is mainly frequented by local anglers. Dense forest, which conceal a few secluded campsites, surrounds the oblong-shaped lake. Above the south end of the lake, a large outcropping—the 8,001-foot Lake Rock—rises high in the air like a small finger.

This is a great destination if you are looking for solitude. Though your entry fee into this area requires traversing deadfall and climbing steep grades without the help of switchbacks. The route to the lake gains over 1,100 feet in 1.5 miles and has one easy ford of Lake Rock Lake's outlet creek. The area near Lake Rock Lake has an abundance of wildlife, so stay alert for moose, elk, deer and black bears. Near the lake, marmots are common in the large rockpiles next to the outlet creek.

Trailhead Directions

The trailhead is directly off Warren Wagon Road but is not marked, so make sure to note your mileage. From downtown McCall, go west on

Lake Rock Lake

Highway 55. At 1.2 miles, turn right onto Warren Wagon Road. Reset your tripmeter and travel north 25.5 miles to a parking area on the right. (The parking area is 0.4 mile north of FR 316 which leads to Josephine Lake.) The trailhead is located at the fringe of the forest, 10 feet from the parking area. There is parking for three or four vehicles.

The Hike

The trail starts in dense forest and traverses south along a hillside. At 0.4 mile, you come within a few yards of Lake Rock Lake's outlet creek. Continue hiking along the steep path and ford two small streams at 0.6 mile. Beyond the last stream, you must negotiate a 15-foot-long marshy area where roots and small rocks assist with the muddy crossing.

At 0.9 mile, cross the modest outlet creek of Lake Rock Lake. The trail stays close to the creek and rises beside granite talus. Look and listen for marmots, also known as whistle pigs, as they communicate with colony members using high-pitched alarm calls.

The trail levels at 1.4 miles to the west of a picturesque boulder field. Continue through forest and arrive at the lake's west edge. Several excellent campsites are found by turning left and following a footpath to the north side of the lake.

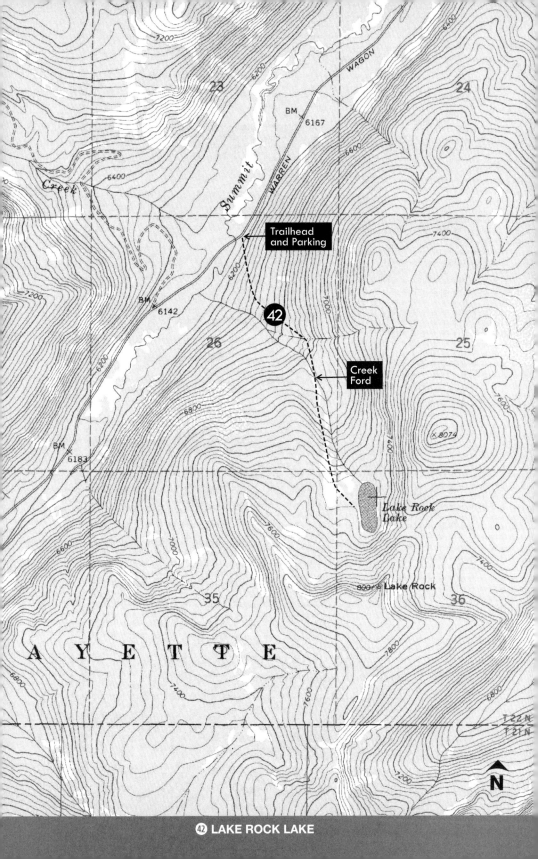

Trailhead
and Parking

Creek
Ford

42 LAKE ROCK LAKE

Loon Lake Loop

Coordinates

Trailhead:

N 45° 12.753'
W 115° 48.538'

Loon Lake:

N 45° 10.038'
W 115° 50.195'

Distance: 10.4 miles

Total Elevation Gain: 1,000 feet

Difficulty: Strenuous

Elevation Range: 5,500 to 6,050 feet

Topographic Map: Loon Lake

Time: 4 to 6 hours

Season: July through mid-October

Water Availability: Loon Lake, Secesh River and many creeks

Cautionary Advice: None

Information: Payette National Forest, McCall Ranger District (208) 634-0400

Pit Latrine: Yes

Loon Lake Loop

By combining three different trails, you can make an outstanding loop hike seeing both Loon Lake and the beautiful Secesh River. The loop has all the ingredients for an epic hike: flower-filled meadows, a large alpine lake, the rugged canyon of the Secesh River, high mountain peaks and thick forest. The half-mile long Loon Lake is one of the larger lakes in the Payette National Forest.

The lake is also known for the B-23 "Dragon Bomber" that landed on it during a heavy snowstorm in the winter of 1943. The plane was returning to Washington State from a training mission in Nevada when the snowstorm forced the pilot to make an emergency landing. The plane landed on the frozen lake but slid off into heavy timber, shearing the wings. Miraculously, none of the eight crew members were killed. In fact, the only injury was a broken kneecap.

What makes the story more dramatic is after a few days with no sign of a rescue, three members of the crew decided to seek help. They hiked down the Secesh River, over the 6,730-foot Lick Creek Summit and finally to the Lake Fork Guard Station. The journey: fourteen days and nearly forty-two miles through deep snow without snowshoes. The remaining crew members were rescued shortly thereafter.

The wreckage of the plane is located about 150 feet from Loon Lake's south edge. A three-quarter-mile footpath meanders along the eastern shore of the lake to the crash site. There are a couple of informative placards near the wreckage describing the plane and crash incident. The area is not developed and is quite remote. When standing among the skeletal remains of the plane, you get an eerie feeling of what these men must have endured.

There are many camping opportunities near Loon Lake including an excellent site near the outlet creek and several more on the west side of the lake. If you decide to visit the plane wreckage on the south side of Loon Lake, the distance of the loop hike is 12.0 miles. The hike to Loon Lake is popular with hikers and mountain bikers.

Bridge over the Secesh River

Trailhead Directions

From downtown McCall, drive west on ID 55 for 1.2 miles. Reset your tripmeter, and turn right onto paved Warren Wagon Road. Drive north 28.4 miles to the Burgdorf Junction. Continue straight, the road surface changes to well-graded dirt road, and proceed another 6.5 miles to a sign "Chinook Campground." Turn right following the single-lane road 1.2 miles to its end where you will find plenty of parking and a pit latrine.

The Hike

There is no clear advantage regarding the direction you complete the loop. The hike is described counter-clockwise. However, there is one slight advantage to hiking the route as described. If you visit Loon Lake and decide you have had enough hiking, you can return via the same trail (out-and-back) and save 1.2 miles as opposed to completing the loop. Unfortunately, you would miss the beautiful canyon hike along the Secesh River.

From the parking area, cross the bridge over the Secesh River. Look for Chinook salmon spawning from late summer to early fall. The trail bends around a hill and climbs a wooded hillside. At 0.8 mile, cross a small creek and ascend a hill with filtered views south to a few high peaks.

Descend to another creek ford, and pass a small meadow at 1.9 miles. The trail continues through dense forest and rises to a saddle with views west to Diamond Ridge and then drops to a signed junction with the Victor and Willow Basket Creek Trails. Continue south, following the sign towards Loon Lake, soon crossing a bridge over Victor Creek. This is an excellent setting for a break or a turnaround spot for a 6.0-miles out-and-back hike.

Beyond the bridge, ascend a steep hillside, ford a small creek and come to an unsigned T-junction. Turn left, hike up a grassy saddle and then descend an open hillside with good views south to Loon Lake. Reach a signed junction at 4.2 miles. The trail east (left) is the one you will take to complete the loop.

To continue to Loon Lake, turn right through a marshy meadow to another junction at 4.4 miles. Turn left and quickly reach another signed junction for the Split Creek Trail. Turn right and head due south for 500 feet to Loon Lake. To find the plane wreckage, cross the outlet creek on a set of rocks and continue south on a footpath about three-quarters of a mile to the wreckage. (The trail to the right at the 4.4-mile junction winds around the west side of Loon Lake to several campsites and continues south through Loon Creek Canyon. You can access the plane wreckage via this trail, too. Once you reach the south side of Loon Lake at 0.9 mile, turn east on a footpath and ford Loon Creek, which can be waist high in early season. Continue east another 150 yards to the wreckage.)

To complete the loop hike back to the trailhead, return to the signed junction at 4.2 miles. Turn east (right) towards the Secesh River. The trail is relatively level and crosses a bridge over a small stream at 0.3 mile (from the junction). The trail undulates over the next half-mile and then makes a steep 200 foot descent through two switchbacks to the bridge over the Secesh River at 1.6 miles. Before crossing the bridge, there is a campsite.

Cross the Secesh River on the steel bridge, and come to a T-junction. (A right turn leads south down the Secesh River nearly 11.0 miles to the Ponderosa Campground on FR 412.) Turn left, passing another camp spot near the edge of the river. From here until you reach the trailhead, the hike takes on an entirely new ambience under the towering canyon walls cradling the Secesh River.

Continue north paralleling the river and ford a couple of small streams. At 2.8 miles, a sign on a tree identifies Victor Creek, which joins with the Secesh River. The beautiful scenery remains similar until 4.4 miles where the canyon opens and the canyon cliffs are not so high. Cross the bridge over Alex Creek at 4.7 miles, and reach the trailhead in just under another mile.

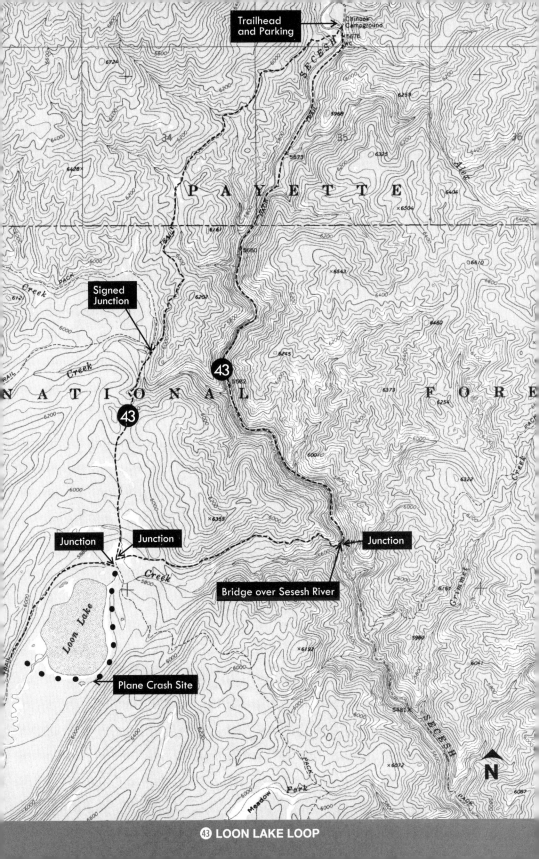

Trailhead
and Parking

Signed
Junction

Junction

Junction

Junction

Bridge over Sesesh River

Plane Crash Site

N

43 LOON LAKE LOOP

Pete Creek Trail

Coordinates

Trailhead:

N 45° 18.183'
W 115° 56.038'

Unnamed Lake:

N 45° 17.371'
W 115° 58.997'

Distance: 9.4 miles out-and-back

Total Elevation Gain: 1,900 feet

Difficulty: Very Strenuous

Elevation Range: 6,200 to 8,000 feet

Topographic Map: Burgdorf

Time: 4 to 6 hours

Season: Late June through mid-October

Water Availability: Pete Creek, several streams, unnamed lake

Cautionary Advice: To reach the unnamed lake, you must hike 0.3 mile off-trail. You should be knowledgable with route-finding.

Information: Payette National Forest, McCall Ranger District (208) 634-0400

Pit Latrine: Yes

Pete Creek Trail

A few miles north of Burgdorf Hot Springs, you will find the Pete Creek Trail. Although known to mountain bikers, it seems to be off the radar of most hikers. This is a beautiful route through dense woods for about 3.5 miles and then up a burned canyon full of gray snags. The trail eventually joins the Bear Pete Trail high on Bear Pete Ridge at 5.0 miles.

Although the enchanting walk through the dense forest is worthy of the hike, the real treat is an unnamed lake—some may call it a large pond—that is found before reaching Bear Pete Ridge. Reaching the lake requires an off-trail hike of a quarter-mile through open woods. The lake sits in a granite-walled amphitheater just north of Bear Pete Mountain. There are a couple of islands, one forested and the other with granite outcroppings, in the center of the beautiful, oval-shaped lake.

Near the lake, which sees very few visitors, several forested knolls allow backpackers to establish a remote campsite. Many lily pads grow along the lake's perimeter. If the hike to the lake is too far, the easy ford of Bear Pete

Creek at 3.3 miles is an excellent destination. There are only a few places to camp along the trail, although a scenic setting is available past the ford of Bear Pete Creek.

Trailhead Directions

From downtown McCall, drive west on ID 55 for 1.2 miles. Reset your tripmeter, and turn right onto paved Warren Wagon Road. Drive north 28.4 miles to the Burgdorf Junction. Reset your tripmeter and turn left, soon passing Burgdorf Campground, Burgdorf Hot Springs and Jeanette Campground. At 4.0 miles, look for a sign "Bear Pete Trhd." on the right side of the road, and turn left on FR 1901. The road passes several dispersed campsites and a pit latrine at 0.1 mile and winds to the trailhead in 0.2 mile.

The Hike

From the signed trailhead, hike west through forest and veer south (left) into a large, beautiful, grassy meadow. Cross the scenic Lake Creek at 0.2 mile via a wooden bridge. The trail enters forest again and meanders through woods over the next mile with little elevation gain. At 1.5 miles, cross a bridge, then a shallow creek and finally the trail nears Bear Pete Creek at 1.8 miles. Over the next mile, the scenery stays similar with open woods, and the elevation gain is modest with only a couple hundred feet of gain.

At 2.7 miles, the trail's grade steepens and gains 400 feet up a rocky hillside. Make an easy ford of Bear Pete Creek at 3.3 miles, and continue to a couple of good, shaded campsites just before entering a large burn area. From here, the hike feels quite different without the dense forest, and the views continually improve as you make your way up canyon. Ford Bear Pete Creek again at 3.8 miles.

Beyond the creek ford, the trail wanders through a stand of trees and rises through two switchbacks. At 4.2 miles, climb through two more switchbacks, and soon the trail levels. Pay attention here for the off-trail hike begins within 1,000 feet of the last switchback. At 4.4 miles, look south (left) for a cairn on a granite rock about waist high. Turn left here (see map). Hike south, first making an easy ascent through a burn area and then through open forest. There are sporadic cairns, but they are not always obvious. Reach the shallow lake in 0.3 mile from the main trail. There are possible campsites along the wooded knolls north of the lake.

If you continue past the granite rock and cairn on the main trail, it rises 300 feet in 0.6 mile to a signed junction with the Bear Pete Trail. The dense forest restricts views, although you can see into the French Creek watershed.

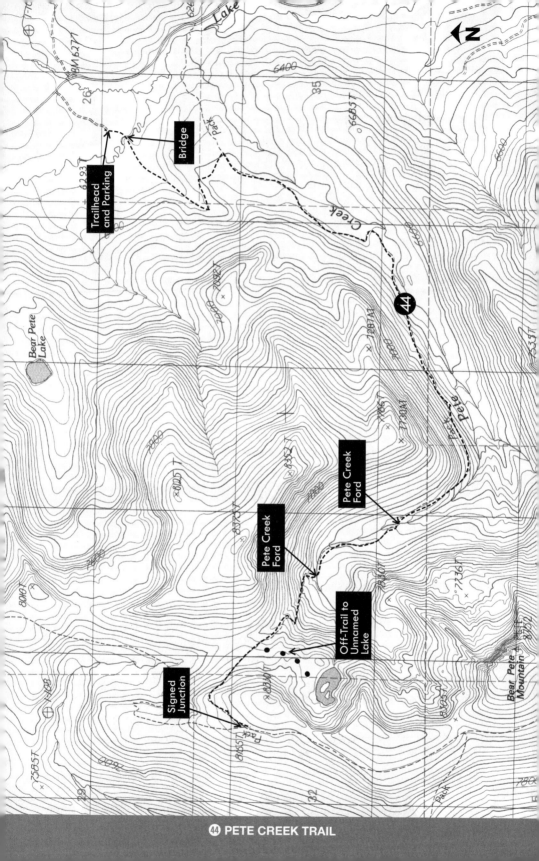

45   Goose Creek Falls Trail

Distance: 3.0 miles out-and-back

Total Elevation Gain: 650 feet

Difficulty: Moderate

Elevation Range: 5,100 to 5,750 feet

Topographic Map: Brundage Mountain, Meadows

Time: 1.5 to 2 hours

Season: Mid-June through mid-October

Water Availability: Goose Creek and several streams

Cautionary Advice: Use caution near the steep ridges above Goose Creek Falls.

Information: Payette National Forest, McCall Ranger District (208) 634-0400

Pit Latrine: Yes

Trailhead:

N 44° 59.994'

W 116° 09.978'

Goose Creek Falls:

N 45° 00.715'

W 116° 09.764'

Goose Creek Falls Trail

There are three trailheads that lead to Goose Creek Falls: one from the Last Chance Campground, one from Brundage Reservoir and this hike, near Brundage Resort. This is the shortest route to the falls although not the most scenic, as that distinction would go to the route from Last Chance Campground. However, this route gets you to the falls in the shortest amount of time and is still a pleasing hike.

The hike starts near its highpoint and descends 600 feet along Goose Creek Canyon's west face to a bridge over Goose Creek. From here, it continues south about a quarter-mile to the falls. The higher elevations of the hike, near the trailhead, provide a bird's-eye perspective of Goose Creek Canyon. The rest of the hike is mainly in dense forest with pockets of wildflower-covered hillsides.

Both Brundage Reservoir and Goose Lake provide the headwaters for Goose Creek. The wide falls are impressive, especially in late spring and early summer when the creek is running high, as they plummet over sixty feet into a large pool. Near the falls, lichen-covered granite boulders surround the creek, and a variety of green shrubs, ferns and conifers complement the

Goose Creek and bridge in January

setting. In winter, this trailhead is kept open for snowmobilers and provides access to an ungroomed and beautiful snowshoe trek to the falls.

Trailhead Directions

From downtown McCall, drive west on ID 55 for 5.5 miles. Turn right onto the paved Brundage Mountain–Goose Lake Road (FR 257). Continue 3.4 miles, and turn left into the Gordon Titus Parking Area. The trailhead is located at the north end of the parking area.

The Hike

Hike 100 feet from the trailhead, and turn left on the Goose Creek Falls Trail. The trail rises 100 feet to the top of a ridge covered with Douglas fir trees. Here, the route descends north along the west-facing canyon wall. Forest, wildflowers, huckleberries, alders and other shrubs shoulder the trail.

At 1.2 miles, cross the bridge over the cascading Goose Creek, which is lined with huge granite boulders. Just beyond the bridge, arrive at a signed junction. (A right turn leads north about 2.5 miles with 1,000 feet of gain to the trailhead near Brundage Reservoir.) Turn south (left) through forest to another junction at 1.4 miles. Turn left again, following the trail southeast through forest. It eventually crosses a granite outcropping near the overlook of the falls. You can follow the trail past the falls to the Last Chance Campground. It is another 2.5 miles and 550 feet of elevation loss to this trailhead. With two vehicles, this would make for a pleasant 4-mile shuttle hike, almost all downhill.

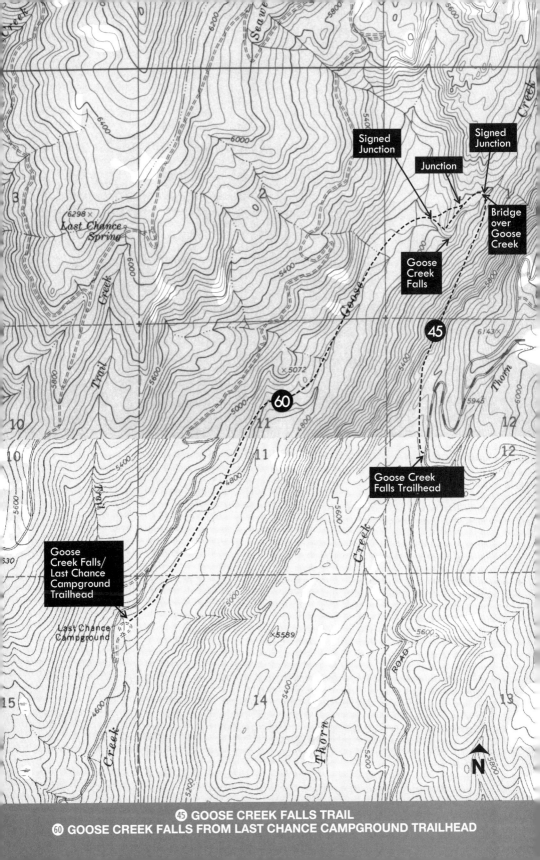

Signed
Junction

Junction

Signed
Junction

Bridge
over
Goose
Creek

Goose
Creek
Falls

45

60

Goose Creek
Falls Trailhead

Goose
Creek Falls/
Last Chance
Campground
Trailhead

Last Chance
Campground

Last Chance
Spring

N

45 GOOSE CREEK FALLS TRAIL
60 GOOSE CREEK FALLS FROM LAST CHANCE CAMPGROUND TRAILHEAD

Fisher Creek

Coordinates

Trailhead:

N 45° 05.564'
W 116° 06.434'

Rock outcropping at 2.0 miles:

N 45° 06.972'
W 116° 07.419'

Distance: 4.0 miles out-and-back

Total Elevation Gain: 250 feet

Difficulty: Easy

Elevation Range: 6,350 to 6,550 feet

Topographic Map: Granite Lake

Time: 1.5 to 2 hours

Season: Late June through mid-October

Water Availability: Fisher Creek, several streams

Cautionary Advice: None

Information: Payette National Forest, McCall Ranger District (208) 634-0400

Pit Latrine: No

Fisher Creek

If you want to experience an easy, crowd-free hike in a beautiful, open canyon, head to Fisher Creek. Although not a long hike, the route provides plenty of serene hiking with flower-covered meadows, dense forest, jagged canyon walls and the boulder-lined Fisher Creek, which finds its headwaters on the southwest face of 8,292-foot Black Tip. In late spring and early summer, the creek flaunts a few mini-waterfalls as it meanders on a leisurly schedule to a confluence with the Payette River.

This hike starts at an unmarked trailhead located at the end of FR 1502, north of Sater Meadows. Although the hike is along an old roadbed, new saplings and plants are retaking the land. The route begins in thick forest and bypasses a beautiful meadow within a quarter-mile. Those with small children will find the nearby Fisher Creek an excellent destination. The hike continues through forest, crossing a few small streams, and at 1.0 mile, enters old burn. Here the hike takes on a new feel as you see steep, granite, canyon walls rising to over 7,000 feet. As you make your way up canyon, you will find many excellent destinations both near Fisher Creek and along the perimeter of several meadows.

The hike description ends at a large, granite outcropping—a perfect perch to observe the triangular Black Tip, the sprawling meadows and towering canyon walls. There is a small waterfall on Fisher Creek about 50 yards east of the outcropping. Off-trail junkies can continue north into the canyon to find secluded backpacking. Because the trail is not maintained, expect deadfall. Although, most of the trees are small and easy to negotiate.

Trailhead Directions

From downtown McCall, drive west 5.5 miles on ID 55. Reset your tripmeter, and turn right onto the paved Brundage–Goose Lake Road. Travel 3.8 miles on paved road and then on an improved dirt road to a signed Y-junction for Granite Lake at 6.6 miles. Turn right, and follow FR 446 for 3.8 miles to the junction of FR 1502 in Sater Meadows. Turn on FR 1502, and follow the road 1.0 mile to its end and the trailhead. There is parking for three or four vehicles.

Outcropping at the end of the hike description

The Hike

From the unsigned trailhead, immediately ford an unnamed creek. In late spring and early summer, a large downed tree provides easy passage across. At a quarter-mile, come to a large boulder on the southwest corner of a lovely meadow. Fisher Creek is located along the meadow's east edge. Continue north, fording a couple of streams and enter burned forest at 1.1 miles. Here, views improve as the landscape is much more open.

The trail now ascends a small hill and continues along a very modest grade to a tree-fringed meadow at 1.5 miles. There are several excellent locations to establish a campsite. Beyond the meadow, the path becomes a bit more cluttered with deadfall but is still very manageable. At 1.9 miles, ford a braided, shallow creek and continue to a granite outcropping to the west (left) of the trail at 2.0 miles. This is the end of the trail description. A beautiful waterfall can be found east of the trail by crossing deadfall and walking about 50 yards down to Fisher Creek. Beyond the outcropping, a faint trail veers east off the roadbed, bisects a meadow and fords Fisher Creek at 2.2 miles. Deadfall is more problematic as you continue north, but the upper canyon is a great place to continue your exploration.

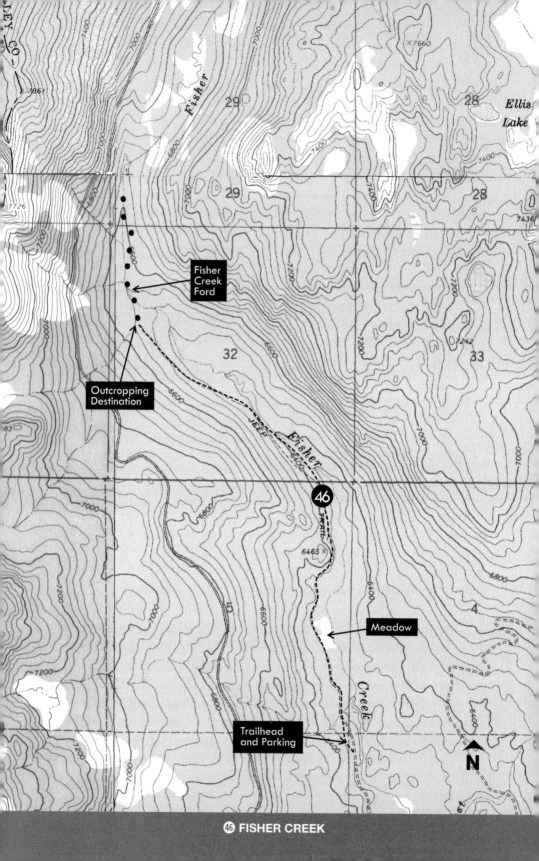

Fisher Creek Ford

Outcropping Destination

Meadow

Trailhead and Parking

Ellis Lake

N

Ellis and Horton Lakes

 Map located on page 146

Coordinates

Trailhead:

N 45° 06.334'
W 116° 05.061'

Ellis Lake:

N 45° 07.703'
W 116° 05.658'

Horton Lake:

N 45° 07.703'
W 116° 05.233'

Distance: 3.6 miles out-and-back (Horton Lake)
3.8 miles out-and-back (Ellis Lake)

Total Elevation Gain: 600 feet (Horton Lake)
700 feet (Ellis Lake)

Difficulty: Moderate

Elevation Range: 6,800 to 7,500 feet

Topographic Map: Granite Lake

Time: 1.5 to 2.5 hours

Season: Late June through October

Water Availability: Ellis and Horton Lakes, several creeks

Cautionary Advice: Beyond the meadow at 1.3 miles, there is no trail and hikers should be experienced with route-finding.

Information: Payette National Forest, McCall Ranger District (208) 634-0400

Pit Latrine: No. There is one near Granite Lake, about a quarter-mile away.

Ellis and Horton Lakes

Ellis and Horton Lakes don't rank high on most hiker's must-see places and for good reason—the trailhead is not identified, and the last half-mile to either lake requires route-finding as there is no trail. However, the adventurous hiker who finds these two gems will have these pristine lakes to themself. The two lakes are located northwest of Granite Lake and are in a magical landscape of granite: rolling ridges, steep ledges and fascinating rock outcroppings. Horton Lake is the closest, but only by 0.1 mile. The smallish, shallow lake contains a tiny island and is bordered by granite slabs, boulders and forest. There are several good campsites. The circular-shaped Ellis Lake is equally pretty and is also a good destination for a backpack outing. The forest near both lakes burned many years ago, although there are patches of green firs near each lake.

The route to the lakes follows an old forest road for 1.3 miles to a tiny meadow resting below a towering, unnamed 7,436-foot granite peak. Although the path begins as a road, it turns into a singletrack at 0.5 mile,

Ellis Lake

crosses a few small creeks through dense forest and eventually fades near the meadow. This is a great destination for those looking for an easy and beautiful walk. Beyond this point, the footpath is difficult to discern so you should be experienced with route-finding.

From the meadow, you can find Horton Lake by hiking northeast up a heavily wooded ravine for about a half-mile to the elongated Horton Lake. From the meadow, Ellis Lake is found by ascending a steep 200 feet up a burned slope and then through open and burned forest to the lake. Both lakes are scenic and certainly off the beaten path. The rolling terrain near the lakes is interesting to explore off-trail.

Trailhead Directions

From downtown McCall, drive west 5.5 miles on ID 55. Reset your tripmeter and turn right onto the paved Brundage–Goose Lake Road. Travel 3.8 miles on paved road and then on an improved dirt road to a signed Y-junction for Granite Lake at 6.6 miles. Turn right and follow FR 446 another 6.8 miles to a sign on the right for Granite Lake and the Cougar Creek Trail. Follow FR 446 another 0.1 mile towards the Cougar Creek Trail. The unsigned trailhead is on the left and is identified by three large granite boulders blocking motorized access to the road. There is parking for several vehicles. Dispersed camping and a pit latrine are located back at the Granite Lake spur road.

The Hike

Beyond the granite boulders at the trailhead, hike north along the roadbed. At 0.5 mile, ford a small stream as the road transitions to a singletrack trail. The vegetation is a bit more lush and the forest is dense. Cross a larger creek at 0.6 mile, and continue along the trail as it veers northeast. At 1.1 miles, the old roadbed ends and looking ahead, you see the south face of an unnamed 7,436-foot peak. Keep walking towards the mountain and at 1.3 miles come to a small clearing near its headwall. Timber, granite rocks and summer wildflowers make this a good destination for an easy hike.

To continue to Horton Lake from the clearing, veer northeast (right) near the base of the ridge. The route—with careful inspection you will locate a faint footpath— gains elevation as it wanders through forest and passes a small pond at 1.5 miles. There are a few spots where you must negotiate dense shrubbery and deadfall. At 1.6 miles, enter burned forest and gain 150 feet to the lake.

To find Ellis Lake from the clearing at 1.3 miles, turn northwest (left) and ascend 200 feet up a steep slope. There is a faint footpath leading to the saddle. At the saddle, a faint trail is visible and veers right

Horton Lake

behind the 7,436-foot peak. The forest is burned here and terrain is open. Continue northwest, gaining another 400 feet, to Ellis Lake in a half-mile. The rolling topography near the lakes makes it easy to become disoriented, so make sure to bring a good map.

Granite Lake to Camp Creek

Distance: 5.0 miles out-and-back

Total Elevation Gain: 850 feet

Difficulty: Moderate

Elevation Range: 6,500 to 6,950 feet

Topographic Map: Granite Lake

Time: 2 to 3 hours

Season: July through mid-October

Water Availability: Lake, Deep and Camp Creeks

Cautionary Advice: None

Information: Payette National Forest, McCall Ranger District (208) 634-0400

Pit Latrine: No. But one is available at the undeveloped campground at Granite Lake.

Map located on page 146

Coordinates

Trailhead:

N 45° 06.387'
W 116° 05.002'

Camp Creek:

N 45° 07.475'
W 116° 02.994'

Granite Lake to Camp Creek

If you are seeking a secluded getaway, look to the Cougar Creek Trail. Located north of Granite Lake, the scenic trail winds through dense forest, across beautiful meadows, and over babbling creeks. Opportunities to see wildlife are plentiful and two of the larger creeks on the hike—Deep and Camp Creeks—offer outstanding destinations for a remote backpack outing.

The nearby Granite Lake is a fine destination if you are looking to disperse camp. There is a primitive camping area, pit toilet included, with several wooded campsites and easy access to Granite Lake. The large, shallow lake is surrounded by forest and by fall dries up to half its early-summer size. There is a granite outcropping near the trail, about a half-mile from the Cougar Creek Trailhead, offering fantastic vistas across Granite Lake.

The hike can be extended beyond Camp Creek as the trail continues northeast over a ridge and intersects with two trails, both of which make a steep descent to Upper Payette Lake (see hikes 33 and 34). If you decide to camp near Granite Lake, there are two other excellent hikes nearby including Fisher Creek and Ellis and Horton Lakes (see hikes 46 and 47).

Trailhead Directions

From downtown McCall, drive west 5.5 miles on ID 55. Reset your tripmeter, and turn right onto the paved Brundage–Goose Lake Road (FR 257). Travel 3.8 miles on paved road and then on an improved dirt road to a signed Y-junction for Granite Lake at 6.6 miles. Turn right and follow FR 446 for 6.8 miles to a sign on the right for Granite Lake and the Cougar Creek Trail. Dispersed camping and a pit latrine are a few hundred feet down the spur road to the right. To find the Cougar Creek Trailhead, continue north on FR 446 another 0.2 mile to its end. There is parking for four or five vehicles.

The Hike

From the trailhead, cross over Lake Creek on a small bridge. The trail is fairly level as it continues northeast. At 0.6 mile, look east through forest for a large granite outcropping. A short walk (off-trail) of 75 feet brings you to it—Mother Nature includes a granite bench—perched high above Granite Lake and offers great vistas.

Back on the main trail, the grade steepens and crests on an open hillside at 1.0 mile. The trail is faint here. Look for a solo tree with a "trail" sign pointing left (northwest). The trail—now more prominent—descends into forest again and winds around the west side of a large meadow. Continue through open forest, across a small meadow with a tiny creek and into another meadow. Here, another tree identifies the trail with a "trail" sign. At the end of the meadow at 1.4 miles, ford the wide but shallow Deep Creek. Early season hikers will find the creek deep enough that they will need to remove their boots. The meadow and creek make for an excellent destination for a short backpack trip or an easy 2.8 miles out-and-back hike.

Beyond the Deep Creek ford, the trail rises 150 feet through forest to a saddle at 1.8 miles. Just past a large outcropping, begin a 350-foot, rocky descent to where the trail starts to flatten at 2.4 miles. A "trail" sign on a tree points left for the continuation of the trail. It is easy to continue north (straight) as it appears the trail goes this way. Don't, for the trail fades within 50 feet. Turn west (left) at the tree with the sign, and descend 50 feet to Camp Creek at 2.5 miles. Beyond the Camp Creek ford, there are several good campsites over the next quarter-mile. If you continue along the Cougar Creek Trail, it rises more than 300 feet and sidehills a steep slope. Within a mile, it enters burned forest and comes to a signed junction for two different trails that descend to Upper Payette Lake (see hikes 33 and 34).

49 Twin Lakes

Coordinates

Trailhead:

N 45° 06.487'
W 116° 10.450'

Twin Lakes:

N 45° 06.126'
W 116° 10.849'

Distance: 1.8 miles out-and-back (east side of lake)

Total Elevation Gain: 450 feet

Difficulty: Easy

Elevation Range: 6,700 to 7,150 feet

Topographic Map: Brundage Mountain

Time: 1 hour

Season: Mid-June through mid-October

Water Availability: Twin Lakes and several creeks

Cautionary Advice: Cattle may be grazing on the first mile of the trail. Please respect the animals and use caution.

Information: Payette National Forest, McCall Ranger District (208) 634-0400

Pit Latrine: No

Twin Lakes

Twin Lakes is actually one lake ringed by granite ridges, hills and lush forest, especially along the lake's west side. The scenery is stupendous with the north face of the 8,479-foot Granite Mountain ascending 1,300 vertical feet from the lake's shore. On the west end of the lake, a crystal-clear creek tumbles over granite slabs, and overnighters will find private campsites.

The half-mile long lake provides plenty of fine campsites all around its perimeter. By mid-to-late summer, the dammed lake is subject to drawdown, which can create the illusion of two lakes due to its figure-eight shape. Depending on the lake's level, the shore can be muddy. Because of the short hiking distance and minimal elevation gain, this is a good hiking choice for those with small children looking for an easy hike or backpack outing.

Trailhead Directions

From downtown McCall, drive west 5.5 miles on ID 55. Reset your tripmeter, and turn right onto the paved Brundage Mountain–Goose Lake Road. Continue 3.8 miles on paved road and then on an improved dirt road. At 6.1 miles, bear left towards Hazard Lake at a signed Y-junction (still on FR 257). Continue past Goose Lake, and at 13.1 miles, turn left at a sign for

Twin Lakes and Granite Mountain

the Granite Mountain/Twin Lake Trailhead. Proceed 0.1 mile to the large parking area and trailhead on the south side of the road.

The Hike

Begin with a prompt crossing of a small creek on a bridge. Continue through a meadow that may have grazing cattle. If you have a dog with you, keep it under control. Try not to surprise the cows, and remove yourself from their area as soon as possible.

Near the end of the meadow, cross the outlet creek of Twin Lakes. At 0.4 mile, the trail enters burned forest and provides outstanding views east to the dark brown Slab Butte. The trail turns west and arrives at a signed junction at 0.6 mile. Turn north (right). (A left turn leads to the Granite Mountain Lookout – see hike 50.) From the junction, ascend 150 feet in 0.3 mile to the east side of Twin Lakes. Footpaths travel on both sides of the lake where you will find a multitude of campsites. The most scenic section of the lake is on its west side. The easiest route is to turn north (right) when you get to Twin Lakes and continue west following a footpath along the lake's perimeter. There is a campsite at 0.3 mile. Continue through burned forest to where the footpath turns south on the lake's west side. At 0.8 mile, come to an inlet creek where a small waterfall tumbles down a granite outcropping. You can continue around the lake, although there is dense foliage on the lake's southwest corner. It is about 1.4 miles to circumnavigate Twin Lakes.

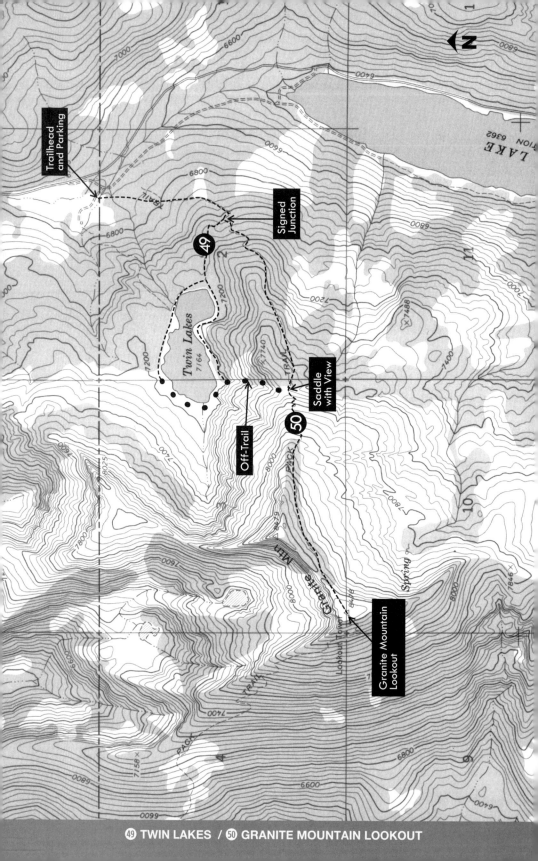

Granite Mountain Lookout

Coordinates

Trailhead:

N 45° 06.487'
W 116° 10.450'

Granite Mountain Lookout:

N 45° 05.622'
W 116° 12.421'

Distance: 5.6 miles out-and-back

Total Elevation Gain: 1,800 feet

Difficulty: Strenuous

Elevation Range: 6,700 to 8,500 feet

Topographic Map: Brundage Mountain

Time: 2.5 to 3.5 hours

Season: July through October

Water Availability: Two creeks near the trailhead

Cautionary Advice: Bring water as there is no reliable source beyond the creeks near the trailhead. Cattle may be grazing along the first mile of the route. Please respect the animals and use caution.

Information: Payette National Forest, McCall Ranger District (208) 634-0400

Pit Latrine: No

Granite Mountain Lookout

The aptly named Granite Mountain looms high on the western edge of the Salmon River Mountains. The broad mountaintop is a half-mile wide and contains two summits with only one foot of difference. The 8,478-foot south summit is home to the Granite Mountain Lookout built in 1954. The higher north summit crests at 8,479 feet with a steep rocky face plunging 1,300 vertical feet to Twin Lakes.

At the mountain's apex, wildflowers carpet the treeless summit with near-perfect views of the surrounding alpine scenery. Looking north and east, the Salmon River Mountains unfold into the Gospel Hump and Frank Church Wildernesses; to the south the views extend thirty miles beyond the town of New Meadows to the 7,715-foot Cuddy Mountain. The views west into the rugged Seven Devils Mountains are equally impressive.

Much of the forest along the lower sections of trail burned in the 1994 fires. Fortunately, shade is provided by a few unscathed Douglas firs, lodgepole pines and subalpine firs. Gazing southeast as you climb to the lookout, enjoy views of Goose Lake and the 8,225-foot Slab Butte. The higher elevations of the trail rise through forest and along granite slabs. If you are

View northwest from Granite Mountain

comfortable hiking off-trail, there is a steep ravine on your return from Granite Mountain where you can descend a thigh-burning 500 feet in less than a half-mile to the southwest corner of Twin Lake. From here, you can complete a semi-loop hike back to the trailhead.

Trailhead Directions

From downtown McCall, drive west 5.5 miles on ID 55. Reset your tripmeter, and turn right onto the paved Brundage Mountain–Goose Lake Road. Travel 3.8 miles on paved road and then on an improved dirt road to a signed Y-junction at 6.1 miles. Bear left towards Hazard Lake (still on FR 257). At 13.1 miles, turn left at a sign for the Granite Mountain/Twin Lake Trailhead. Proceed west another 0.1 mile to the large parking area and trailhead on the south side of the road. There is dispersed camping near the trailhead, but you may have bovines joining you at your campfire.

The Hike

The hike starts with a prompt crossing of a small creek on a little bridge. Pass through a meadow, which may have grazing cattle, and cross downed logs over the outlet stream of Twin Lakes at 0.1 mile. The trail fords a small stream and at 0.4 mile enters burned forest. Looking east, there are outstanding views to the dark brown Slab Butte. The trail turns west and arrives at a signed junction. Turn south (left). (A right turn leads to Twin Lakes in 0.3 mile – see hike 49.)

Beyond the junction, the trail continues through burned forest. Alpine knotweed is prolific on the open hillsides, making for a beautiful hike in the fall when the plant turns bright shades of burgundy. At 1.0 mile, look south to see the dammed two-mile long Goose Lake.

The trail continues its gradual climb past granite boulders and plenty of wildflowers, including lupine, Indian paintbrush, penstemon, sulphur buckwheat and aster. At 1.7 miles, you will come to a grassy saddle—marked with a cairn—which if you hike a few yards to the north provides a picturesque vista of Twin Lakes and the rugged peaks beyond. If you are looking for a shorter hike, this destination is a fine turnaround spot for a 3.4 miles out-and-back hike with 1,000 feet of gain. This is also the start of the very steep descent to Twin Lakes to make a semi-loop. (To do so from here, head north (right). Within 20 yards, the steep ravine down to Twin Lakes is visible. There is a faint footpath at times as the route crisscrosses from the east side of the ravine to the west side as it descends. It is 0.4 mile with a very steep 500 feet of elevation loss to the lake. From the lake, you can follow a footpath around the west side of Twin Lake for a longer hike, or head east to the trailhead for a short hike.)

View southeast to Goose Lake

From the grassy knoll, the trail's grade steepens as it twists and turns over rock slabs. On the open granite slabs, the trail is easy to lose, but there are many cairns to assist with route-finding. At 2.2 miles, the lookout is visible if you look west to the top of Granite Mountain. With each step the views improve, with the 8,126-foot Council Mountain dominating the skyline from over twenty-five miles away. Reach the broad mountaintop of Granite Mountain, between its two summits, at 2.6 miles. Looking down the steep north face of the peak, you can see an unnamed small lake. Continue a gradual ascent another 0.2 mile to the base of the lookout. The fire lookout is usually occupied from late June through September. Please respect the lookout staff's privacy.

51 Lake Serene

Distance: 4.4 miles out-and-back

Total Elevation Gain: 1,300 feet

Difficulty: Strenuous

Elevation Range: 6,850 to 7,350 feet

Topographic Map: Hazard Lake

Time: 2 to 3 hours

Season: Late June through mid-October

Water Availability: Lake Serene, several creeks

Cautionary Advice: There is very little shade on this hike, so plan accordingly.

Information: Payette National Forest, McCall Ranger District (208) 634-0400

Pit Latrine: No

Coordinates

Trailhead:

N 45° 10.612'
W 116° 10.728'

Lake Serene:

N 45° 11.670'
W 116° 11.603'

Lake Serene

It was the Hungarian psychiatrist, Thomas Szasz, who said it best: "Boredom is the feeling that everything is a waste of time, serenity, that nothing is." Perch yourself on one of the surrounding boulders at Lake Serene, and this thought will certainly ring true.

Lake Serene is located less than 2 miles south of the rugged Hazard Creek Canyon, nestled in a small glaciated bowl below an unnamed 8,124-foot granite peak. Steep slopes covered with dark green firs, gray snags, willows, bright green grass and talus surround the lake. Near the outlet stream, huge boulders provide flat platforms to allow you to immerse yourself in the beauty of this small gem.

Plenty of gray snags surround the lake, specifically the west side, as the fires of 1994 ravaged this area. The recovery has been gradual, and willows and native grasses now surround the lake. Backpackers will most likely have the lake to themselves and will find a couple of campsites in the gray snags to the west of the outlet creek. En route to the lake, you will see a few stands of burned forest from the Tepee Springs Fire of 2015. Fortunately, the fire did not impact the terrain directly around Lake Serene.

Trailhead Directions

From downtown McCall, drive west 5.5 miles on ID 55. Reset your tripmeter, and turn right onto the paved Brundage Mountain–Goose Lake Road. Continue 3.8 miles on paved road and then on gravel. At 6.1 miles, bear left at a signed Y-junction towards Hazard Lake (still on FR 257), and continue north to the Grassy Mountain Trailhead at 18.6 miles. The large parking area is located on the right side of the road. The trailhead is located across the road from the parking area.

The Hike

The trail makes an immediate rise through a small meadow to a signed junction at 0.2 mile on a burned ridge. Continue straight, following the sign to Lake Serene. (A left turn takes you to Grass Mountain Lakes and Coffee Cup Lake – see hike 52.) Under a canopy of dense forest, the path descends alongside a small meadow and fords an unnamed creek at 0.5 mile.

The trail veers west on an open hillside as the grade steepens and gains 200 feet to where is becomes moderate at 0.8 mile.

Lake Serene

As the trail gains elevation, views looking northeast into the Vance Creek drainage improve. In July and early August, wildflowers are plentiful and include Indian paintbrush, mountain bluebells, lupine, phlox and penstemon. At 1.0 mile, wind through a section of burned trees, pass below a granite ridge and come to a little knoll only a few feet east of the trail at 1.4 miles. A little scramble to a tree at the end of the knoll is a good destination to enjoy a snack and take in the views.

Past the knoll, make a final gain of 100 feet to a saddle at 1.7 miles. You cannot see Lake Serene as it is tucked directly below the ridge to the left. On both sides of the saddle, you can ascend the treed ridgeline to improve your vistas. From the saddle, descend a steep 400 feet to where the trail levels at 2.1 miles. Veer south, and ascend 100 feet beside Lake Serene's outlet creek to the lake's north side.

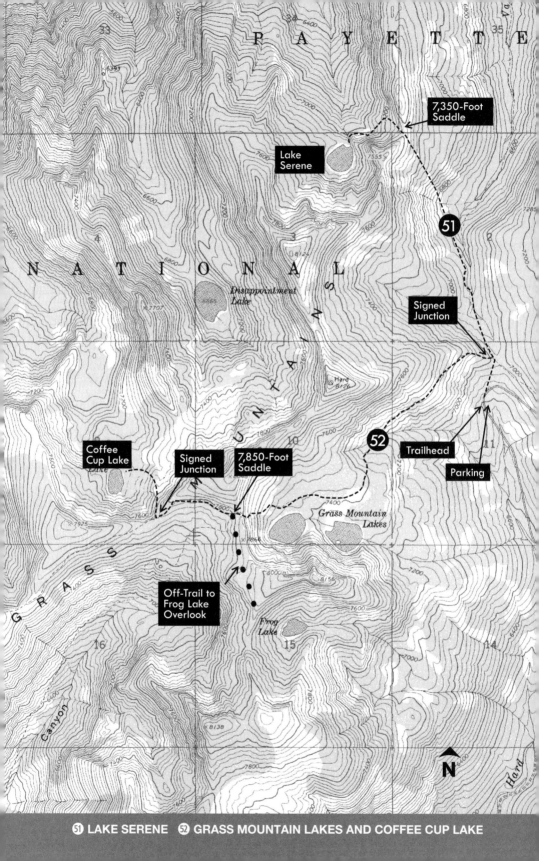

P A Y E T T E

7,350-Foot
Saddle

Lake
Serene

N A T I O N A L

Disappointment
Lake

51

Signed
Junction

52

Trailhead

Parking

Coffee
Cup Lake

Signed
Junction

7,850-Foot
Saddle

Grass Mountain
Lakes

Off-Trail to
Frog Lake
Overlook

Frog
Lake

G R A S S

Canyon

N

51 LAKE SERENE   **52** GRASS MOUNTAIN LAKES AND COFFEE CUP LAKE

Grass Mountain Lakes and Coffee Cup Lake

Coordinates

Trailhead:

N 45° 10.612'
W 116° 10.728'

Coffee Cup Lake:

N 45° 10.295'
W 116° 13.057'

Distance:
3.8 miles out-and-back (Grass Mountain Lakes)
6.4 miles out-and-back (Coffee Cup Lake)

Total Elevation Gain:
750 feet (Grass Mountain Lakes)
1,800 feet (Coffee Cup Lake)

Difficulty: Easy to Strenuous

Elevation Range: 6,850 to 7,850 feet

Topographic Map: Hazard Lake

Time: 2 to 4 hours

Season: Late June through October

Water Availability: Grass Mountain Lakes, Coffee Cup Lake, several streams and creeks

Cautionary Advice: The lakes are bordered by a few marshy areas and mosquitoes are plentiful in early July.

Information: Payette National Forest, McCall Ranger District (208) 634-0400

Pit Latrine: No

Grass Mountain Lakes and Coffee Cup Lake

If you are looking for scenic, high mountain lakes, the two Grass Mountain Lakes and Coffee Cup Lake don't disappoint. The easily accessed Grass Mountain Lakes are less than a quarter-mile apart and are appropriately named: both lakes are bordered on their north side by a field of tall brilliant green grass. Dramatic granite cliffs sprinkled with green grass and fir trees rise dramatically from the lakes' perimeters. If you happen to be at the lakes in June and early July, lingering snowfields make for postcard photography.

The hike to the circular Coffee Cup Lake is more rigorous. You must first ascend 400 feet to a 7,850-foot saddle west of the Grass Mountain Lakes. The vistas looking over the Grass Mountain Lakes to the distant mountains are exceptional. Beyond the saddle, you continue west another half-mile and finally descend 400 feet to Coffee Cup Lake. In early summer, wildflowers are a constant on most of the hike. All of the lakes offer good campsites.

Looking east from the 7,850-foot saddle

Outstanding scenery, modest elevation gain and a short hiking distance, make the Grass Mountain Lakes an excellent choice for backpackers with small children. The Tepee Springs Fire did burn some of the forest in the area, although much of the burn is mosiac. It is most obvious in the forest just before reaching the lower Grass Mountain Lake and beyond the saddle to Coffee Cup Lake.

Trailhead Directions

From downtown McCall, drive west 5.5 miles on ID 55. Reset your tripmeter, and turn right onto the paved Brundage Mountain–Goose Lake Road. Continue 3.8 miles on paved road and then on an improved dirt road. At 6.1 miles, bear left towards Hazard Lake at a signed Y-junction (still on FR 257). Continue past Goose Lake, and reach the Grassy Mountain Trailhead at 18.2 miles. A large parking area is located on the right side of the road. The trailhead is located across the road from the parking area.

The Hike

The trail makes a quick climb through a small meadow to a signed junction at 0.2 mile. The north fork trail leads to Lake Serene (see hike 51). Turn left as the trail's grade steepens and winds through a switchback on an open slope at 0.3 mile. Views are very good looking down to the canyon containing Goose Creek Road and beyond to several high peaks.

At 0.6 mile, the trail levels and then descends below a steep granite wall through partially burned forest. Over the next quarter-mile, the wildflowers are often spectacular and include Indian paintbrush, sego lily, lupine, penstemon, spirea and horsemint. Enter burned forest again at 1.0 mile, and cross a small creek along a slope blanketed with granite boulders. At 1.3 miles, the trail levels in a grassy meadow and continues to an unsigned junction at 1.4 miles. (The right fork continues to Coffee Cup Lake.) To access the two Grass Mountain Lakes, take the left fork, which leads to the highest lake in a quarter-mile. There is a footpath between the two lakes.

To continue to Coffee Cup Lake at the 1.4 mile junction, turn west (right). The trail enters forest and rises through a scenic setting of granite boulders, wildflowers, seasonal creeks and fir trees. At 1.9 miles (from the trailhead), leave the forest behind on an open slope and reach the signed saddle at 2.1 miles. You can turn south (left) at the saddle and follow the flat ridge a half-mile to an overlook of Frog Lake.

From the saddle, continue west along an undulating, open slope to a signed junction for Coffee Cup Lake at 2.6 miles. Four hundred feet below, Coffee Cup Lake glistens, and the Seven Devils Mountains are in the far distance. Turn right. (If you continue west, the trail continues approximately 6 miles to a trailhead near Hard Creek.) The spur trail to Coffee Cup Lake makes a steep descent below a talus-covered slope. At 2.9 miles, the trail levels in a tiny

The easternmost Grass Mountain Lake

meadow, and the lake will no longer be visible due to dense forest. Look to your left for a cairn near a small stream. Turn left and descend through open forest to the northeast side of Coffee Cup Lake. There are several shaded campsites on its north side.

Hidden and Hard Creek Lakes

Coordinates

Trailhead:

N 45° 10.469'
W 116° 10.031'

Hard Creek Lake:

N 45° 10.364'
W 116° 08.815'

Hidden Lake:

N 45° 08.973'
W 116° 09.079'

Distance: 3.2 miles out-and-back (Hard Creek Lake)
4.8 miles out-and-back (Hidden Lake)

Total Elevation Gain: 550 feet (Hard Creek Lake)
600 feet (Hidden Lake)

Difficulty: Moderate

Elevation Range: 6,900 to 7,400 feet

Topographic Map: Hazard Lake

Time: 1.5 to 2.5 hours

Season: Late June through mid-October

Water Availability: Upper Hazard and Hidden Lakes, several creeks

Cautionary Advice: None

Information: Payette National Forest, McCall Ranger District (208) 634-0400

Pit Latrine: Yes

Hidden and Hard Creek Lakes

From the Hard Creek Trailhead, hikers can access two beautiful, but very different, mountain lakes. The figure-eight-shaped Hard Creek Lake is closest to the trailhead. Although the vast majority of trees were burned in the 1994 fires, the lake is stunning. Gray snags, a sprinkling of green firs and a multitude of granite slabs fringe the lake. In midsummer, many wildflowers bloom in the meadows near the lake.

Along the way to Hard Creek Lake, a maintained spur trail travels due south over 1.0 mile to Hard Creek Basin and the fittingly named Hidden Lake. Even though the 1994 fires burned in the basin, the fire's effects are not as noticable. Most of Hidden Lake is surrounded by dark green firs and is bordered on its south side by an attractive, fluted, granite ridgeline. Both lakes offer good campsites.

The hike to the lakes offers meadows, open hillsides covered with wildflowers and lots of granite terrain. Hidden Lake offers a greater sense of seclusion. The hike to Hard Creek Lake can be extended with an easy trek to Upper

There are many granite outcroppings along the trail to Hidden Lake

Hazard Lake. Both Hard Creek and Upper Hazard Lakes offer good fishing for cutthroat, brook and rainbow trout.

Trailhead Directions

From downtown McCall, drive west 5.5 miles on ID 55. Reset your tripmeter, and turn right onto the paved Brundage Mountain–Goose Lake Road FR 257). Travel 6.1 miles to a signed Y-junction. (At 3.8 miles the road changes to an improved dirt road.) Take the left fork at the junction, and continue north towards Hazard Lake (still on FR 257). At 18.7 miles, turn right onto a short spur road. Follow it 0.1 mile into the Hard Creek Campground. The trailhead is located next to a large information sign.

The Hike

From the trailhead, follow the trail east as it traverses a small meadow with several streams. In July, many wildflowers bloom here including Indian paintbrush, fireweed and pearly everlasting. At 0.4 mile, the trail veers south and descends 100 feet along a grassy hillside. Arrive at a signed junction at 0.9 mile for either Hidden Lake or Hard Creek Lake. (If you are hiking to Hidden Lake, see next page.) To find Hard Creek Lake, turn left, and ascend a moderate grade weaving between lichen-covered boulders. As you ascend the open hillside, the scenery improves looking east to steep granite ridges rising 700 feet to the top of a 7,975-foot unnamed peak. Wildflowers are a constant in this area, too.

At 1.5 miles, make an easy ford of Hard Creek, and reach the long, narrow Hard Creek Lake. There are a handful of campsites scattered around its perimeter. To visit the much larger Upper Hazard Lake in three-quarters of a mile, follow the trail east around the south side of Hard Creek Lake and ascend 100 feet to a saddle (see map). From here, make an easy descent of 100 feet to the large twenty-acre lake.

Hidden Lake

To find Hidden Lake, continue straight (south) at the 0.9 mile junction. Make an easy ford of Hard Creek at 1.0 mile, and continue through an area with many granite boulders. Over the next half-mile, the trail makes a gradual descent weaving past boulders and beautiful granite outcroppings. There are very good views south to Granite Mountain. After an elevation loss of 200 feet, the trail levels in a grassy meadow at 1.8 miles. You could establish a tent site here. In the meadow, veer southeast into forest. Make a

Hard Creek Lake

ford of Hidden Lake's outlet creek at 2.3 miles. Beyond the creek ford, make one final gain of 50 feet and arrive at Hidden Lake's wooded north side. There are good campsites here and on the opposite side of the lake. (About 500 feet *before* the ford of Hidden Lake's outlet, there is a tree blaze identifying a vague trail heading east.

This route rises more than 1,000 feet to a saddle at 7,850 feet and decends to Hard Creek Lake. The trail has not been maintained and is difficult to follow. It is much easier to access Hard Creek Lake by returning back to the junction at 0.9 mile and hiking north to the lake.)

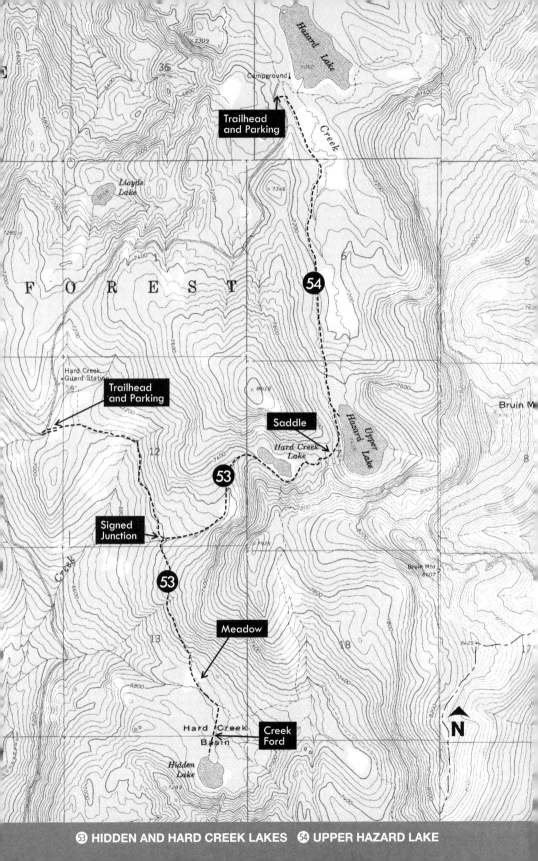

Trailhead
and Parking

Trailhead
and Parking

Saddle

54

53

53

Signed
Junction

Meadow

Creek
Ford

N

FOREST

Lloyds
Lake

Hazard Lake

Campground

Creek

Upper
Hazard
Lake

Hard Creek
Guard Station

Hard Creek
Lake

Bruin M

Bruin Mtn

Hard Creek
Basin

Hidden
Lake

Upper Hazard Lake

Coordinates

Trailhead:

N 45° 12.004'
W 116° 08.615'

Upper Hazard Lake:

N 45° 10.608'
W 116° 08.277'

Distance: 3.8 miles out-and-back

Total Elevation Gain: 350 feet

Difficulty: Easy

Elevation Range: 7,050 to 7,400 feet

Topographic Map: Hazard Lake

Time: 1.5 to 2 hours

Season: Late June through mid-October

Water Availability: Upper Hazard Lake and Hazard Creek

Cautionary Advice: None

Information: Payette National Forest, McCall Ranger District (208) 634-0400

Pit Latrine: No. But one is available at the Upper Hazard Campground.

Upper Hazard Lake

If you seek lush meadows, spectacular granite mountains and a storybook alpine lake, look no further than the hike to Upper Hazard Lake. Upper Hazard Lake is one of the prettier lakes in the area with a sheer granite ridge extending 600 feet above its south edge. In midsummer, a carpet of green grass and wildflowers dot the lake's perimeter.

The easy hike starts near Hazard Lake and continues south about 2 miles through a wide, scenic canyon. One of the highlights is the half-mile long meadow near the trailhead, jam-packed with colorful wildflowers from July to early August. Beyond the meadow, much of the forest was burned in the 1994 Corral Fire, although new saplings are taking hold. The fire's impact near Upper Hazard Lake is minimal and plenty of green forest thrives. Overnighters will find several campsites along the lake's north and west side.

You can find a smaller but equally beautiful lake, Hard Creek Lake, by taking an easy half-mile hike over a wooded ridge. If you have two vehicles, an outstanding shuttle hike would be to leave a car at the Hard Creek Campground (see hike 53) and hike one-way (about 4.5 miles) from Hazard Lake to your other vehicle at Hard Creek Campground.

Upper Hazard Lake

Trailhead Directions

From downtown McCall, drive west 5.5 miles on ID 55. Reset your tripmeter, and turn right onto the paved Brundage Mountain–Goose Lake Road (FR 257). Continue 3.8 miles on paved road and then on a well-graded dirt road. At 6.1 miles, bear left at a signed Y-junction towards Hazard Lake (still on FR 257). At 21.5 miles, look for a sign on the right side of the road "Upper Hazard Lake Trail." Turn right and follow the short spur road to the trailhead and parking.

The Hike

From the trailhead, the trail veers southeast for 400 feet to a junction with a side trail coming from Hazard Lake Campground. Continue south and enter a large grassy meadow where Hazard Creek snakes its way north. In July, countless wildflowers including red Indian paintbrush, pink elephant head, blue lupine, white American bistort, purple shooting star and yellow lousewort explode in a kaleidoscope of color.

At the end of the meadow, the trail makes a modest elevation gain through subalpine fir and gray snags. Cross a quarter-mile-long meadow at 1.0 mile and then ford a small creek and ascend a steep 200 feet. The trail levels at 1.6 miles and reaches the lake at 1.9 miles.

To visit Hard Creek Lake, follow the trail around the west (right) side of Upper Hazard Lake and ascend 100 feet in a quarter-mile to a saddle (see map). From here, descend through burned forest and a hillside meadow to the east side of Hard Creek Lake.

Upper and Lower Twin & Hard Butte Lakes

Coordinates

Trailhead:

N 45° 15.265'
W 116° 09.693'

Hard Butte Lake:

N 45° 15.935'
W 116° 12.564'

Distance: 7.0 miles out-and-back

Total Elevation Gain: 800 feet

Difficulty: Moderate

Elevation Range: 7,300 to 7,750 feet

Topographic Map: Patrick Butte

Time: 2.5 to 4 hours

Season: July through mid-October

Water Availability: Twin and Butte Lakes, creeks, pond

Cautionary Advice: None

Information: Payette National Forest, McCall Ranger District (208) 634-0400

Pit Latrine: Yes

Upper and Lower Twin & Hard Butte Lakes

The Twin Lakes (Upper and Lower) and Hard Butte Lake are set in a large granite amphitheater surrounded on three sides by steep granite walls. The three lakes string together for about a mile nestled directly below the north wall and are suprisingly off the radar of most hikers. Hard Butte and Upper Twin are the largest of the three and are also the most scenic. All three lakes offer wooded campsites and see a profusion of colorful wildflowers in July.

A bit of trail irony unfolds on this trek. ATVs are permitted on the first couple of miles to the lake basin. Rutted and dusty from the ATVs, the trail is similar to a small road, and you might wonder why you are on this journey. But a funny thing happens at a marked junction. ATVs are only allowed on the trail (344) south to Rainbow Lake. The right fork trail (347) continues west and turns into a narrow singletrack. It is as though you went from a major freeway to a lovely country road in the middle of nowhere.

The one-mile long footpath through the lake basin is not maintained, but its tread is apparent for most of the route. If you decide to backpack to the lakes, you can dayhike to a dilapidated lookout on Hard Butte—one of the highest peaks in the area at 8,659 feet—for some of the best views in the

Upper Twin Lake

Salmon River Mountains. Although the Tepee Springs Fire burned near here, it is mainly confined to a half-mile segment of trail. There is minimal sign of the fire near the lakes. There are many open meadows along this hike and wildflowers are a constant from the second week of July until early August.

Trailhead Directions

From downtown McCall, drive west 5.5 miles on ID 55. Reset your tripmeter, and turn right onto the paved Brundage Mountain–Goose Lake Road. Continue 3.8 miles on paved road and then on a well-graded dirt road. At 6.1 miles, bear left at a signed Y-junction towards Hazard Lake (still on FR 257). At 24.8 miles, arrive at a signed junction with FR 308. Continue straight (north) to the end of the road and Clayburn Trailhead in 1.4 miles. The trailhead is to the left of the large information sign in the parking area.

The Hike

Two trails depart from the Clayburn Trailhead. One travels east to Lava Ridge. The other heads north to Rainbow, Hard Butte and Upper Twin Lakes. The dusty, wide trail starts on level ground and makes a short descent to an old fence. At 0.7 mile, ford a small muddy creek, and turn northwest through open forest. At 1.3 miles, the trail enters a sagebrush meadow with outstanding views west to Hard Butte and the steep, granite walls shouldering Hard Butte and Upper and Lower Twin Lakes.

At 2.1 miles, arrive at a signed junction. The left fork trail goes south 1.2 miles to Rainbow Lake (see hike 57). Take the right fork and hike into burned forest, a result of the Tepee Springs Fire. The trail rises to a ill-defined junction at 2.4 miles. A vague trail goes southeast from the junction and descends 150 feet in a quarter-mile to another unsigned junction. If you turn right, you can continue south to Rainbow Lake in another 0.9 mile.

At the 2.4-mile junction, turn north (right) and proceed through burned forest. As you gradually make your way north, the burn is not so bad the further you hike. Soon, ford the outlet creek from Lower Twin Lake and come to a pond (east side of trail) at 2.8 miles. For a great perspective of the intensity of the Tepee Springs Fire as it moved north, walk to the east edge of the pond, and look north down to Partridge Creek Lake and beyond. This fire was very hot and left little in its wake. Back on the main trail near the pond, look to your left for a footpath leading west into open forest. Arrive at Lower Twin Lake within 400 feet. There is a good campsite here near the lake's outlet creek.

Lower Twin Lake and the distant Hard Butte Peak

To find the other two lakes, cross Lower Twin's outlet creek, and hike west on a footpath (vague in sections) through open forest to Upper Twin Lake in 0.4 mile. There are several good campsites on the lake's north, south and east side. From Upper Twin Lake, follow the footpath as it veers southwest to Hard Butte Lake in a quarter-mile. There are many campsites on the lake's north and east side.

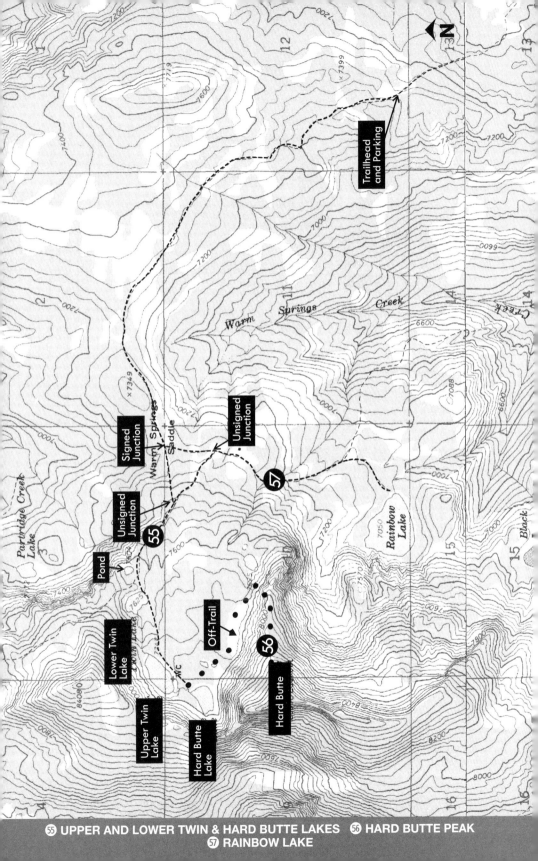

N

Trailhead and Parking

Warm Springs Creek

Creek

Signed Junction

Unsigned Junction

Warm Springs Saddle

Unsigned Junction

57

Rainbow Lake

55

Pond

Partridge Creek Lake

Off-Trail

Black

Lower Twin Lake

56

Hard Butte

Upper Twin Lake

Hard Butte Lake

**55 UPPER AND LOWER TWIN & HARD BUTTE LAKES 56 HARD BUTTE PEAK
57 RAINBOW LAKE**

Hard Butte Peak

Coordinates

Trailhead:

N 45° 15.265'
W 116° 09.693'

Hard Butte Peak:

N 45° 15.635'
W 116° 12.602'

Distance: 9.2 miles out-and-back

Total Elevation Gain: 1,700 feet

Difficulty: Strenuous

Elevation Range: 7,300 to 8,650 feet

Topographic Map: Patrick Butte

Time: 4 to 5.5 hours

Season: July through mid-October

Water Availability: Several unnamed creeks, Hard Butte Lake and Upper and Lower Twin Lakes

Cautionary Advice: The lookout on top of the peak has collapsed and is unstable. Use caution around the structure. This route requires experience reading maps and route-finding. Do not attempt the hike if snowfields are still present.

Information: Payette National Forest, McCall Ranger District (208) 634-0400

Pit Latrine: Yes

Hard Butte Peak

This is a mandatory hike for those who like off-trail challenges and destinations rarely seen. The 8,659-foot Hard Butte is one of the highest peaks in the area, and from the top of this juggernaut, you experience sweeping vistas that extend for fifty miles. These include the Salmon River Mountain's extremes: sage to conifer forests, barren summits to alpine lakes and deep canyons to pristine meadows.

The 900-foot ascent from the base of the mountain to the lookout provides a bird's-eye view north of Hard Butte Lake, Upper and Lower Twin Lakes and the higher 8,841-foot Patrick Butte. At the peak's apex, views southeast to Rainbow Lake and Black Lake and beyond to Big Hazard and Hazard Lakes are equally compelling. Far in the distance, the panoramic Idaho-sized vista includes ridge after ridge of pointy peaks.

There was a fire lookout on top of the peak, but it was abandoned many years ago, and the structure (built in 1933) collapsed in 2002. Although no longer maintained, the rocky trail along the steep ridgeline to the top of Hard Butte is still in reasonable condition. This trek is for experienced hikers with route-finding skills. The biggest challenge is finding the abandoned trail leading to Hard Butte's apex. If you make this hike, don't forget to bring your camera.

Trailhead Directions

From downtown McCall, drive west 5.5 miles on ID 55. Reset your tripmeter, and turn right onto the paved Brundage Mountain–Goose Lake Road. Continue 3.8 miles on the paved road and then on a well-graded dirt road. At 6.1 miles, bear left at a signed Y-junction towards Hazard Lake (still on FR 257). At 24.8 miles, arrive at a signed junction with FR 308. Continue straight (north) to the end of the road and Clayburn Trailhead in 1.4 miles. The trailhead is to the left of the large information sign in the parking area.

The Hike

View north from Hard Butte Peak

Follow hike 55 to Hard Butte Lake at 3.5 miles. From the east side of Hard Butte Lake, look for a footpath that leads southeast. Follow the faint tread southeast past a shallow pond. Continue east along the base of the rocky north face of Hard Butte. About a half-mile from Hard Butte Lake, look south (right) for the trail cut into the steep hillside. (Make sure to reference the included map.) There are a few small cairns near the edge of the meadow and at the base of the mountain to help with route-finding. The coordinates for where the trail starts up Hard Butte are N 45° 15.745', W 116° 12.088'.

From the base of the mountain, the trail rises steeply through a switchback and reaches the top of the ridge after a gain of 300 feet and a quarter-mile of hiking. Here, the route veers west (right) on level ground for about 500 feet. The trail makes one final assault to the ridgetop, ascending a very steep 600 feet in 0.4 mile to the collapsed lookout.

57 Rainbow Lake

Coordinates

Trailhead:

N 45° 15.265'
W 116° 09.693'

Rainbow Lake:

N 45° 15.241'
W 116° 11.617'

Distance: 6.6 miles out-and-back

Total Elevation Gain: 700 feet

Difficulty: Moderate

Elevation Range: 7,050 to 7,350 feet

Topographic Map: Patrick Butte

Time: 2.5 to 3.5 hours

Season: July through mid-October

Water Availability: Rainbow Lake, several creeks

Cautionary Advice: None

Information: Payette National Forest, McCall Ranger District (208) 634-0400

Pit Latrine: Yes

Rainbow Lake

When peering across the large Rainbow Lake, it isn't hard to understand the lake's magnetism—it is a real beauty with a series of granite, stairstepped cliffs rising nearly 1,700 feet to the apex of 8,659-foot Hard Butte. The lake is framed with dark green forest, and in midsummer, yellow-flowering water lillies and a lime-colored grassy shoreline make for superb, early morning photography.

Unfortunately, you might be disappointed if you expect a singletrack trail. ATVs are allowed on the entire route to the lake, and the trail turns into a dusty, moon walk by the end of summer. Mid-week visitors are likely to have the area to themselves, but expect to see a few motorized vehicles on the weekend. Mid-July to early August sees an abundance of wildflowers along most of the route. If you decide to camp at Rainbow Lake, you could make an easy day hike to Twin Lakes and Hard Butte Lake.

Overnighters will find a few campsites but not as many as you would think for such a large lake. This is an excellent choice for a modest backpack trip with small children. The west side of the lake is a wonderful place to explore off-trail and you can ascend a few of the rocky knolls for a bird's-eye perspective of Rainbow Lake. The Tepee Springs Fire burned hot in the forest near the last half-mile of the hike and burned some of the trees on the steep cliffs below Hard Butte. With all that said, is Rainbow Lake worthy of your time? Absolutely!

Trailhead Directions

From downtown McCall, drive west 5.5 miles on ID 55. Reset your tripmeter and turn right onto the paved Brundage Mountain–Goose Lake Road (FR 257). Continue 3.8 miles on paved road and then on a well-graded dirt road. At 6.1 miles, bear left at a signed Y-junction towards Hazard Lake (still on FR 257). At 24.8 miles, arrive at a signed junction with FR 308. Continue straight (north) to the end of the road and Clayburn Trailhead in 1.4 miles. The trailhead is to the left of the large information sign in the parking area.

The Hike

From the trailhead, hike north on the wide trail as it descends slightly through open forest. At 0.4 mile, ford a muddy creek and continue in and out of forest to a large meadow at 1.0 mile. The trail veers west offering great views of the large granite amphitheater containing Twin and Hard Butte Lakes. At 1.7 miles, enter forest again and arrive at a signed junction at 2.1 miles. (The right fork continues west to Lower Twin Lake in 0.8 mile.)

At the signed junction, veer south (left) as the trail stays in open forest and remains fairly level. At 2.4 miles, come to an unsigned, obscure junction. This faint trail travels northwest (right) and gains 150 feet in a quarter-mile to another junction with the trail to Twin and Hard Butte Lakes.

Back on the main trail, ford a good-sized creek. The trail starts a descent of 150 feet to another creek ford at 2.7 miles and enters burned forest. Continue south, soon fording another creek, to a poorly marked junction at 3.1 miles. The trail straight ahead (160) is infrequently maintained and is difficult to follow. Veer right and arrive at the east edge of Rainbow Lake in 0.2 mile where there are several overused campsites. You can locate a couple of less-trodden sites in forest along the lake's north perimeter. If you want to access the west side of the lake, the easiest route is to turn right at Rainbow Lake and continue along the lake's north side to its west side. There is a faint footpath, but you will need to negotiate deadfall and a few muddy sections through dense forest.

58 Big Dave Trailhead to Lava Butte Lakes

Coordinates

Trailhead:

N 45° 14.248'
W 116° 08.155'

Upper Lava Butte Lake:

N 45° 16.788'
W 116° 07.401'

Distance: 7.2 miles out-and-back

Total Elevation Gain: 1,600 feet

Difficulty: Strenuous

Elevation Range: 7,150 to 8,000 feet

Topographic Map: Hazard Lake, Patrick Butte, Hershey Point

Time: 3 to 4.5 hours

Season: July through mid-October

Water Availability: Big Dave Creek, Lava Butte Lakes and several creeks

Cautionary Advice: None

Information: Payette National Forest, McCall Ranger District (208) 634-0400

Pit Latrine: No

Big Dave Trailhead to Lava Butte Lakes

If you time this hike during July, prepare yourself for a constant walk among wildflowers—shooting stars, arrowleaf balsamroot, Indian paintbrush, mountain bluebells and sego lily. And even if the flowers aren't out, the spectacular views along most of the route, always are. Starting from the Big Dave Trailhead, you walk through meadows and along open hillsides and ascend to Lava Ridge where you are rewarded with spectacular views west of Patrick Butte, one of the highest peaks in the area, and to the distant Seven Devils Mountains. The views are equally stunning east as Elk Meadows sprawls along the valley floor while the rugged Salmon River Mountains unfold as far as the eye can see.

After a short traverse on Lava Ridge, you descend below black and brown cliffs to the three Lava Butte Lakes. The trail winds between the first two lakes where the 1994 fires burned most of the trees. However, the contrast between the burned vegetation, towering gray cliffs, green grassy slopes and glistening lakes blaze an unforgettable image. The final destination is the largest lake—located off-trail about a quarter-mile. The lake's surrounding timber partially escaped the fire's wrath and has pockets of trees. The Lava Butte Lakes can be accessed from several trailheads; although not the shortest (try hike 59), this route is arguably the most scenic.

Trailhead Directions

From downtown McCall, drive west 5.5 miles on ID 55. Reset your tripmeter, and turn right onto the paved Brundage Mountain–Goose Lake Road (FR 257). Continue 3.8 miles on paved road and then on a well-graded dirt road. At 6.1 miles, bear left at a signed Y-junction towards Hazard Lake (still on FR 257). At 24.8 miles, reach a road junction. There will be a sign "Elk Lake Trail 1, Elk Mdws. Tr. 9." Turn right towards Elk Meadows, and continue 0.8 mile to a couple of pullouts on both sides of the road. Park here. To find the trailhead, walk back down the road 100 feet to the signed trailhead on the north side of the road.

The Hike

From the trailhead, ascend an open hillside to the west of Big Dave Creek. In late June and July, there are many wildflowers blooming here. As you ascend the ridge, take the time to glance over your shoulder to Big Hazard Lake just a mile away. At 0.6 mile, descend into open forest and cross a lava-covered gully. Continue uphill reaching a saddle and flower-filled meadow at 1.0 mile. To the west, you can see two of the highest mountains in the area—8,659-foot Hard Butte and 8,841-foot Patrick Butte.

Over the next mile, the trail continues north through open forest and past hillside meadows gaining nearly 300 feet. At 2.2 miles, reach a signed junction with Trail 505, which heads west and descends to the Clayburn Trailhead in another 2.7 miles. (This is the longest route to Lava Butte Lakes.) Continue north (straight) and quickly come to a second junction. (The trail to the right—a continuation of Trail 505—descends 450 feet and continues through forest in 2.0 miles to FR 308.) Beyond the junction, make a modest ascent along Lava Ridge, and reach an unsigned junction at 2.5 miles. For spectacular views of the area and Lava Butte Lakes, continue along the ridge another half-mile to its end.

Turn right at the unsigned junction, and descend through two switchbacks directly below a towering black ridge. The trail crosses a saddle and winds between the two lower lakes at 3.2 miles. There are a couple of campsites near the trail. To visit the largest lake, continue to another junction at 3.4 miles. Turn west (left) and ascend 100 feet off-trail to the lake in 0.2 mile. There are a couple of campsites on the east side of the lake and an excellent site in timber on the lake's north side.

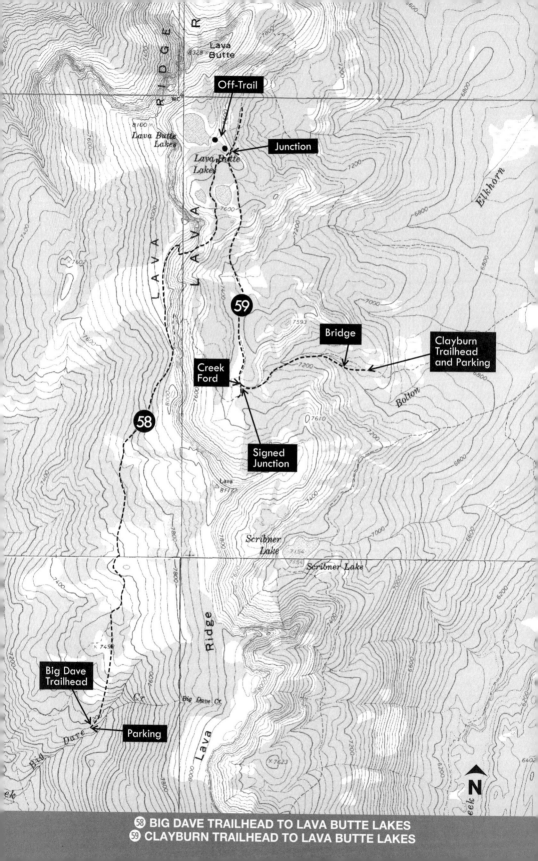

Off-Trail

Junction

Bridge

Clayburn
Trailhead
and Parking

59

Creek
Ford

58

Signed
Junction

Big Dave
Trailhead

Parking

N

58 BIG DAVE TRAILHEAD TO LAVA BUTTE LAKES
59 CLAYBURN TRAILHEAD TO LAVA BUTTE LAKES

Clayburn Trailhead to Lava Butte Lakes

Distance: 4.6 miles out-and-back

Total Elevation Gain: 850 feet

Difficulty: Moderate

Elevation Range: 7,050 to 7,700 feet

Topographic Map: Hershey Point, Patrick Butte

Time: 2 to 3 hours

Season: July through mid-October

Water Availability: Lava Butte Lakes, several creeks

Cautionary Advice: None

Information: Payette National Forest, McCall Ranger District (208) 634-0400

Pit Latrine: No

Coordinates

Trailhead:

N 45° 15.787'
W 116° 06.481'

Upper Lava Butte Lake:

N 45° 16.788'
W 116° 07.401'

Clayburn Trailhead to Lava Butte Lakes

The three enchanting Lava Butte Lakes sit directly east of the stunning Lava Ridge. Although much of the forest burned near the lakes in 1994, the setting is a bit surreal with the east-facing, fluted, gray cliffs of Lava Ridge towering over the circular lakes. There are a few stands of forest near the largest lake, and all three lakes offer campsites.

There are actually two Clayburn Trailheads—a single trail (505) that extends between the two trailheads—one from the west on FR 257 (the longest hiking route to the lakes) and another from the east on FR 308 (this hike description). The hike from FR 308 is the shortest route, and the scenery is spectacular. It includes old-growth forest, several creek-laced meadows and the Lava Butte Lakes. In July, wildflowers explode in a riot of color near the trailhead and along the open, burned slopes approaching the lake basin. Wildlife is abundant in the area, and this route offers you the best chance to see it. Although the lakes are good destinations for backpackers, the outskirts of the meadows on the approach to the lakes are equally good.

Of the three routes to the lakes, this is the least-used trail since the trailhead is another 8 miles past the Big Dave Trailhead (see hike 58). The drive is spectacular as FR 308 climbs over a high pass and dishes out a bird's-eye view down to Upper Hazard and Hazard Lakes, the Little French Creek watershed and beyond to the imposing, surrounding mountains. About a mile before reaching the Clayburn Trailhead, there is a short trail (about a quarter-mile long) from FR 308 that provides access to Scribner Lake.

Trailhead Directions

From downtown McCall, drive west 5.5 miles on ID 55. Reset your tripmeter, and turn right onto the paved Brundage Mountain–Goose Lake Road (FR 257). Continue 3.8 miles on paved road and then on a well-graded dirt road. At 6.1 miles, bear left towards Hazard Lake at a signed Y-junction (still on FR 257). At 24.8 miles, arrive at a signed junction with FR 308. There will be a sign "Elk Lake Trail 1, Elk Mdws. Tr. 9" on the right side of the road. Turn right (east) towards Elk Meadows, and drive 8.5 miles to the signed trailhead on the left side (west) of the road. There is parking for three or four vehicles.

The Hike

From the trailhead, hike west, and cross a bridge over Bottom Creek at 0.1 mile. From here, ascend 100 feet through a switchback to where the trail levels. In late July, the open slopes in the area are awash with Indian paintbrush, fireweed, pearly everlasting and many other wildflowers. At 0.5 mile, enter dense forest with an understory of ferns, and ascend to a signed junction at 0.8 mile. (By continuing west, the trail leads into a meadow and rises a steep 500 feet to the top of Lava Ridge in about 1.2 miles where it intersects with other trails.)

From the junction, turn north (right). Over the next half-mile there are plenty of level spots to establish a campsite as you hike along the edge of a long meadow. Ford a creek at 0.9 mile, and continue in forest. At 1.3 miles, ford Elkhorn Creek, and enter a badly burned area. The trail rises 250 feet along a talus-covered slope weaving between gray snags and midsummer wildflowers. At 1.8 miles, crest a ridge, and look north to see the lowest Lava Butte Lake. Northeast of the lake, is a burned hill and just beyond it, sits the largest Lava Butte Lake although you cannot see it from here.

From the ridge, descend about 100 feet, soon passing to the east of the lowest lake. Ford the lake's outlet creek where you will come to a trail junction at 2.1 miles. The trail to the left bisects the two lower lakes in a quarter-mile and continues to the top of Lava Ridge. To find the largest and most scenic lake from the junction, head west (off-trail) and ascend 100 feet to the top of the burned hill and lake at 2.3 miles. There is an excellent campsite located in forest on the northeast side of the lake.

Goose Creek Falls from Last Chance Campground

Map located on page 181

Coordinates

Trailhead:

N 44° 59.435'
W 116° 11.283'

Goose Creek Falls:

N 45° 00.715'
W 116° 09.764'

Distance: 5.0 miles out-and-back

Total Elevation Gain: 550 feet

Difficulty: Moderate

Elevation Range: 4,650 to 5,100 feet

Topographic Map: Brundage Mountain, Meadows

Time: 2 to 3 hours

Season: June through early November

Water Availability: Goose Creek and several streams

Cautionary Advice: Use caution near the steep bank above the falls.

Information: Payette National Forest, New Meadows Ranger District (208) 347-0300

Pit Latrine: Yes

Goose Creek Falls from Last Chance Campground

Starting from the Last Chance Campground, this easy hike is an excellent choice for families or anyone looking for a fairly level walk through forest. Evergreens shade the trail as it weaves between lichen-covered boulders and small meadows and over tiny creeks. An added bonus: morels in late May, wildflowers in June and July, and huckleberries in late August. The final destination—Goose Creek Falls—is a wide waterfall that plummets nearly 60 feet into a large pool. The falls are surrounded by granite outcroppings, shrubs, ferns, and dense forest.

There are three trails providing access to the falls. The shortest route is from Brundage Mountain–Goose Lake Road near Brundage Mountain Resort. Access from this trailhead (see hike 45) is shorter by 2 miles roundtrip but has more elevation gain along a steeper grade. There is another route from the trailhead near Brundage Reservoir.

The best view of the falls is from its base. This requires a scramble down a steep, rocky pitch and is not recommended for young children. The Last Chance Campground is usually open from Memorial Day weekend until mid-September and features over twenty campsites.

Trailhead Directions

From downtown McCall, drive west on ID 55 for 7.8 miles, and turn right onto the well-graded Last Chance Road (FR 453). This road is located between mile markers 151 and 152. Follow the road 2.2 miles to a Y-intersection. Turn right into the Last Chance Campground and drive 0.3 mile to the trailhead. There is parking for three or four vehicles.

The Hike

From the trailhead, enter thick forest of spruce, lodgepole pine and Douglas fir. The trail crosses several small creeks on footbridges and passes a few large granite rocks. Picnic

Look for morel mushrooms along the trail to Goose Creek Falls

opportunities abound during the first mile of hiking as the crystal-clear Goose Creek is always near.

At 1.0 mile, the trail rises high above the creek. Pass another large boulder at 1.3 miles and cross several more footbridges. Arrive at a signed junction at 2.4 miles. Turn right, passing a small waterfall and ascend 100 feet to a granite outcropping that provides a scenic overlook of Goose Creek Falls.

For a longer hike from the falls, continue north along a footpath a short distance to a junction on the main trail. Turn right and arrive at a signed junction (about a quarter-mile from the falls), just a few feet west of the bridge over Goose Creek. Huge boulders line the creek and make for a scenic

Goose Creek Falls

setting. You can cross Goose Creek and ascend a steep 600 feet in 1.2 miles to the trail's end at Brundage Mountain–Goose Lake Road (FR 257). The views are sensational on the climb. The trail north (from the signed junction near the bridge) rises more than 1,000 feet in about 2.5 miles to the trailhead near Brundage Reservoir.

Cow Camp Trail to Squirrel Creek

Coordinates

Trailhead:

N 45° 09.613'
W 116° 22.769'

Squirrel Creek:

N 45° 11.974'
W 116° 22.377'

Distance: 7.6 miles out-and-back

Total Elevation Gain: 1,600 feet

Difficulty: Moderate

Elevation Range: 4,550 to 5,000 feet

Topographic Map: Pollock Mountain, Indian Mountain

Time: 3 to 4.5 hours

Season: Late May through early November

Water Availability: Pony Creek, Squirrel Creek and several streams

Cautionary Advice: The total elevation gain is much greater than the elevation range would suggest.

Information: Payette National Forest, New Meadows Ranger District (208) 347-0300

Pit Latrine: No

Cow Camp Trail to Squirrel Creek

The late Steve McQueen once quipped, "I would rather wake up in the middle of nowhere than in any city on earth." This legendary quote will likely resonate with you on this secluded trek. The Cow Camp Trail—an insipid name at best that hardly inspires a hike—cuts through beautiful, old-growth forest and ambles over a multitude of ridges. Along the way are huge ponderosa pines and grand firs, a dense understory of thimbleberries, mountain ash and other flora. There are several scenic creeks, and opportunities to see wildlife are good. Solitude is a given; although think twice during hunting season when the trail sees considerable foot traffic.

Because the trail traverses the side of steep hillsides, backpackers will find very few flat areas for camping. However, an excellent campsite is located near Pony Creek, about 2.5 miles from the trailhead. Beyond Pony Creek, the trail rises over a ridge and descends to Squirrel Creek, a wonderful end to the hike. Here, Squirrel Creek meanders through thick forest and cascades over moss-covered rocks. A small footbridge provides a fantastic seat to dangle your feet above the creek's glistening water.

Trailhead Directions

From downtown McCall, drive west on ID 55 for 11.8 miles to the intersection with US 95. Turn north onto US 95. Travel 11.1 miles, and turn left, just past the bridge over the Little Salmon River, onto Smokey Boulder Road (FR 074). Reset your tripmeter, and travel west 2.3 miles on the dirt road to a fork. Take the right fork, and travel another 4.2 miles to the bridge across Boulder Creek. The signed trailhead is located 50 feet beyond Boulder Creek. There is no parking at the trailhead. There is parking before the bridge over Boulder Creek on both sides of the road.

The Hike

From the road, the trail enters dense forest and parallels Boulder Creek. It then rises about 100 feet to a ridge and descends to an easy ford of Pollock Creek. At 0.6 mile, cross a tiny stream on a small bridge, and come to an unsigned junction. Turn right, ascending through partially burned forest. The trail enters old-growth forest and is relatively level as it marches north over several tiny streams.

At 1.6 miles, cross a small knoll with engaging views to the Little Salmon River and beyond to the Salmon River Mountains. Continue hiking through forest and at 2.3 miles, descend 250 feet to Pony Creek. Immediately before the creek there is an excellent campsite. Cross Pony Creek on a downed log and ascend a steep 400 feet to another ridge at 3.1 miles.

Bridge over Squirrel Creek

Beyond the ridge, make a long descent along a forested hillside, and reach the small bridge spanning Squirrel Creek at 3.8 miles. The terrain is not level, but a creative backpacker might find enough level ground for a small two-person tent. You can extend the hike as the trail continues past Squirrel Creek. The trail's grade is very steep and rises more than 500 feet in 1.2 miles to a signed junction. From here, you can hike north nearly 3.0 miles to other connecting trails near Campbell's Cow Camp or descend a couple of miles to Boulder Creek.

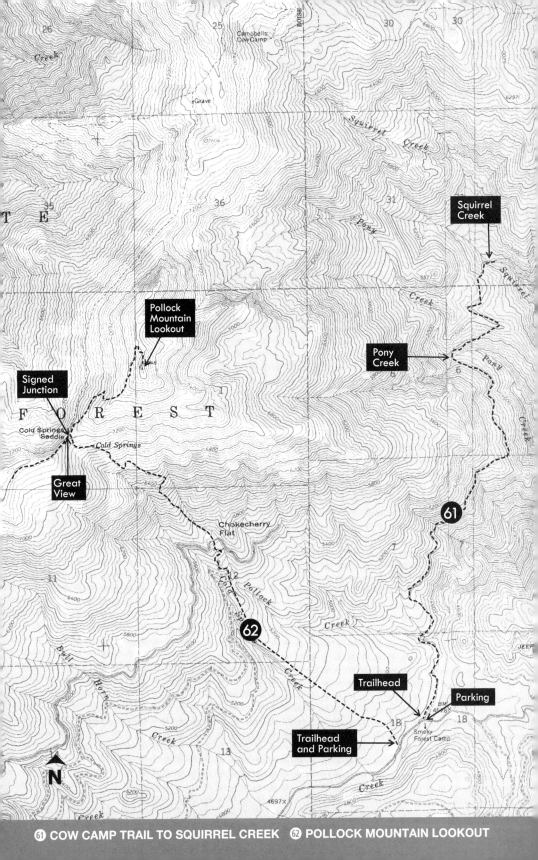

Campbells
Cow Camp

+Grave

Squirrel Creek

Squirrel Creek

Pony

Pollock Mountain Lookout

Pony Creek

Signed Junction

FOREST

Cold Springs Saddle

Cold Springs

Great View

61

Chokecherry Flat

Pollock

62

Creek

Bull Horn

Creek

JEEP

Trailhead

Parking

BM

Smoky Forest Camp

Trailhead and Parking

Creek

N

Creek

Creek

4697×

Pollock Mountain Lookout

Distance: 9.2 miles out-and-back

Total Elevation Gain: 3,450 feet

Difficulty: Very Strenuous

Elevation Range: 4,600 to 8,050 feet

Topographic Map: Pollock Mountain

Time: 4.5 to 6.5 hours

Season: Early July through mid-October

Water Availability: None

Cautionary Advice: Be aware of thunderstorm activity along the higher elevations of the hike.

Information: Payette National Forest, New Meadows Ranger District (208) 347-0300

Pit Latrine: Yes

Coordinates
Trailhead:
N 45° 09.475'
W 116° 23.018'
Pollock Mountain Lookout:
N 45° 11.367'
W 116° 24.774'

Pollock Mountain Lookout

Is it a cliché to rant about the views on another hike to a lookout? Well, most clichés have some origins in truth. Yes, the ascent is a lung-busting 3,400 feet gain, but the jaw-dropping vistas are worth every footstep.

The lookout is on top of the 8,048-foot Pollock Mountain, one of the highest peaks in the area. It is about seven miles east of the Hells Canyon Recreation Area. The vistas here are exceptional in all dirctions. Looking northwest, the deep canyon containing the Rapid River is just three miles away. Beyond the canyon, the rugged hills rise to the dark peaks of the Hells Canyon Wilderness. To the east, the Salmon River Mountains unfold with a captivating perspective of the appropriately named 8,479-foot Granite Mountain and to the deep gorge containing Hazard Creek. To the south, Meadows Valley and Long Valley spread out as far as the eye can see.

Although the views from Pollock Mountain are the highlight of the hike, the lower sections of trail are scenic, too. Along the way, you pass many massive grand fir trees, some of the largest in Idaho. Beyond Chokecherry Flat, outstanding views of the surrounding canyons and mountains are always on stage. Before reaching the lookout, the trail traverses a barren ridge of oversized granite talus.

Trailhead Directions

From downtown McCall, drive west on ID 55 for 11.8 miles to the intersection with US 95. Reset your tripmeter and turn north onto US 95. Travel 11.1 miles, and turn left onto Smokey Boulder Road (FR 074), which is just past the bridge over the Little Salmon River. Reset your tripmeter again and travel west 2.3 miles on the dirt road to a junction. Take the right fork in the road and travel another 4.4 miles to a sign "Pollock Mtn. Trail." Veer right and look for the trailhead on the right in 0.1 mile.

The Hike

From the trailhead, head north through dense forest. At 0.4 mile, the trail empties onto an old Jeep road. Turn right, walking up the road about 600 feet to an unsigned junction that is easy to miss. The road continues to the right, but look west (left) for the trail to the lookout. Veer left here and ascend through forest.

At 1.8 miles, you arrive at Chokecherry Flat, the end of FR 158. FR 158 is an extremely rough road that leads back to Boulder Creek Road in 8 miles and is mainly used by ATV traffic who park at Chokecherry Flat and hike to the lookout. ATV use is prohibited on the trail to the lookout.

Beyond Chokecherry Flat, the trail's grade is very steep. Reach the first of seven switchbacks at 2.2 miles as the views to the south continue to improve. This section of trail meanders past a few stands of enormous grand fir trees. At 2.8 miles, cross an open hillside covered with sagebrush and wildflowers, and climb through four more switchbacks. Pass beside Cold Springs, and make one final climb to a signed junction at 3.6 miles where four trails intersect at Cold Springs Saddle.

At the junction, several signs point to different destinations. The sign "Pollock Mtn. L. O. Trail" is deceptive in that it points north in the direction of a trail that travels below the west face of Pollock Mountain, paralleling the Rapid River. Do not take this trail. Instead, look for a cairn and take the trail that heads northeast.

The trail rises through a couple of switchbacks in open forest. Leave the trees behind on an open hillside. If you look northeast, you can see the white lookout near the apex of Pollock Mountain. At 4.2 miles, traverse through a field of granite boulders. Reach the broad ridge north of Pollock Mountain's apex and turn south (right) to the lookout. The fire lookout is utilized during the summer months, so please respect the occupant's privacy. If you have the time, walk Pollock Mountain's broad summit, which extends more than a half-mile north from the lookout.

63 Hazard Creek Falls

Coordinates

Trailhead:

N 45° 11.109'
W 116° 16.844'

Hazard Creek Falls:

N 45° 12.087'
W 116° 14.668'

Distance: 5.8 miles out-and-back

Total Elevation Gain: 1,000 feet

Difficulty: Moderate

Elevation Range: 3,600 to 4,400 feet

Topographic Map: Indian Mountain

Time: 2.5 to 3.5 hours

Season: Late April through mid-November

Water Availability: Hazard Creek

Cautionary Advice: Use caution around the waterfall as there are steep drop-offs.

Information: Payette National Forest, New Meadows Ranger District (208) 347-0300

Pit Latrine: No

Hazard Creek Falls

Big Hazard and Hazard Lakes give birth to Hazard Creek, a tributary to the Little Salmon River. The creek flows west through a steep-walled canyon, which in early summer is decorated by a brilliant display of wildflowers. This hike starts along the lower section of the creek and rises nearly 3 miles to a rocky overlook of Hazard Creek Falls. Although scenic, the rocky overlook only allows for a partial view of the falls.

The low elevation of the trailhead at 3,600 feet enables hikers to access the area while higher elevations are still covered in snow. Indeed, late spring hikers will find the falls a raging torrent with the fresh snowmelt. The trail starts as an old Jeep road, eventually transforming into a singletrack trail. From here, the hike to the overlook is along a moderate grade through thick forest.

The Tepee Springs Fire did burn in the canyon, and signs of the fire are more evident the further along the trail you hike. However, much of the dense brush in the canyon is now gone and the views to the steep canyon walls are much better. Backpackers will find a couple of small sites near the overlook. En route to Hazard Creek Falls, about 400 feet off-trail, there are two small, steep waterfalls that you can hike to the base of. Beyond the overlook, the fire burned hot, and the trail is difficult to negotiate due to deadfall.

Trailhead Directions

From downtown McCall, drive west on ID 55 for 11.8 miles to the three-way intersection of ID 55 and US 95 in New Meadows. Reset your tripmeter and turn right onto US 95. Travel 15.4 miles, and look for a sign "Hazard Creek Road" between mile markers 176 and 177. Reset your tripmeter, and turn right onto the well-graded FR 287. Travel 0.9 mile to a fork in the road. Go left, uphill, another 0.4 mile to the unsigned trailhead on the right (south). If you continue on FR 287, there are several dispersed campsites at higher elevations.

The Hike

The hike starts on the wide road and veers east to a rocky knoll with good views down to Hazard Creek and beyond to patches of burned forest on the north facing canyon wall. The trail descends 100 feet and passes a possible campsite at 0.7 mile. At 1.1 miles, the road ends and the route narrows considerably as it ascends a rocky tread.

At 1.3 miles, pass a granite outcrop that extends into Hazard Creek and offers excellent views. The trail continues to rise steadily through the rugged canyon under a canopy of dense forest and shrubs and crosses over a small creek at 2.1 miles. To the left, about 400 feet through burned forest, walk off-trail to a steep, unnamed waterfall (see map). The

Hazard Creek in October

grade steepens from here and bisects a hillside of granite boulders. The base of Hazard Creek Falls lies to the right of this boulder field, an ankle-twisting proposition not worth the effort.

The trail levels at 2.8 miles where a cairn (south side of trail) identifies a footpath leading 50 feet to a flat ledge perched high above Hazard Creek Falls. Although the ground is rocky here, there are a couple of locations in the area for a small tent. Beyond the falls, the trail has not been maintained and is difficult to follow.

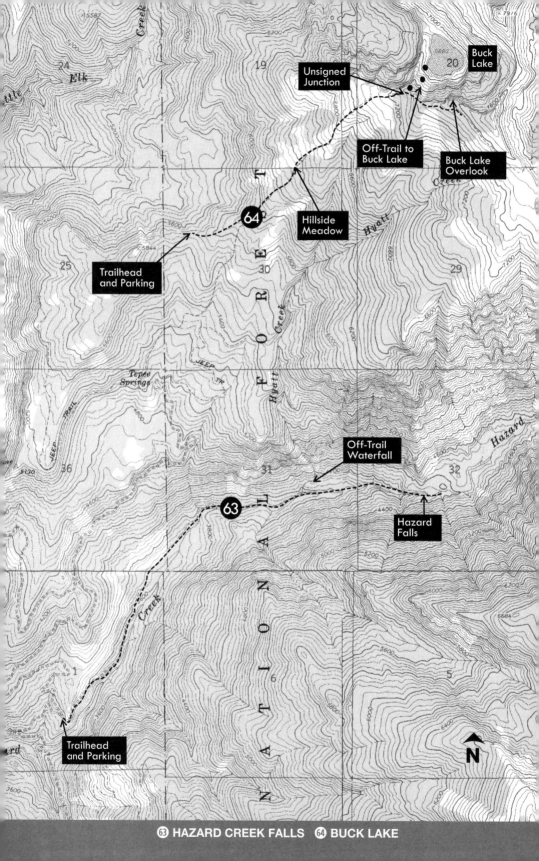

Buck Lake

Unsigned
Junction

Off-Trail to
Buck Lake

Buck Lake
Overlook

64

Hillside
Meadow

Elk

Trailhead
and Parking

Tepee
Springs

Off-Trail
Waterfall

63

Hazard
Falls

Creek

Trailhead
and Parking

N

63 HAZARD CREEK FALLS 64 BUCK LAKE

64 Buck Lake

Coordinates

Trailhead:

N 45° 13.169'
W 116° 16.009'

Buck Lake Overlook:

N 45° 13.741'
W 116° 14.378'

Distance: 3.8 miles out-and-back

Total Elevation Gain: 1,850 feet

Difficulty: Strenuous

Elevation Range: 5,700 feet to 7,500 feet

Topographic Map: Hazard Lake, Indian Mountain

Time: 2 to 3 hours

Season: Late June through mid-October

Water Availability: None, unless you descend the unmaintained trail down to Buck Lake

Cautionary Advice: Bring adequate water as there are no reliable water sources along the trail.

Information: Payette National Forest, New Meadows Ranger District (208) 347-0300

Pit Latrine: No

Buck Lake

It's difficult to decide which is a greater wonder—the spectacular scenery near Buck Lake or the fact that so few hikers venture here. Other than hunting season, and maybe not even then, you are unlikely to see other people. This beautiful trail is about 22.0 miles northeast of New Meadows and explores the rugged topography on the extreme west edge of the Salmon River Mountains.

The route to the lake includes hillside meadows, open forest and plenty of summer wildflowers. Outstanding views are a constant. One noteworthy destination is the open meadow about a mile into the hike that offers breathtaking views into the deep canyon containing the Little Salmon River, and beyond to 8,048-foot Pollock Mountain and the serrated Seven Devils Mountains skyline. The final segment of the hike ascends to a granite outcropping perched 700 feet above the beautiful Buck Lake, challenging the meadow for "best of scenery."

Although there is no official trail down to Buck Lake, there is a user-created footpath. It is steep and faint in spots, but those who make the journey will be one of the few who actually have the opportunity to dip their toes in this

Buck Lake in late October after an early fall snowstorm

hidden oasis. The lake is surrounded by steep scree slopes, so backpacking is not an option.

The dirt road to the trailhead is good except for the last 0.4 mile, which requires a high-clearance vehicle. Passenger cars can park where the road gets rocky and hike to the trailhead, adding 0.8 mile (out-and-back) to the trip. The trail does travel through sections of burned forest from the Tepee Springs Fire of 2015.

Trailhead Directions

From downtown McCall, drive west on ID 55 for 11.8 miles to the three-way intersection of ID 55 and US 95 in New Meadows, and turn right onto US 95. Continue north another 15.4 miles, and look for a sign "Hazard Creek Road" between mile markers 176 and 177. Reset your tripmeter, and turn right onto the well-graded FR 287 (Hazard Creek Road). Travel 0.9 mile to a Y-junction. Take the left fork of the road, and proceed another 6.2 miles to the signed trailhead. A high-clearance vehicle is recommended for the last 0.4 mile of the road. If you have a passenger car, there is adequate parking along the road before it gets rocky.

The Hike

From the signed trailhead, head north onto an open slope with many summer wildflowers and then into forest. The trail enters burned forest from the Tepee Springs Fire at 0.3 mile and makes a steep rise of more than 300 feet to a hillside meadow at 0.6 mile. The trail is ill-defined here. Make sure not to cross the meadow. Instead turn east (right) and ascend along the edge of burned forest. As you ascend, the trail will become more apparent. Over-the-shoulder views are spectacular looking west.

At 1.0 mile, the trail turns northeast up a steep hillside and winds behind a little knoll that blocks views looking west. After a bit more elevation gain, the trail levels in a patch of old-growth evergreens at 1.4 miles. Enter burned forest again, and climb a little over 100 feet to an unsigned juction at 1.6 miles more than 400 feet above Buck Lake (see map).

Veer left here if you want to descend down to Buck Lake. The route is very steep and requires a bit of route-finding. The footpath weaves through forest and over rocky knolls to the south side of the lake. There are no campsites near the lake due to the steep canyon walls surrounding the lake.

Past the unsigned junction, the trail makes a final rise of 250 feet over the next quarter-mile to a granite outcropping (about 50 feet off-trail) sitting high above Buck Lake. The views are phenomenal especially looking south and west.

View looking west from the hillside meadow

65 Rapid River and the West Fork of the Rapid River

Coordinates
Trailhead:

N 45° 21.179'
W 116° 23.862'

Potter's Flat:

N 45° 18.603'
W 116° 26.056'

Distance: 10.8 miles out-and-back

Total Elevation Gain: 1,800 feet

Difficulty: Strenuous

Elevation Range: 2,250 to 3,200 feet

Topographic Map: Heaven's Gate

Time: 4 to 6.5 hours

Season: All year

Water Availability: Rapid River and the West Fork of the Rapid River

Cautionary Advice: Watch for rattlesnakes during the summer months. The canyon can be very hot in July and August.

Information: Nez Perce National Forest, Salmon River Ranger District (208) 839-2211

Pit Latrine: Yes

Rapid River and the West Fork of Rapid River

The Rapid River is one of the more scenic river canyons in Idaho. Exposed bluffs, grassy ridges, steep canyon walls, and the lucid river make for an excellent locale for exploration. The river was designated a Wild and Scenic River in 1975.

The water quality of the river is exceptional and supports Chinook salmon, steelhead, and rainbow and bull trout. Raptors abound with the possibility of seeing peregrine falcons, golden eagles, red-tailed hawks, American kestrels, Cooper's and sharp-shinned hawks and northern harriers. Wildlife flourishes too, especially along the West Fork of the Rapid River. Look for deer, elk, cougar, wolves and black bear.

The best times to hike the trail are April through May and September through October when temperatures are mild. In late spring, wildflowers are prolific on the green hillsides. In October, be aware of hunters along the West Fork. The low elevation of the trail can make midsummer hiking extremely hot with temperatures often soaring above 100°F. You can hike during the winter months but be cautious of ice on the trail. The narrow canyon gets little direct sunlight.

The rugged canyon cradling the Rapid River

The first 4 miles of the hike are in a narrow canyon, often only feet from the Rapid River. There are sections of the trail that are cut into the steep hillsides, sometimes 150 feet above the river. From the confluence of the Rapid River and the West Fork of the Rapid River, the trail rises 400 feet to Potter's Flat. Camping opportunities exist at the confluence and near Potter's Flat. The hike can be extended another 3 miles past Potter's Flat to McCrea Place where the canyon is wide. The setting is beautiful with steep grassy hillsides, McCrea Creek and old-growth ponderosa pines. It is an excellent destination for a remote backpacking trip.

Trailhead Directions

From downtown McCall, drive west on ID 55 for 11.8 miles to its intersection with US 95. Turn right onto US 95. Travel 29.7 miles, past mile marker 191 and turn left onto paved Rapid River Road. Continue 2.9 miles, and veer right into the large parking area and trailhead.

The Hike

From the parking area, follow the singletrack trail as it veers south along a grassy hillside. The trail is high above the river and you should watch children closely along this short section.

At 0.5 mile, pass below orange and gray cliffs and come to an unsigned junction. A side trail veers west up the steep mountainside to Mount Sampson and Cannon Ball Mountain. Continue on the main trail as it rises to a rocky ridge perched high above the river and descends to a beautiful bridge spanning the Rapid River at 1.1 miles.

Beyond the bridge, the trail stays close to the river and meanders through a dense understory and, at 2.7 miles, rises more than 150 feet up a steep hillside. In May and June, hikers will find plenty of colorful wildflowers. The trail stays high above the river for the next half-mile and finally drops to the river again. In this area, look for the Pacific yew, a conifer tree more commonly found along the Pacific Coast Ranges. The tree can be identified by its reddish-brown bark.

At 4.2 miles, cross the Rapid River on another bridge. The trail rises 100 feet on an open hillside, covered with wildflowers in late spring. Reach a signed junction at the confluence of the West Fork of the Rapid River and the Rapid River. Camping is possible down below on a grassy flat area next to the West Fork. The trail along the Rapid River continues south over 15 miles to its headwaters near the Lick Creek Lookout. Many sections of this trail are overgrown with dense vegetation.

Turn right at the signed junction, heading west up the canyon. The trail rises 400 feet on an open hillside below brown and gray cliffs. Views down to the

Rapid River

West Fork and beyond to the steep ridges on the south side of the river are beautiful. At 5.1 miles, when the trail begins to level, look to your left for a faint footpath to a wooden headstone for J. Jones, a miner killed in 1899.

Reach Potter's Flat at 5.4 miles. Here the river is wide and tranquil with excellent campsites near its grassy banks. This is the end of the hike. The hike can be extended by following the main trail further west. It rises 900 feet through dense forest in 3.2 miles to McCrea Place. The canyon is wide here and an old cabin—McCrea's cabin—still stands near McCrea Creek. In late spring, the grassy hillsides usually attract many elk and deer. Backpackers will find this location to be an excellent destination.

Trailhead and Parking

Trailhead

Bridge

65

Bridge

Signed Junction

Potter Flat

N

65 RAPID RIVER AND THE WEST FORK OF THE RAPID RIVER

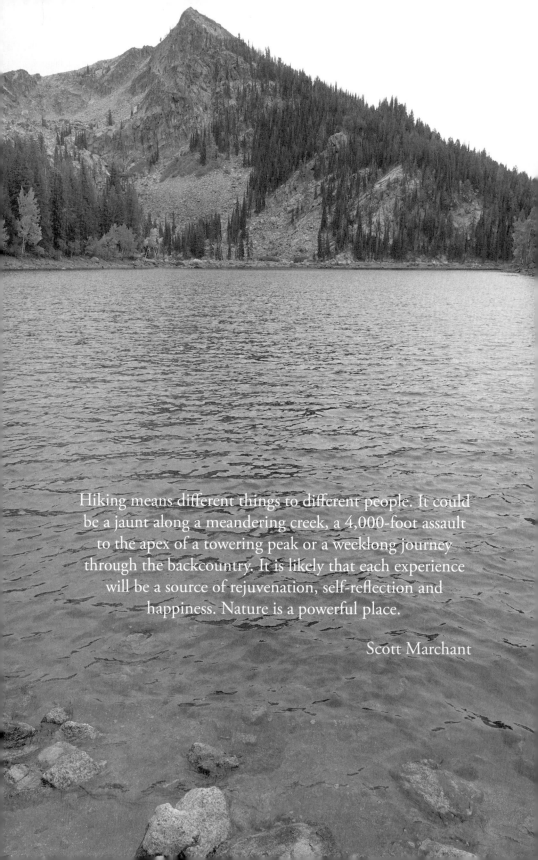

Hiking means different things to different people. It could
be a jaunt along a meandering creek, a 4,000-foot assault
to the apex of a towering peak or a weeklong journey
through the backcountry. It is likely that each experience
will be a source of rejuvenation, self-reflection and
happiness. Nature is a powerful place.

Scott Marchant

ABOUT THE AUTHOR AND PHOTOGRAPHER

Although Scott Marchant grew up in Florida and did not see his first snowfall until he was in college, he has been a hiker and enthusiast of the high mountains from the first time he saw the Sierra Nevada Mountains. This is his sixth Idaho hiking guidebook, and he spends the vast majority of his time wandering and sleeping in Idaho's beautiful landscape, lugging pen, paper and camera. In addition to hiking guidebooks, Scott produces a yearly Idaho wilderness calendar. Although he likes to sequester himself in the woods as much as possible, Boise is his permanent residence.